Identity and Foreign Policy in the Middle East

Edited by
Shibley Telhami and
Michael Barnett

CORNELL UNIVERSITY PRESS
ITHACA AND LONDON

First published 2002 by Cornell University Press
First printing, Cornell Paperbacks, 2002

Printed in the United States of America

Library of Congress Cataloging-in-Publication Data
Identity and foreign policy in the Middle East / edited by Shibley
Telhami and Michael Barnett.
    p. cm.
Includes bibliographical references and index.
ISBM 0-8014-3940-X (cloth) — ISBN 0-8014-8745-5 (pbk.)
    1. Middle East—Foreign relations.   2. Middle East—Politics and
government—20th century.   3. Group identity—Political aspects—Middle
East.   4. National state.   I. Telhami, Shibley. II. Barnett, Michael
N., 1960–   .
    JZ1670 .134 2002
    327'.0956—dc21

                                2001004561

Cornell University Press strives to use environmentally responsible suppliers and materials to the fullest extent possible in the publishing of its books. Such materials include vegetable-based, low-VOC inks and acid-free papers that are recycled, totally chlorine-free, or partly composed of nonwood fibers. For further information, visit our website at www.cornellpress.cornell.edu.

Cloth printing   10 9 8 7 6 5 4 3 2 1
Paperback printing   10 9 8 7 6 5 4 3 2 1

Contents

CONTRIBUTORS

Michael Barnett, University of Wisconsin, Madison
Adeed Dawisha, Miami University, Ohio
Ibrahim A. Karawan, University of Utah
Marc Lynch, Williams College
Suzanne Maloney, Brookings Institution
Yahya Sadowski, American University of Beirut
Stephen Saideman, Texas Tech University
Shibley Telhami, University of Maryland, College Park

Acknowledgments

This book resulted from a conference hosted by the Sadat Chair program at the University of Maryland, College Park, which addressed the relationship between communal/national identities and the foreign policies of Middle Eastern states. All of the papers were original and were prepared to address a common theme. They have undergone several revisions in response to comments by the two editors, by three Press reviewers, and by an additional reviewer solicited by the editors. The chapter on Iran was not part of the conference but was solicited later on the recommendation of one of the reviewers. The project was partly funded by the Carnegie Corporation of New York.

The project benefited from the participation, presentations, and comments of scholars other than contributors to this volume. In particular we acknowledge the insightful presentations by Richard Herrmann; Kemal Kirisci and Martin Sampson; Mona Makram-Ebeid; Mahmood Sariolghalam; and Hakan Yavuz. Helpful comments were made by Amatzia Baram, Avner Cohen, Milton Esman, Benjamin Frankel, Graham Fuller, Joshua Goldstein, Ted Gurr, Barbara Harff, Michael Hudson, George Irani, Hisham Melhem, Henry Nau, Andrew Parasiliti, Jerome Segal, Ehud Sprinzak, Jonathan Wilkenfeld, and William Zartman. We also are grateful to Hellmut Lotz and Jennifer Skulte for research help and to Hillary Brandt, Raquel Fontanes, and, especially, Aysha Ismail for administrative support.

S. T. and M. B.

Identity and Foreign Policy in the Middle East

1. Introduction

Identity and Foreign Policy in the Middle East

SHIBLEY TELHAMI

MICHAEL BARNETT

Much of the political history of the Middle East has been told with reference to political identities. Certainly from World War II to the 1970s, debates among students of Middle East politics focused on the rise and decline of the pan-Arab movement, on the early weakness of states in the region, or on the lack of fit between the boundaries imposed by colonial powers and existing identities.[1] Recent debates have examined the Islamic trend in Middle East politics and the extent to which it challenges the domestic legitimacy and political stability of these states. Since the Gulf War of 1991, the revival of the Kurdish national movement and the decline in

---

[1] On the impact of colonialism and the creation of weak states for understanding the primacy of Arab nationalism and regional dynamics, see Michael Hudson, *Arab Politics: The Search for Legitimacy* (New Haven: Yale University Press, 1977); Gabriel Ben-Dor, *State and Conflict in the Middle East* (New York: Praeger Press, 1983); and Paul Noble, "The Arab System: Opportunities, Constraints, and Pressures," in *The Foreign Policies of the Arab States*, ed. B. Korany and A. Hillal Dessouki (Boulder: Westview Press, 1984): 41–78. On the changing alliance patterns among Arab states, see Y. Evron and Y. Bar-Siman-Tov, "Coalitions in the Arab World," *Jerusalem Journal of International Relations* 1 (winter 1975): 71–108; Alan Taylor, *The Arab Balance of Power System* (Syracuse: Syracuse University Press, 1982); Roger Owen, *State, Power, and Politics in the Making of the Modern Middle East* (New York: Routledge, 1992): 90–92; P. J. Vatikiotis, *Conflict in the Middle East* (London: George Allen and Unwin, 1971): 18–22, 92, and *Arab and Regional Politics in the Middle East* (New York: St. Martin's Press, 1984); and Elie Kedourie, "The Chatham House Version," in his *The Chatham House Version and Other Middle-Eastern Studies* (London: Weidenfeld and Nicolson, 1970). On the decline of Arab identities, see Bernard Lewis, "Rethinking the Middle East," *Foreign Affairs* 71, no. 4 (1992): 99–119; Ghassan Salame, "Inter-Arab Politics: The Return to Geography," in *The Middle East: Ten Years after Camp David*, ed. W. Quandt (Washington, D.C.: Brookings Press, 1988): 319–56; George Corm, *Fragmentation of the Middle East: The Last Thirty Years* (London: Hutchinson Books, 1983); Fouad Ajami, "The End of Pan-Arabism," *Foreign Affairs* 57 (winter 1977/78): 355–73; Mohammed Sid-Ahmed, "The Arab League and the Arab State," *Al-Ahram Weekly*, April 6–12, 1995, 8; and Salame, "'Strong' and 'Weak' States: A Qualified Return to the *Muqaddimah*," in *The Arab State*, ed. G. Luciani (Berkeley: University of California Press, 1990): 29–64.

the sovereign authority of the Iraqi state over some of its territory have resurrected questions about Iraq's political identity. A key question in the much-anticipated regime transitions that have begun to occur with the exit of long-serving Arab leaders is whether their departures will unleash a clash among rival ethnic, sectarian, and religious groups. Nearly all discussions in the aftermath of September 11th, and in regard to the United States's strategy to fight terrorism, highlight whether Middle Eastern states will be able to align with the United States because of their Islamic character. The boundaries of group loyalty and membership have demonstrated considerable fluctuation during the past century and will continue to do so. No student of Middle Eastern international politics can begin to understand the region without taking into account the ebb and flow of identity politics.

Although scholars of the region cannot escape the salience of identity, a powerful trend in contemporary international relations theory has proceeded as if identity mattered little for our understanding. Post-World War II international relations theorizing became increasingly systemic. Moving away from classical realist models of international politics that recognized some variations in national interest because of variations in national cultures, international relations theory drifted toward largely unvarying systemic properties to deduce what were sometimes assumed to be uniform national interests.[2] Kenneth Waltz's *Theory of International Politics* christened this development and launched a thousand studies that refined his theoretical model. Such refinements, however, rarely broached the possibility that state interests might vary because of variation in national politics and culture. Such considerations were the stuff of domestic politics, which threatened the sin of reductionism. It was never Waltz's intention to develop a theory of foreign policy; he was clearly aware that states could have domestic motives in the conduct of foreign policy. But many scholars of foreign policy employed his work as if all state interests can be derived from the relative position of the state in international politics.

The important point here is that scholars made assumptions about state interests and motivations rather than treating them as objects of investigation. Although they did not in principle exclude domestic sources of interests,[3] in practice many assumed that international politics holds a monopoly on the state's interests. Whether Waltzian systemic theory demands a materialist definition of the international system and allows no variation in state interests is a matter of debate,[4] but little doubt

[2] Kenneth Waltz, *Theory of International Politics* (Reading, Mass.: Addison-Wesley, 1979).

[3] Stephen Krasner's *Defending the National Interest* (Princeton: Princeton University Press, 1978) defined the national interest inductively and reflecting the view of central policy makers, without assuming that these views originate in international politics.

[4] For recent contributions to this debate, see Randall Schweller, "Neorealism's Status-Quo Bias: What Security Dilemma?" in *Realism: Restatements and Renewal*, ed. B. Frankel (Portland: Frank Cass, 1996): 90–112; Shibley Telhami, "An Essay on Neorealism and Foreign Policy," presented at the American Political Science Association, Atlanta, Georgia, September 4, 1999;

exists that during the last two decades many scholars working in the systemic tradition assumed that the homogeneity of state interests was a logical starting point.

Scholars of international politics were quick to adopt and to develop these systemic models for the Middle East. Stephen Walt's *Theory of Alliances* modified Waltz's model to suggest that the "balance of threat" provided a better predictor of the origins and shifts in alignment patterns.[5] He daringly tested that model in a place that was thought to be dripping with identity politics, namely the Arab Middle East. Specifically, he argued against the prevailing wisdom that inter-Arab politics was roiled by identity and religious politics and in favor of the view that inter-Arab politics was just like any other interstate politics because the properties of the system were the same as anywhere else. Arab leaders might saturate their policies in the language of Arabism and Islam, but realists and neorealists had long recognized that self-interested state leaders would use local legitimation principles to justify foreign policies driven by power politics. Similarly modifying neorealist tenets, Shibley Telhami argued that the road to Camp David was driven by a shift in the regional and international balance of power, a shift that caused participants to recalculate which policies would best enable them to pursue their long-standing security interests.[6] Like Walt, Telhami took issue with regional scholars who argued that ideological politics explains the policies of Israel, the United States, and Egypt. Good old-fashioned power politics was, he suggested, the most powerful explanation for this rupture in the Arab-Israeli conflict. Some of the most contrarian and interesting contributions to the scholarship on the international relations of the Middle East set out to debunk the conventional wisdom.

Other factors also influenced this move toward systemic and rationalist theorizing. The tendency among scholars of Middle Eastern politics to focus on identity-based movements led to the field's self-exclusion from broader theoretical debates. Because the content of these identity-based movements was particular to the region, the region appeared to be unique. Systemic-oriented scholars, by contrast, could build an analytic bridge between the Middle East and theory-building. In addition, rationalist precepts provided a haven from the sometimes latent orientalism and ethnocentrism that characterized scholarship on the region. Rational-choice theories presumed that Arab leaders were like their counterparts elsewhere, and that their base interests and instincts were driven by the familiar, fundamental goals of power, security, and survival. The view that Middle Eastern populations were somehow irrational and were driven

Colin Elman, "Horses for Courses: Why Not Neorealist Theories of Foreign Policy?" *Security Studies* 6 (autumn 1996): 7–53; and Kenneth Waltz, "Reply to Elman", *Security Studies* 6, no. 1 (1997).

[5] Stephen Walt, *The Origins of Alliances* (Ithaca: Cornell University Press, 1987).

[6] Shibley Telhami, *Power and Leadership in International Bargaining* (New York: Columbia University Press, 1990).

into the streets in acts of self-destruction was now replaced by the view that social mobilization could be effected by long-standing grievances and collective-
action problems familiar to students of protest politics. Although this move toward rationalism had the effect of denying any explanatory significance to
culture, religion, and identity politics, it was welcome in a field that frequently
made unwarranted, reified, and non-falsifiable claims regarding Arab or Middle
Eastern culture.

This systemic and rationalist perspective has many virtues that we admire
and explains many important events in the Middle East, but it cannot account
for much of the *foreign policies* of states in the region.[7] Our aim in this volume is
to explore the role of identity politics in foreign policy. The challenge, as we see
it, is not to presume that because the specific content of identity-based claims
are particular to the region, therefore their forms and effects are particular. Indeed, an impressive spate of research over the last several years has built models
regarding the relationship between identity politics and regional politics that
are potentially transferable across regions. Much of this work has derived from
constructivist international relations theory (though some realist theory also aspires to identify the cultural and national roots of foreign policy).[8] Constructivism posits that social (and international) structures are alloyed with normative
and material elements, that social structures constitute actors' identities and interests, and that the practices of actors embedded in that social structure
not only reproduce the structure but also sometimes transform it. This broad
ontology, generally borrowed from sociological theories, has been applied to international and regional politics to address an impressive range of empirical
phenomena.[9]

[7] An additional body of literature begins with domestic rather than systemic politics to understand how Arab politics is shaped by states whose lack of legitimacy forces them to use Arabism as an ideological prop. See Michael Hudson, *Arab Politics*; F. Gregory Gause III, "Sovereignty, Statecraft, and Stability in the Middle East," *Journal of International Affairs* 45 (winter
1992): 441–67; Paul Noble, Rex Brynen, and Bahgat, "Conclusion: The Changing Regional
Security Environment," in *The Many Faces of National Security in the Arab World*, ed. Korany,
Noble, and Brynen (New York: St. Martin's Press, 1993): 275–302; and Avraham Sela, *The Decline of the Arab-Israeli Conflict: Middle East Politics and the Quest for Regional Order* (Albany:
SUNY Press, 1997); and Ali Hillal Dessouki and Korany, "The Global System and Arab For-
eign Policies," in *The Foreign Policies of Arab States*, ed. Korany and Dessouki (Boulder, Colo.:
Westview Press, 1991).

[8] See, for instance, Samuel Huntington's "American Creed" and its role in American foreign policy.

[9] For theoretical statements, see Nicholas Onuf, *World of Our Own Making* (Columbia: University of South Carolina Press, 1989); Alexander Wendt, *Social Theory of International Politics*
(New York: Cambridge University Press, 1999); Emanuel Adler, "The Middle Ground: Constructivism in World Politics," *European Journal of International Relations* 3, no. 3 (September
1998): 291–318. For empirical statements, see Peter Katzenstein, ed., *The Culture of National Security* (New York: Columbia University Press, 1996); Rodney Bruce Hall, "Moral Authority as

Various scholars have developed theories derived from constructivism to explain Middle Eastern politics over the decades. Arabism constituted Arab states with Arab national interests, which enabled constructivists to explore the impact of identity and to challenge realist propositions that interests are homogeneous in all contexts because they derive from unwavering anarchy. Constructivists took aim at various considerations: the social construction of Arab national interests; the emergence of sovereignty as the organizing principle of interstate politics; the effect of Arab and sovereignty norms on interactions among survival-seeking Arab leaders; and the shift in interests of Arab states caused by transformations in national identities. One important conclusion is that a shared identity can be tied to conflict or cooperation.[10] If, as some realists now claim, the region has become more realist, then we have to explain these emergent properties rather than assume their existence.[11]

In many respects, the editors of this volume represent these two theoretical camps. Telhami has developed systemic theories of international relations to explain important developments in Middle Eastern politics; Barnett has developed constructivist-inspired models to explain central features of inter-Arab politics. Although still lauding systemic theorizing, over the past several years Telhami has incorporated issues of transnational legitimacy and identity-based claims to add perspective to important features of inter-Arab dynamics.[12] Barnett's early study of the sociological character and organization of the region has been recently amended to include the relationship between identity politics and power in regional politics.[13] We do not want to give the appearance of a happy convergence between neorealist and constructivist approaches. After all, important differences exist between systemic and sociological models of international politics, including the definitional properties of a social structure. We also are skeptical of additive models that presume that systemic and ideational variables

a Power Resource," *International Organization* 51, no. 4 (autumn 1997): 591–622; Mlada Bukovansky, "American Identity and Neutral Rights from Independence to the War of 1812," *International Organization* 51, no. 2 (spring 1997): 209–44; and Margaret Keck and Kathryn Sikkink, *Activists beyond Borders* (Ithaca: Cornell University Press, 1998).

[10] See Michael Barnett, *Dialogues in Arab Politics: Negotiations in Regional Order* (New York: Columbia University Press, 1998); Marc Lynch, *State Interests and Public Spheres: The International Politics of Jordan's Identity* (New York: Columbia University Press, 1999); and Dalia Dassa Kaye, *Multilateralism in the Middle East* (New York: Columbia University Press, 2001).

[11] See Malik Mufti, *Sovereign Creations: Pan-Arabism and Political Order in Syria and Iraq* (Ithaca: Cornell University Press, 1996), and F. Gregory Gause III, "Sovereignty, Statecraft, and Stability in the Middle East."

[12] Telhami, "Power, Legitimacy, and Peace-making in Arab Coalitions" in *Ethnic Conflict and International Politics in the Middle East*, ed. Leonard Binder (Gainesville: University Press of Florida, 1999).

[13] Barnett, *Dialogues in Arab Politics*.

can be combined to account for more variance in international dynamics. Still, this healthy debate between constructivist and systemic theories has led to a shifting of positions and to greater clarification and appreciation of each approach's strengths and weaknesses.

This book furthers our understanding of how the formation and transformation of national and state identities affect the foreign policy of Middle Eastern states. Specifically, we hope to make several theoretical and substantive contributions. The first is to advance our theoretical understanding of the relationship between identity and foreign policy. Over the last several years an impressive amount of research has examined the relationship between identity and foreign policy.[14] But tremendous debate remains regarding the effects of identity and the methods used to evaluate those effects. Given the centrality and prominence of identity in the Middle East, such debate deserves clarification. Scholars of the Middle East have produced a trove of good descriptive studies of how identity politics affects regional politics. But these studies, like many others based on a systematic approach to identity politics, would benefit from sharper concepts, greater awareness of how identity can affect foreign-policy outcomes, and more analytical comparisons of hypotheses. The payoff would be greater clarity regarding theoretical alternatives.

We see two important theoretical contributions. The first is a greater understanding of which identity emerges and why. Communities and societies can be understood as engaging in a continuous debate over their collective identity.[15] As Edward Said observes, "We need to regard society as the locale in which a continuous contest between adherents of different ideas about what constitutes the national identity is taking place."[16] Debates over national identity highlight the menu of choices regarding that identity, which includes not only alternative categories (Arabism vs. Islam) but also different interpretations of a particular identity (conservative vs. radical Arabism). Further, the interpretations themselves sometimes contain alternative categories (Zionist-religious vs. Zionist-secular Israeli). International relations scholars have not been quick to examine these debates, probably because they have spent much time simply attempting to convince the field that national identity warrants attention. But different categories are possible at any moment, and one of our concerns is how a particular formulation becomes momentarily fixed. One of our goals is to think systematically about the regional, international, and domestic forces that advance one identity over another.

[14] Katzenstein, ed., *Culture of National Security.*

[15] William Connolly, *Identity/Difference* (Princeton, N.J.: Princeton University Press, 1991): 204; and Samuel Kim and Lowell Dittmer, "Whither China's Quest for National Identity?" in *China's Quest for National Identity*, eds. Dittmer and Kim (Ithaca: Cornell University Press, 1993): 241.

[16] "The Phony Islamic Threat," *The New York Times Magazine* (November 21,): 62.

Our second theoretical goal is to provide greater understanding of how identity affects foreign policy. Here the important point is that identity appears at different places in the causal chain. For some, identity appears most prominently as an ideological device to justify self-interested politics. This has been the null hypothesis in many studies of the Middle East—presuming, for instance, that Arabism is nothing more than an ideological prop in the hands of self-interested, power-seeking Arab leaders. Many contributions in this volume also recognize that governmental officials can be expected to grab onto any weapon that serves their immediate interests, and ideology is almost always unsheathed. For others, identity is part of the cultural terrain and thus conditions the possible and the actual. This dynamic is noted by Barnett and Lynch, who discuss how identity conditions what government leaders can entertain and is considered legitimate by their societies. For others, still, identity provides a direct link to a discrete foreign policy preference or outcome. Would Egypt have intervened in the Yemeni civil war in the 1960s had it not had a republican Arabist identity? Can we understand why Syria rejected a bilateral deal similar to the Egyptian-Israeli deal for more than twenty years without reference to Syria's political identity?[17] Can Iran's role in Lebanon be understood without reference to Iran's Islamic identity? The relationship between foreign policy and identity need not always be so direct, however. Identity politics can raise the cost of some policy options for governments. One payoff for explicating identity's place in the overall story being advanced is an understanding of whether identity challenges or complements materialist theories.

Finally, this volume aspires to enhance our understanding of the Middle East in general and the countries covered in this volume, four Arab and two non-Arab: Egypt, Syria, Jordan, Iraq, Iran, and Israel. We are well aware that identity politics has been on the research agenda of the Middle East for decades. But by being clearer about how we use the concept of identity, by giving greater consideration of the menu of choice, and by carefully considering how that choice leads to a particular foreign policy outcome, we can enhance our understanding of these countries and of regional politics. In all of our cases the question of state identity has been a central part of the political debate. In Syria, the rise of the Ba'ath and the advocacy of Arabism over nationalism or Islamism has led to the definition of state as an Arab republic without reference to the Islamic character, as many had insisted. In Jordan, the severing of ties with the West Bank in 1989 signaled a further detachment of the Palestinian component of the Jordanian identity. The meaning of Israel's Jewishness has been hotly contested in Israel's internal and external debates. Iraq's identity, always a part of the Arabist-statist debate, now has the amplified dimension of subnational debate. Iran,

[17] For a discussion of this issue, see Shibley Telhami, "Why Israel and Syria Have Come to the Table Now," *The Washington Post* (Dec. 19, 1999).

which witnessed a genuine revolution in the ascendance of the Islamic regime, has been the subject of internal and external debates. And Egypt, which had led the pan-Arab movement in the 1950s and 1960s, was the first to abandon it in the 1970s, much to the shock of many Egyptians and Arabs.

In the remainder of this chapter we want to lay out our views regarding some basic issues that routinely follow discussions concerning the link between identity politics and foreign policy. Specifically, in the next section we sketch competing perspectives on identity formation and change; we then briefly survey the choices among identity politics in the Middle East; after that we discuss different concepts about how identity shapes foreign policy; we then offer an overview of how identity politics at the regional level has ebbed and flowed during the century. This overview discusses the relationship among shifts in material conditions, namely technology, national identity debates and their regional effects, and future possibilities given the region's ongoing information revolution.

Competing Perspectives on Identity Formation and Change

Part of our collective goal is to understand the emergence and construction of particular definitions of state or national identity. But before we outline a range of analytic alternatives, we want to discuss our take on some conceptual issues. Although many definitions of identity exist, most begin with the understanding of oneself in relationship to others.[18] Identities, in short, are not only personal or psychological, but are also social, profoundly influenced by the actor's interaction with and relationship to others. Through interacting and participating in an institutional context, the actor ascribes to an identity. Similarly, national and state identities are formed in relationship to other nations and states; those corporate identities are tied to residents' relationships to those outside the boundaries of the community and the territory, respectively. State identity can be understood as the corporate and officially demarcated identity linked to the state apparatus; national identity can be defined as a group of people who aspire to or have a historical homeland, share a common myth and historical memories, have legal rights or duties for all members, and have markers to distinguish themselves from others. In this view, the nation and the state are analytically distinct. As Anthony Smith aptly notes,

> The [state] refers exclusively to public institutions, differentiated from and autonomous of, other social institutions and exercising a monopoly of

[18] See Dittmer and Kim (1993), Smith (1991), Bloom (1990), and Wendt (1994) for discussions of national and state identities that build on this definition.

coercion and extraction with a given territory. The nation, on the other hand, signifies a cultural and political bond, uniting in a single political community all who share a historic culture and homeland. This is not to deny some overlap between the two concepts, given their common reference to a historic territory and (in democratic states) their appeal to the sovereignty of the people. But, while modern states must legitimate themselves in national and popular terms as the states of particular nations, their content and focus are quite different.[19]

The distinction between state and national identity is designed not only to offer analytical nuance but also to provide greater historical and conceptual clarity. In the Middle East the state's identity can be quite distinct from national identities of the local population, generating the domestic insecurities apparent to even the most casual observer.

At one time the need to distinguish between state and national identity would have struck international relations scholars as unnecessary. The working assumption during much of the Cold War was that the state represented a rather homogeneous community within its borders that could be referred to as a nation. But the end of the Cold War and the unleashing of ethnic and identity-based civil wars led international relations scholars to revise their assumptions and to recognize that the state and the nation are not coterminous in much of the world. In fact, the lack of overlap between state and national identity can generate an inherently unstable and precarious situation, one that results in political, economic, and symbolic exercises by the state in order to shift subnational loyalties to the symbols of the state. These exercises often have resulted in clashes between rivals for power and in the spillover of conflict from the national to the international realm. These outcomes have attracted the attention of international scholars, who have begun to widen their theoretical aperture to examine subnational processes and their foreign policy international implications.

That state and national identity are not coterminous is no surprise to those working in the Middle East (or anyone who worked outside the West, for that matter). Indeed, a state-building project can be understood as a social engineering exercise intended to generate the very state-national conflation assumed by international relations theorists. The critical difference between Middle Eastern state-building projects and those in other parts of the Third World has been that Arab leaders have attempted to shrink the national imagery from its transnational status to the confines of the state, whereas other Third World leaders have attempted to fill up the state with a national identity derived from subnational particles. An important consequence of this dynamic for the Middle

[19] Anthony Smith, *National Identity* (Las Vegas: University of Nevada Press, 1991): 14–15.

East is that national and state-building projects have been played out on a regional—and not simply a domestic—stage.

Any discussion of national identity and state-building immediately raises the suspicion that we are simply introducing the concept of identity in place of the more familiar concept of ideology. Such suspicions can run particularly high in the context of Middle Eastern scholarship, where for decades the debates focused on Arab nationalist ideology and the tendency among many noted and diverse scholars, including Elie Kedourie, P. J. Vatikiotis, and Stephen Walt, to speak of an Arab ideology. We can differentiate between ideology and identity by asking about the roots and functions of both. The concept of ideology was introduced in Marxist scholarship to explain how relations of domination are reproduced with minimal resort to direct force.[20] According to this view, individuals had objective interests that typically derived from their position within a (material) social structure, and the ideology led them to act in ways that were inconsistent with those interests. This sort of claim is famously associated with the concept of false consciousness. Studies of ideology, therefore, typically noted that the ideas articulated by subordinate classes were not in their objective interests but instead worked to the advantage of the dominant class.[21]

International relations scholars and students of the Middle East have typically treated ideology in a similar way. The general tendency has been to assume that interests derive objectively from the international distribution of power. This realist approach posits that states promote certain ideas as in the interests of humanity or the "international community" that, in fact, are in the interests of the dominant classes. Great powers forward certain ideas, think of various "civilizing missions," as justification for policies intended to further their own interests. To the extent that the subordinate states accept these ideas, the ideology propagates their subordination. When scholars like Ajami, Vatikiotis, and Kedourie refer to Arabism, for instance, they typically portray the ideology as an instrumental idea in the hands of self-interested leaders. Arabism depends on the prior material interests of Arab states—that is, governments—and its sole function is to further those interests and to make their continued domination acceptable to lesser powers.

Academic discussions about identity have become increasingly fashionable since the 1970s because of attempts to understand how individuals occupy social locations that are not reducible to material structures, how these locations generate action, and how they can be altered. In contrast with ideology studies that attempt to understand how language masks social reality and occludes *real* inter-

---

[20] Trevor Pervis and Alan Hunt, "Discourse, Ideology, Discourse, Ideology, Discourse, Ideology . . . ," *British Journal of Sociology* 44, no. 3 (September 1993): 474–75.

[21] Ibid.

ests, many studies of identity begin with the function of language in constituting social subjects and their relations.[22] Studies of identity, therefore, take pains to demonstrate how interests are not objectively derived but rather are socially constructed and dependent on historically bounded social roles occupied by knowledgeable actors.

Scholars of international relations and the Middle East who favor the concept of identity over ideology, therefore, begin with a very different view of social reality. These scholars, including those in this volume, are interested in understanding how a historically constructed concept of Arab identity, for instance, leads to certain interests and practices. Such study acknowledges that the social forces that shape identity and conceptions of group boundaries are susceptible to change at rare moments. Further, these forces can lead to different interpretations of the interests that define the nation or state, and changes in the underlying normative structures shape state action in particular ways. In general, students of ideology and identity typically begin with very different view of social reality and thus expect their concepts to do very different sorts of analytic work.

But how might we explain national and state identity formation? While scholars of international relations have not spent much time discussing the emergence of national identities, the field has been highly mined by scholars of comparative politics. As Steve Saideman notes in the concluding chapter, primordial views of nationalism have fallen out of favor and variants of constructivism are widely accepted. Although some politicians and political activists might offer a primordial view of identity to create firm boundaries between otherwise fluid categories, at best this simply represents their attempt to construct ideational boundaries using criteria that are deemed primordial and essential. The history of the region—and the history of all nationalism—reveals a debate over what constitutes national or state identity. The contributors to this volume attempt to uncover this social construction process and note that national identity is rarely hegemonic; in fact, at best it merely receives a reprieve from assaults from alternative definitions. We are interested, for example, in explaining why Egypt became the "United Arab Republic" in the 1950s and why it changed into the "Arab Republic of Egypt" in the 1970s. How do we understand the movement in Jordan away from a pan-Arab identity and toward a territorial-nationalist identity? Why did Arab nationalism trump a strong Syrian nationalist movement in the pre-1970s?

Since our primary interest is in the causal relationship between identity and foreign policy, we are not aiming to forward a theory of identity formation. In-

[22] See Pervis and Hunt, "Discourse, Ideology, Discourse, Ideology, Discourse, Ideology . . . ," and Rogers Brubaker and Frederick Cooper, "Beyond Identity," *Theory and Society* 29, no. 1 (2000): 1–47.

stead, we hope that by addressing the sources of political identity, we identify possible causes of winning identities. Nor are we aspiring to identify a master cause for the emergence of a particular national identity. No single explanation can account for the emergence of a particular national identity. Saideman charts the three primary sources of political identity, so we need only summarize them here as power elite/instrumental forces, societal forces, and international forces.

Power elite and instrumental arguments have long been popular, contending that nationalism is manufactured and manipulated by politically savvy and power-hungry political elites. Variants of these arguments have been quite influential in Middle Eastern scholarship, particularly in explanations of the rise of Arabism and its association with urban notables and the State elite.[23] But even the most die-hard instrumentalists typically incorporate other factors in their analyses and recognize an existing cultural fabric that is available for manipulation. Astute politicians understand that not all identities are equally plausible or politically desirable and thus tailor their message so that it manipulates what already exists.

In contrast to instrumentalist arguments that typically rely on a top-down approach, societal explanations suggest bottom-up factors. Sometimes governmental leaders are caught off-guard by an undertow of nationalism. This has been evident in various places where Arab leaders were late to recognize Arabism's emerging presence, cultivated by social movements, political activists, intellectual undercurrents, and new ideas. This societal dimension also is evident where both state and societal groups agree on a national identity but differ over its meaning and expectations. This is famously demonstrated in several instances in the Arab Middle East, where the palace or government articulated one vision of Arab nationalism while the streets advocated an alternative. During the 1950s the young King Hussein thought himself to be protectively wrapped in the symbols of Arab nationalism, only to find that various societal groups demanded a more radical version, leaving him isolated at home. Upon coming to power in Egypt in 1970, Sadat attempted to bolster Egypt's Islamic identity for political reasons, only to discover that religious groups violently opposed his version of that identity.

Finally, international factors can shape national identity. Sometimes the international system is simply a catalyst for local discussions and debates. The ends of empires are typically associated with wide-ranging debates over the boundaries of the political community.[24] The collapse of the Ottoman Empire triggered a region-wide debate over what would fill the power vacuum. The end

---

[23] Kedourie, "Chatham House Version."

[24] Charles Tilly, "States and Nationalism in Europe, 1492–1992," *Theory and Society* 23 (1995): 131–46.

of the Cold War and the demise of the Soviet Union similarly instigated a discussion over the boundaries of the region and its various components, including a Mediterranean community, a Middle Eastern community, an Arab community, and a pan-Turkic community. At other times the effects of the international system are more direct. For example, debate continues over whether nationalism in the Third World and the Middle East represents the export of a Western political form. Forms of colonialism and imperialism have triggered a domestic backlash and caused a growing demand for national self-determination. Contemporary globalization, particularly forms that are viewed as containing elements of Western culture, has precipitated a defense of local cultures that are supposedly threatened. This response is most closely associated with the emergence of certain strands of Islamism. "Great Power" intrusions have a history of forcing discussions concerning the boundaries of the political community. For instance, during the Cold War the attempt by the West to pressure Arab countries to subscribe to its containment policy fanned the flames of Arab nationalism, most famously in the case of the Baghdad Pact.

We conclude with two points. First, we are unlikely to find a monocausal explanation of state or national identity formation. And we are not aiming for one here. At best we are likely to find that certain explanations dominate in a particular region or for a particular period. This rather mundane conclusion is supported by the contributions here. Second, we are unlikely to find a single master variable operating in any one case. Although one variable is likely to account for a greater part of the story, additional factors usually influence the outcome. All of the contributors to this volume recognize the mixture of factors that affect development of a particular national identity at a particular time.

The Menu of Choices of "National Identities" in the Middle East

Even those who emphasize the power of rulers in shaping identities acknowledge that the menu of options is limited. One does not have to take a primordial view of identity to recognize that there are limited, historically contingent possibilities. Neither of us is likely to adopt a "North American" identity in the foreseeable future. Nor can we imagine the emergence in contemporary Israeli or Arab politics of a mass movement favoring a "Middle Eastern" identity. The contemporary possibilities in the Middle East are limited by history and have typically revolved around one of three influences: statism, Islam, and Arabism. In contrast to the histories of nationalism in many other parts of the world, in the Middle East some of the most viable alternatives have been transnational. This dynamic is best understood as a result of several factors—the emergence of a Germanic definition of nationalism (one that views language as an essential characteristic of nationalism), widening networks of association, and the external effects of colonialism, imperialism, and Zionism. In Israeli politics identity largely has been limited to different strands of Zionism, though in this supposedly post-Zionist age religious and secular identities vie for contention.

Few subnational groups have successfully contended to define the national identity. One principal exception has been the Kurds in Iraq; other notable efforts include the contemplation of a small "Christian/Maronite" state in Lebanon and the Arab/non-Arab division (north/south) in the Sudan. We do not mean to suggest that subnational identities have not been important factors in the emergence of a particular national identity, however. In Syria and Iraq, for example, the advocacy of an Arab identity over an Islamic identity may suit Allawites, Christians, and Druze Syrians, who cannot hope to advance their own subnational identities for the state but who have quickly latched onto those transnational or national identities because they were viewed as more accepting and protective of their minority status. This highlights how the choice of a national identity is not only an expression of affective and emotional allegiances but also an instrumental feature of associational politics.

The practical possibilities for national-state identities are, perhaps, more limited. In contemporary Middle Eastern politics the state has gained the upper hand and is increasingly viewed as legitimate by its society. One consequence of the state's institutionalization and legitimation is that rival views of the national identity have attempted to fix a meaning of the identity that accommodates their own vision of the legitimate political community. A saga in Egyptian politics, nicely surveyed by Ibrahim Karawan, involves national identity and its inclusion of Islamic and Arab associations. Egypt's saga has become part of the drama of the region as a whole. In many other Arab states the contemporary debate has not focused on a state-national identity versus Arabism but on the meaning of state that has a territorial-national identity *and* an Arab identity. Even when Anwar Sadat changed Egypt's name from the United Arab Republic to the Arab Republic of Egypt, he kept the Arab identity in the name. Another telling example of this duality was the PLO's conception of self after the 1982 Israeli invasion of Lebanon. A Saudi student's letter to the editor of *Falastine Althawra*, the central organ of the PLO, requested an explanation for the choice of Cyprus as the center for Palestinian publications and asked: "Why did you not choose an Arab state as your center, as we all would have expected? . . . I had not expected that the PLO would be so ungrateful for all the aid provided to it by the Arabs . . . especially since the liberation of Palestine is the primary Arab concern." The editor's reply was telling. "The PLO is not ungrateful," the editor replied. "The deposits of one Arab state in the United States provide a sufficient budget for the liberation of Palestine in a year. Payment in blood cannot be compared with monetary payments. This revolution is indeed Arab, but Palestinian decisions shall remain independent regardless of the cost." Yet the same *Falastine Althawra*, in considering the debate on Qawmiyya (Arab nationalism) vs. Wataniyya (statism) concluded in its leading article that the Palestinian considers himself "first Arab, second Arab and third Palestinian."[25]

The discussion of a "menu of choice" might suggest that these identities are exclusive and therefore are incapable of being melded. But that clearly is not so, especially in the Middle East. As most students of nationalism and identity politics have observed, individuals, nations, and states can hold multiple identities; in fact, sometimes these identities can be integrated in a relatively harmonious way. For many Egyptians at various times being an Egyptian and an Arab nationalist was smoothly accomplished and did not unleash any identity conflicts. Sometimes this could lead to a national chauvinism—what is good for Egypt is good for the Arab world—but sometimes it could mean that the Arab national identity would help define what it meant to be an Egyptian. At other times it makes more sense to think of a hierarchy of identities, one that constitutes the core and others that are "activated" during certain social situations and do not undermine the pillar.

The history of the region, however, suggests that these identities sometimes conflict because certain environmental developments force actors to choose between demands imposed by one identity and those imposed by another. In this respect, states can have an "identity conflict,"[26] which is likely to emerge under two conditions. The first is whenever competing definitions of the collective identity call for contradictory behaviors, or roles. Thus, identity conflict might be seen to exist

> when there are contradictory expectations that attach to some position in a social relationship. Such expectations may call for incompatible performances; they may require that one hold two norms or values which logically call for opposing behaviors; or they may demand that one [identity] necessitates the expenditure of time and energy such that it is difficult or impossible to carry out the obligations of another [identity].[27]

Identity conflict can also exist whenever definitions of the "collective self are no longer acceptable under new historical conditions."[28] In other words, a crisis might emerge whenever the state's collective identity (or the debate over that identity) is at odds with the demands and defining characteristics of the broader

---

[25] See Shibley Telhami, "The Evolution of Palestinian Sovereignty," in *Problematic Sovereignty*, ed. Stephen Krasner (New York: Columbia University Press, 2001).

[26] Lowell Dittmer and Samuel Kim, "In Search of a Theory of National Identity," in *China's Quest for National Identity* (Ithaca: Cornell University Press, 1993): 6–7.

[27] Sheldon Stryker, *Symbolic Interactionism: A Social Structural Perspective* (Reading, Mass.: The Benjamin/Cummings Publishing Company, 1980): 73.

[28] Dittmer and Kim, "In Search of a Theory of National Identity," 7.

community (which represents an additional source of the state's identity). This possibility has been noted by various scholars of the Middle East, who have characterized these moments of competing expectations and internal debate as "role conflicts."[29] Although a menu of choice might exist, the categories inherent in the choice might be blurred and interpolated in new ways, might be arranged hierarchically, and might occasionally conflict.

The Difference Identity Makes: How Identity Affects Foreign Policy

Ultimately, our aim is to discuss the link between identity and foreign policy. Therefore, the central question is: Does the introduction of identity inform us about the foreign policies of Middle Eastern states in ways that we otherwise would not understand them? Simply put, what difference does identity make? Is it possible that the debate concerning identity, important within the state, is not especially relevant for the foreign policies of states? Although we believe that identity must be added to the mix, we would be remiss if we did not discuss the rival hypothesis, that identity is parasitic on material structures, which has in fact been the null hypothesis.

Perhaps scholars have had difficulty evaluating, and even conceptualizing, the possibility that identity might shape foreign policy because of the strength of existing theoretical dispositions. The typical realist proposition is about the dominance of calculations of the "national interest" (or, more accurately put, focuses on calculations of regime survival) in the pursuit of foreign policy, over all other considerations, including ideological ones. The notion, for example, that Arab unity was the central factor driving Nasser's foreign policy or the foreign policies of Ba'thist Syria and Iraq in the 1960s has been eloquently refuted by Malcolm Kerr, who showed the central weight of self-interest. But to say that most foreign-policy issues force such trade-offs on politicians, or that a state's national interests are the same in nearly all cases where survival is at stake, would be highly inaccurate.[30] Even if one envisioned pan-Arabism as an instrument of policy for Nasser, we still have to ask why it was such a useful instrument. A convincing answer must refer to the prevalent societal norms that made this issue resonate.

Scholars also have tended to pose their research questions and to organize their research designs to answer the following question: Do identities or interests shape the state's foreign policy? Among the various problems conjured by this formulation, we see two as most central. The first is that sophisticated realists and neore-

---

[29] Michael Barnett, "Nationalism, Sovereignty, and Regional Order in Arab Politics," *International Organization* 49, no. 3 (summer 1995); Korany, "Egypt," in *Echoes of the Intifada*, ed. R. Brynen (Boulder, Colo.: Westview Press, 1991): 195–214.

[30] Malcolm Kerr, *The Arab Cold War* (New York: Oxford University Press, 1970).

alists recognize that interests are not driven by brute material forces; therefore, their conception of interests often includes references to ideational factors. A second problem is that this formulation fails to recognize that identities can be a source of interests. Therefore, posing the question as interests vs. identities is misleading.[31] Scholars of the region have recognized that identity can be an important source of the state's national interest. This phenomenon is most evident where an Arab state rarely refers to the state's interest but rather to the Arab national interest, which presumably comes from a transnational Arab nation and not from the territorially defined state. Only by noting how Arabism shapes the Egyptian national interest are we able to explain many significant foreign-policy events, including its intervention in Yemen in the 1960s or its unity with Syria. Conversely, a pan-Arabist Egypt could not have made bilateral peace with Israel. Marc Lynch argues that changes in the Jordanian national identity shaped the definition of the Jordanian national interest. The national identity is an important source of the state's interest.

Similar examples of the relationship between national identity and foreign-policy orientation are readily available. Consider the transformation of the Palestinian priority once the PLO was recognized as a national movement. As a movement aiming to bring Palestinian refugees justice and a return to Palestine, the PLO had interests that were mutually exclusive with Israel's interests: a Palestinian return would undermine Israel's Jewish majority and thus the state's Jewish identity. Becoming a national movement, however, transformed the PLO's aims, catapulting its goal of establishing a state over its original goal of reclaiming Palestine. One implication of this transformation was a decrease in the use of violence as an instrument of policy.[32]

Still, any conclusion regarding the significance of viewing "identity" as a variable in foreign policy rests on whether such an approach enhances our understanding of outcomes. This book goes some distance in substantiating this claim. But we want to suggest a cautious approach to the identity-as-variable perspective. Saying that we are interested in understanding the difference that identity makes does not mean that we that we see identity as being fixed. This view begins with the notion that identity can be treated as a variable, can take on different values, and can be accurately measured on some scale. Then it attempts to establish an association between changes in the independent variable of identity and changes in the dependent variable—for instance, foreign-policy orientation. In this example, a typical hypothesis is that the more pan-Arab the Arab state, the more antipathy and conflict it will express toward Israel. This was, in fact, the sort of hypothesis that has been typically forwarded to test the claim that Arab nationalism affects

[31] Wendt, *Social Theory of International Politics*, chapter 3.
[32] Telhami, "The Evolution of Palestinian Sovereignty."

inter-Arab and Arab-Israeli dynamics. Although this approach generates clear, testable hypotheses, it has at least two serious epistemological flaws.

The first is that identity has a constitutive and not a causal standing in the positivist sense. By asking a constitutive question, as John Ruggie quipped, we are interested in what makes the world hang together, or, as Alexander Wendt put it, "how are things in the world put together so that they have the properties they do."[33] Explanation is not mere description since understanding the constitution of things does essential work in explaining how those things behave and what causes outcomes. As Barnett and Finnemore observe: "[U]nderstanding how the double helix DNA molecule is constituted materially makes possible causal arguments about genetics, disease, and other biological processes."[34] Similarly, understanding how national identity is constituted allows us to make certain claims regarding what is possible. In other words, constitutive claims do not attempt law-like statements such as: If X happens, then Y must follow. Constitutive claims regarding identity and foreign-policy outcomes, therefore, will not proffer a one-to-one relationship between identity and behavior. Instead, we should consider how a particular identity makes certain kinds of state behavior possible or probable, and why.[35] To say that the shift in Egypt's identity from Arabist to statist made possible the Camp David accords is not to say that all Arab states with a statist identity will make peace with Israel. Rather, the Arab identity as previously inscribed had treated peace with Israel as nearly taboo, and the shift toward a state-national identity made peace with Israel thinkable. To write, as Barnett does in this volume, that a shift from a revisionist to a liberal Zionist identity makes a territorial compromise with the Palestinians possible does not mean that it will happen. To say that an Islamic identity makes an alliance with the West difficult is not to say that it is inconceivable. We should avoid slipping into deterministic claims when probabilistic statements are warranted.

Second, we need to know more about how particular identity claims are inscribed with different meanings at different historical moments. As many have argued, Arabism has been associated with different historical projects during the past century, and to presume that Arabism has one particular meaning—for instance, unification—misses the central fact that Arabism has been attached to different projects at different moments. Arabism has had different meanings for different actors at different times—in fact, a central debate in Arab politics has concerned the

[33] John Ruggie, "What Makes the World Hang Together," *International Organization* 52, no. 3 (1998): 855–86; Alexander Wendt, "Constitution and Causation in International Politics," *Review of International Studies* 24, no. 4 (1998): 101–17.

[34] Michael Barnett and Martha Finnemore, "The Politics, Power, and Pathologies of International Organizations," *International Organization* 53, no. 4 (autumn 1999): 701.

[35] Wendt, "Constitution and Causation in International Politics."

meaning of Arabism.[36] Therefore, we need to be attentive not only to how deeply felt is the Arab identity in relationship to alternatives but also to the shifting of meanings and practices attached to that identity. The same can be said of Islam.

This imposes the additional demand that we move away from an either-or view of national identity. As many students of the Middle East have recognized, national identities can be fluid and entangled in different ways. Though it is tempting to assume that national identities are mutually exclusive and have clearly differentiated boundaries, and Middle Eastern politics suggests that national identities are more fluid than frequently acknowledged.[37] Even those who emphasize the role of elites in shaping identity believe that identity changes, though they typically perceive it as a dependent variable. This observation reinforces our earlier point about the possibility of multiple identities. Indeed, the chapter contributions are rife with examples of the fluidity of identity politics, the capacity of national and corporate identities to morph and to interpolate with one another.

The Information Revolution, Collective Identities, and Regional Politics

One obvious way in which the Middle East differs from most other regions is that the national identity has had a transnational character. Indeed, one of the striking features of the Middle East has been a reversal in the archetypical modernist assumption regarding the movement of identity from highly localized to more transnational settings. Changes in material factors, including technology and economic exchange, increased density of interactions; these interactions, in turn, made possible the widening and deepening of mutual identification. Beginning with the pioneering work of Benedict Anderson, the field of international studies now recognizes that the evolving national imagery was made possible because of changing material conditions and expanding information networks. Although a matter of considerable debate, the factors that generated Arab political consciousness can be briefly enumerated. One factor was the common Arab language, which provided not only the media of communication but also nascent symbols of identity (particularly as they pertained to Islam). The introduction of new print and media technologies made it possible to communicate to all Arab-speaking audiences for the first time. The new political vocabulary of nationalism flowered in the late nineteenth century and then got a caffeinated injection from colonialism and Zionism; these represented the threats upon which all nationalism thrives.

State-centered nationalism competed evenly with Arab nationalism as the premier language of political mobilization and protest until just after World

[36] Barnett, *Dialogues in Arab Politics.*
[37] Barnett, "Nationalism, Sovereignty, and Regional Order," 510.

War II. The scales then tipped in favor of Arab nationalism because various seminal events, mainly those revolving around the fight for independence and creation of the Israeli state, signaled to Arab populations that they faced common threats because of their common identity. But perhaps the most important force in creating transnational Arabism was the competition among Arab leaders for political prestige. Arab leaders gained tremendous symbolic and political capital by demonstrating that they were the fiercest defenders of Arabism, demonstrations made possible through new means of communication, most famously radio broadcasts such as Nasser's *Sawt al-Arab* (Voice of the Arabs). Although the historical record suggests that few Arab leaders were genuine champions (at least to the extent that they always were ready to sacrifice for the cause), their symbolic competition on a regional stage left them more accountable to all Arab citizens on issues defined as "Arab." This competition was the root of the regional instability.

Although considerable debate surrounds the reasons for the decline of Arabism and the rise of statism, the state's near monopolization of the means of communication probably contributed to this outcome. Although few studies have demonstrated the salience of this argument, our intuition, anecdotal evidence, and studies of other state-building experiences suggests that control of communications was highly important. More certain is the role that information technologies played in the rise of Islam in general and in the spreading fame of particular clerics. In the 1970s Khomeini was able to spread his message from his sanctuary in Paris to his growing followers in Iran through cassette tapes. These tapes were easily copied and smuggled across borders, as the Iraqi and other Arab Gulf governments discovered to their collective horror. Information technologies have grown much more sophisticated and more widely available in the Middle East since the late 1970s with the advent of videotapes, pirate satellite cable stations, and web-based technology.[38]

The end of Arabism can be observed not only in the shift in discourse—that is, the watering down of Arabism and the growing references to Islam and the state—but also in a changing pattern in inter-Arab politics. Specifically, once Arab leaders no longer found it useful to compete over the symbols of Arabism (largely because these symbols had lost resonance with their populations), their interactions began to stabilize around sovereignty norms, and the regional state system began to resemble other regional systems. This shift led to debates among inhabitants regarding whether the change was good; many of the debates focused on what was left of Arabism, the concept of Middle Easternism, and the normalization of Israel. Once again, the debates took place not only on a national stage but also on a regional stage.

[38] See Dale Eikelman and Jon Anderson, eds., *New Media in the Muslim World* (Bloomington: Indiana University Press, 1999).

Likewise, the 1990s information revolution in the Middle East affected collective identities in the region. Although states remained dominant players in the information arena in much of the region, actors outside the state and market forces driven by intense competition for audience attention challenged states' capacity to control information even on core political issues. In particular, the proliferation of satellite technology altered the viewing habits of much of the Middle East and gave some newspapers an edge over others. The proliferation of the Internet among elites (for now) has been another growing influence. Most important, ease of access and lower costs have led to the emergence of many competing sources of information, often not directly controlled by the government, and sometimes driven by commercial, not political, interests. This increased competition has drawn more attention to market considerations in attracting audiences for political or commercial purposes.

The information "market" in the Arab world has been defined by one central factor: language. Arabic defines the maximal size of the market and differentiates the regional from the global media. *Al-Hayat* newspaper, out of London, Al-Jazira satellite TV out of Qatar, and ART TV out of Rome all attempt to reach the widest Arabic market. Although they have links to specific states, their target is mostly outside these states. To secure the largest audience among Arabs, they cater to Arab tastes and interests, not uniquely Egyptian, Saudi, or Qatari tastes. And although some, especially Al-Jazira, have begun addressing controversial domestic issues in the Arab world, most focus on issues involving common Arab interests, especially in the foreign policy arena, and Arab-Israeli issues. Granted, some programs and media outlets cater to local tastes in the Arab world. But the dominant media typically cover the entire Arabic-speaking audience in the region (and beyond, for many of these outlets produce broadcasts and publications for the Arab population in North America and Europe).

This trend arguably is creating an increasingly common world view in the Arab world, especially on foreign policy questions. Although the media are not harmonious and do not have uniform agendas, their market orientation and need to focus on common interests within the market are shaping a more common regional perspective.

How is this consequential? One example may have been the common elite and public reaction to the Doha conference on multilateral Arab-Israeli cooperation in 1996, after the election of Benjamin Netanyahu as prime minister of Israel. Universal opposition to this conference among elites across the region, perpetuated by a common position in the "new media," may have been the reason for Saudi and Egyptian opposition to it despite U.S. pressure. Obvious historical parallels exist between this development and the emerging focus by various Arab newspapers on Arab issues revolving around Palestine and colonialism during the 1930s and 1940s. During this period the emergence of an Arab political consciousness enabled individuals to mobilize more easily along issues that had come to be defined as threatening the interests of all Arabs regardless of their citizenship.

We see other spillover possibilities from the framing of discrete events and issues as Arab. Some possibilities are negative to the extent that they can be the harbingers of regional instability. To suggest that citizens across the Arab Middle East might be mobilized along an Arab identity for issues defined as central to all Arabs suggests the growth of an Arab identity that might, once again, encourage Arab leaders to compete with each other over these politically valuable symbols. Whether this competition would lead to a repetition of the regional instability that haunted Arab politics during the 1950s and 1960s is an open question. But we are doubtful because Arab states have greater legitimacy now, thus making it less likely that Arab leaders would need to rely on the prop of Arab nationalism to manufacture their legitimacy. More important, symbols of Arabism have changed, especially with the emerging Arab-Israeli peace and the absence of expectations of unity among Arab states.

Could this growing mutual identification around Arab issues have positive spillover consequences? A recurring claim (dare we say hope?) among pan-Arabists is that these material changes will produce a vibrant and self-sustaining Arab nationalism. It is difficult for us to see the information revolution alone resuscitating any drive for political integration among Arab states. Serious discussions concerning political unification are a thing of the past. But it is quite possible that mutual identification could sustain conversations regarding economic and political cooperation. For example, secular governments in the region may find it difficult to confront the Islamist challenge individually but may see in the new collective self-consciousness in the Arab world (which is largely led by a secular media) a foundation for a new ideology and alliances, especially following an Arab-Israeli peace.[39]

We only can speculate about the future link among changes in information technologies, shifts in group boundaries, and regional dynamics because of historical precedents. The regionally specific point is that scholars of the Middle East have long considered the relationship between identity and foreign policy and will continue to do so. Sometimes the identity in question is Arab, at other times, Islamic. By examining the complex relationship among informational networks, domestic political and economic practices, transnational forces, and interstate interactions, they understand how the emergence of a national and state identity contributes to foreign policy and to regional dynamics. The more general point is that the Middle East provides an important reservoir for theorizing and for contributing to broader debates in international relations. Rather than constructing hypotheses and theories that derive from recent experiences and processes, theorists should be drawn to the Middle East for the obvious reason that we have a century of experiences.

[39] Telhami, "Power, Legitimacy, and Peace-making."

Overview of the Chapters

This volume contains studies of six countries: Egypt, Syria, Iraq, Iran, Jordan, and Israel.[40] The first three of these cases represent leaders of the pan-Arab movement in the 1950s and 1960s and thus provide excellent examples of the relevance of transnational identity. Iran provides the most dramatic case of the revival of Islamic political identity in the region in the 1970s and 1980s. Israel and Jordan represent two states whose identity was linked to an important territory, the West Bank, and more broadly, to the dominant Palestinian issue. But these cases can be grouped not only in terms of different historical dimensions and relationship to different transnational and subnational projects; they also can be organized along different theoretical claims regarding the relationship between identity and foreign policy.

Two of the authors (Barnett and Lynch) fit broadly into a constructivist view of identity that sees the cultural context of the state as defining the boundaries of what governments can entertain. Karawan and Dawisha place the weight of explanation on ruling elites whom they see as able to construct identities in ways that best suit their interests. Maloney situates herself between constructivist and instrumental approaches, noting a recursive process whereby Iran's post-revolutionary leaders were both constituted by and appropriated a religious identity for reasons involving both self-understanding and power. Sadowski emphasizes process, both internal (modernization) and external (interactions with other states) as shaping the state's identity. We have a range of historical cases and theoretical approaches.

In chapter 2, Marc Lynch sees the rise of a dominant Jordanian identity for the Hashemite Kingdom of Jordan that stems from several key factors—public debate involving rival Arabist, Palestinian, and Jordanian identity frames, the definition of what "Jordanian" identity is not, and the strategic interests of the Jordanian state itself, particularly in defending its vulnerable sovereignty. By engaging "both rationalist and constructivist theoretical approaches," Lynch focuses "on the role of domestic and international public spheres in shaping the strategic contestation of identity and interests." Lynch does not regard identities to be in a postmodern state of constant flux; rather, he sees collective identities—state and national—as relatively stable over time, most often changing only when domestic and/or international crises occur. For Lynch, state identity is a key component in the articulation of national interests in foreign policy, and the foreign-policy realm "serves as a particularly potent symbolic battlefield for defining state identity," as well as a rival to existing material interests of the state.

[40] We would like to thank Jennifer Skulte for preparation of excellent background materials and for helping prepare the summaries.

Barnett argues in chapter 3 that in politicized, democratic Israel, where state identity is highly contested and foreign-policy issues are central to political and societal debates, foreign policy and state identity are linked intricately and dynamically. Barnett makes the following claims: First, national identity does not cause behavior but rather makes some behavior possible and legitimate and others not so. Second, to understand how this historical process is constructed at a particular moment requires consideration of the relationship between ideational and institutional variables; ideational variables include the related concepts of identity, historical narratives, and frames, while the institutional variables refer to the political and electoral system. Third, actors strategically attempt to shift the cultural landscape in order to make possible and to legitimate certain foreign-policy actions, and they do so within a political-institutional context. Barnett explores this conceptual architecture in the context of Rabin's efforts to legitimate the Oslo peace process and the ideological response by his critics and Netanyahu to that process.

In chapter 4, Suzanne Maloney argues that identity plays both a "constructivist" and a utilitarian role in shaping Tehran's international agenda. On the one hand, Iranian identity is a multidimensional force emanating from the country's lengthy historical tradition and geo-strategic influence that bears remarkable continuity despite the upheaval of the past two decades. Even so, the adoption of explicitly religious rhetoric and policy goals since the Islamic Revolution has steered Iran's foreign policy; the imagery of a transnational Muslim cause has been invoked to legitimize the ambitions of the clerical leaders, who have established ideological "red lines" that constrain Tehran's present and future choices. At its most basic level, the Islamic Revolution represented a bid to reconstruct the Iranian identity, and the continuing differences within the leadership thrust identity and foreign policy to the center of a fractious struggle for power.

Dawisha contends in chapter 5 that the emergence of a dominant Arab identity in Iraq is largely due to manipulation by the political elite of the history of the territory and people—a history that includes cities in modern Iraq that were renowned Arab centers of their time. Significant tension exists between Iraqi identity and the predominant Arab one, however, which can be seen over time in the domestic and international politics of the country. Iraqi President Saddam Hussein and his associates have been able to choose from among the "various and competing identities [of Iraq]" and take advantage of the "countless opportunities to define and redefine the country's identity in accordance with their own interests and the dictates of policy at any given time." In sum, Dawisha places his views on state identity somewhere between the constructivist and primordial theories and believes that political leaders, while unable to impose an identity that does not resonate with their public, nevertheless choose from a variety of identities that are acceptable to their societies. As such, Dawisha believes that political elites have a central role in defining and redefining state identity, especially where the state predominates.

In chapter 6, Sadowski maps out in the case of Syria what many scholars have observed to be a pattern in Arab politics in general: the increasing strength of state identity. He sees the historical emergence of a proto-Syrian identity as the dominant state identity and, increasingly, the national identity as well. While pan-Arabism continues to be both the official identity of the state and to have some resonance among the various groups and classes in Syria, its dominance has declined since peaking in the 1970s. Sadowski explains this in two ways. First, the processes and effects of modernization in Syria have taken hold, homogenizing the country and enabling a territorial and common cultural identity—a Syrian identity. Second, the interaction of Syria with other states (especially Israel and Lebanon) in the regional state system has strengthened the legitimacy of the state itself apart from the decreasing legitimacy of the Assad regime. The strengthening proto-Syrian and waning pan-Arab identity of Syria affects the country's foreign policy to the extent that national interests have increasingly replaced the transnational interests associated with a weakly institutionalized state and strong pan-Arab identity.

Unlike the other countries discussed in this volume, Egypt can be correctly described as a "nation-state" with a high level of ethnic homogeneity and a historical Egyptian identity. Karawan contends in chapter 7 that while Egyptians at all levels of society hold multiple identities concurrently, the political elite decides on the identity that it wants to predominate. Karawan sees the political elite using identity as a central tool to legitimate foreign policy, but foreign policy itself is often based on more realpolitik calculations. The public affects this process significantly only at times of crisis, when the political elite is not as able to make its desired identity for the state predominate. Also, Egypt's political elite has wanted the country to play a central role in the Arab world since its creation as a modern state. To this end, Egypt's foreign policy often makes important references to the state identity as understood by the political elite and accepted by the public.

Saideman's concluding chapter ties the empirical cases to the major debates on identity and foreign policy. He outlines "four possible relationships between communal identities and foreign policy: no relationship; ethnic conflict inhibits foreign policy; ethnicity serves to construct reality; and finally, ethnic conflict influences foreign policy as strategic politicians attempt to use foreign policy for domestic political purposes." In his analysis of their strengths and weaknesses, he draws on examples from the Middle East to illustrate some of the "questions and puzzles created by the foreign policies of countries in the region." He concludes by raising provocative questions to help structure the debates about identity and foreign policy for the Middle East and beyond.

2. Jordan's Identity and Interests

MARC LYNCH

Jordan offers an important and intriguing case for the study of the relationship between identity and foreign policy.[1] Jordan is a small, weak state with a highly centralized foreign policy system, in a hostile international environment, and so its foreign policy should be expected to be highly conditioned by international power and threat. Many of Jordan's most significant foreign policy decisions cannot be explained convincingly by theories that emphasize such variables, however. Jordan's behavior toward Israel, toward key Arab states, and toward Palestinians exhibits contradictions between imputed strategic interests and publicly avowed identity. Jordan's very existence as a state long clashed with certain versions of Arabism, which suggested that Jordan represented a particularly illegitimate example of colonial divisions of the Arab world. Jordan's attempts to assimilate the West Bank, its competition with the PLO for the right to represent the West Bank, and its decision to sever ties with the West Bank involved both international strategic interaction and deeply contested questions of state identity. Jordan's functional cooperation with Israel clashed with Arabist norms of exclusion. Its foreign-policy choices constitute ongoing answers to a question eloquently posed by Tariq al-Tal: "Is the East Bank a Hashemite state or a Jordanian state?"[2] The salience of identity concerns does not mean, however, that Jordan followed the dictates of identity at the expense of its interests. Jordan's foreign policy can best be explained by incorporating public contestation of identity, in which the interests of the state came to be defined rather than simply pursued.

Identity forms the backdrop to the formation of conceptions of threat, opportunity, and interests. Neither immutable nor infinitely malleable, state identity can change during periods of crisis through public contestation. State

---

[1] The arguments and analysis in this chapter draw on Marc Lynch, *State Interests and Public Spheres: The International Politics of Jordan's Identity* (New York: Columbia University Press, 1999).

[2] Tariq al-Tal, "Legends and Misunderstandings in Jordanian-Palestinian Relations," *al-Siyasa al-Filastiniyya* 12 (Beirut, 1996, in Arabic).

interests cannot simply be derived from identity, any more than they can be directly derived from international structure or economic concerns. Instead, actors come to understand their interests through the process of competitive, public interpretation of collective identity. The debate over identity and international relations in the Middle East, pitting advocates of Islamic or Arab cultural uniqueness against realists who deny any distinctiveness to inter-Arab politics, has often seemed divorced from the robust debates in the wider literature. Recent contributions more directly engage the international relations debates.[3] Telhami's sophisticated instrumentalism places Arabist identity within the context of strategic interaction: Regimes invoke collective identities and norms in a competitive fashion to increase their power in the regional order and to protect themselves against similar bids by their rivals. Barnett places dialogues over regional order at the center of inter-Arab relations, making debates over identity a crucial dimension of power relations. Barnett and Telhami each offer sophisticated readings of the relationship between identity and behavior that draw, respectively, on constructivist and rationalist approaches to international relations. In this chapter I re-examine the case of Jordan, drawing on and extending my earlier work, to demonstrate the role of domestic and international public spheres in shaping the strategic contestation of identity and interests.

This volume's discussion of the paths by which identity affects behavior follows the contours of the rationalist-constructivist debate over the origin and stability of interests. Rationalism generally posits that state identity and interests can be held constant, and that state behavior can be modeled based on these exogenously specified preferences.[4] Rationalists distinguish between preferences—goals that can be determined only exogenously and may be influenced by identity—and strategies chosen by actors in response to the strategic situation and beliefs about the preferences of others. Changing strategies—behavior—does not imply changing preferences. Actors choose among multiple possible identities based on their material self-interest and the context of the

---

[3] Shibley Telhami, "Power and Legitimacy in Arab Alliances," paper presented to American Political Science Association annual meeting, 1994; Michael Barnett, *Dialogues in Arab Politics: Contestations in Regional Order* (New York: Columbia University Press, 1998) and "Identity and Alliances in the Middle East" in *The Culture of National Security: Norms and Identity in World Politics*, ed. Peter Katzenstein (New York: Columbia University Press, 1996): 400–447. Also see F. Gregory Gause III, "Systemic Approaches to Middle Eastern International Relations," *International Studies Review* 1, no. 1 (1999): 12–31.

[4] Jeffrey Legro, "Culture and Preferences in the International Cooperation Two-Step," *American Political Science Review* 90, no. 1 (1996): 118–37. For an overview of rationalist approaches, see Robert Powell and David Lake, eds., *Strategic Choice and International Relations* (Princeton, N.J.: Princeton University Press, 1999).

interaction—in other words, the structure of incentives cause the choice of identity, rather than identity constituting actors' preferences.[5] Therefore, interdependent choice by predefined actors under changing structural conditions, rather than culture or public discourse, drives the translation of identity into interests, behavior, and outcomes. Depending on the level of analysis, then, either "Jordan" or "Jordanians" and "Palestinians" represent coherent collective actors with shared interests; their conflict or cooperation derives from the structure of their strategic interaction.

Constructivism builds on the insight that the interests pursued by strategic actors are informed by identity, in that norms and identities give meaning to social action.[6] The identity of "Jordan" rather than only the behavior of Jordan becomes problematic. As Wendt has argued, before knowing what "we" want, it is necessary to know who "we" are; "we" want certain things and behave in certain ways based on a logic of appropriateness.[7] In the place of methodological individualism, constructivism employs a social ontology, in which deeply constitutive networks of relations and discourse shape actor identities and interests.[8] This is not simply a domestic level theory, since the contestation of identity takes place in both national and international arenas. In Arab politics, the identity of "Arabism" rendered relations among Arab states fundamentally different from relations between Arab and non-Arab states—not just competitive, to be sure, but also constitutively different. The identity demands of Arabism ruled out Israel as a legitimate alliance partner, irrespective of the strategic merits of such a relationship; such an alliance would simply be inappropriate for an Arab state. For constructivists, identities shape the conception of interests both through deep structures of discourse and institutions and through the social process of public contestation.[9] Interests—underlying preferences involving

[5] David D. Laitin, *Identity in Formation: The Russian-Speaking Populations in the Near Abroad* (Ithaca: Cornell University Press, 1998).

[6] Alexander Wendt, "Anarchy Is What States Make of It," *International Organization* 46, no. 2 (1992): 391–425; Wendt, "Collective Identity Formation and the International State," *American Political Science Review* 88, no. 2 (1994): 384–96; Emanuel Adler, "Constructivism: Seizing the Middle Ground," *European Journal of International Relations* 3, no. 3 (1997): 319–63.

[7] James Fearon, "What is Identity (As We Now Use the Word)?" unpublished paper (March 1997); Alexander Wendt, *Social Theory of International Politics* (New York: Cambridge University Press, 1999).

[8] Friedrich Kratochwil and Rey Koslowski, "Understanding Change in International Politics," *International Organization* 48, no. 2 (1994): 215–47.

[9] On the need to incorporate interaction into constructivist approaches, see Jeffrey Checkel, "The Constructivist Turn in International Relations Theory," *World Politics* 50, no. 2 (1998): 324–48. For a useful typology of approaches to preferences, see Masato Kimura and David Welch, "Specifying Interests," *International Studies Quarterly* 42, no. 2 (1998): 213–44.

outcomes—can then change as interaction produces new collective identities. The goal of theory should be to identify those points at which change in preferences is more or less likely, the direction of change, and the significance of such change for subsequent behavior.

This version of constructivism shares the rationalist interest in strategic interaction and accepts that actors pursue their self-interest once it has been defined. This approach departs from rationalism, however, by also considering the constitutive effects of strategically driven behavior. While actors choose certain behaviors to demonstrate their adherence to a strategically useful identity or norm, these may become internalized when maintained over time. Viewed from a traditional, rationalist approach, state policy is *constrained* by institutionalized conceptions of identity: "the King could not ignore the powerful Arabist convictions of the Jordanian street."[10] From a constructivist approach, state preferences are *constructed* through public struggles over identity.

The constructivist hypothesis that state identities can change in the process of interaction should not be conflated with the postmodernist claim that identity is always in flux or easily malleable. Like Barnett in this volume, I argue that identity is subject to change during periods of "identity conflict" in which a formerly stable, collective identity becomes the subject of open political debate during a crisis. Where Barnett generally assumes the existence of a public sphere in which these identities can be openly contested, I argue that the institutional foundations for public discourse should be seen as a crucial variable for a generalizable theory. Introducing the public sphere should better allow constructivists to specify not only the conditions under which identity conflict is likely to produce change in conceptions of interests but also hypotheses about the likely direction of change.

I argue that the relationship between identity and interests is forged in the public sphere, and that the institutional structure of the public sphere shapes the potential for change and continuity in identity and interests.[11] The public sphere refers to those institutional sites in which actors debate political issues before an audience, to identify solutions to common problems. The concept of the public sphere adds balance to the focus on civil society and democratization that characterized Middle East studies in the 1990s.[12] Many of the moves toward democratization in Arab states have been tentative and controlled from above as

[10] For example, see Laurie A. Brand, "Liberalization and Changing Political Coalitions: The Bases of Jordan's 1990–1991 Gulf Crisis Policy," *Jerusalem Journal of International Relations* 13, no. 4 (1991): 1–46.

[11] Craig Calhoun, ed., *Habermas and the Public Sphere* (Cambridge, Mass.: MIT Press, 1992).

[12] See Michael C. Hudson, "Obstacles to Democratization in the Middle East," *Contention* 5, no. 2 (1996): 81–105.

a strategy for regime survival.[13] The public sphere concept better captures the dimension of public discourse and debate, independent of the extent of institutional change. The existence of media is not alone sufficient to constitute a public sphere. For a public sphere to be said to exist, actors must use these media to engage in public arguments. Where the institutional capacity for mediated public discourse exists, actors can invoke competing interpretations of collective identity in the attempt to shape public conceptions of the state's interests. Behavior consistent with and justified in terms of a dominant conception of national identity reinforces that identity. At the same time, opposition groups can strategically deploy avowed identities to publicly challenge the government's interpretation of state interests. A wide range of political identity groups—Transjordanian nationalists, Palestinian nationalists, liberals, Islamists, Arabists, Hashemites—compete to define Jordan's identity and thus to articulate an attendant set of state interests. Non-Jordanian actors also participate in these struggles: Israel, for example, ascribes various identities to Jordan—"Jordan is Palestine" or "Jordan is a tacit ally"—and acts toward Jordan on the basis of these assumed identities and interests. The state mediates between overlapping domestic and international debates.

The Arab case offers an important example of an international system in which state borders do not necessarily bound political public spheres.[14] In the traditional understanding of the public sphere as it emerged in Europe, the public sphere was composed of citizens engaged in rational–critical discourse aimed at influencing state policy. In an international context, public discourse aims to affect both state policies and international public opinion. An inter-Arab public sphere has long coexisted with and often overwhelmed domestic public spheres.[15] Where Arab public spheres dominate state public spheres, collective identities and interests tend to take an Arabist form; as Barnett demonstrates, this does not end competition between Arab states but rather establishes the terms of that competition. Only when Jordan developed an active and compelling domestic public sphere could Jordan's interests be articulated openly in terms of Jordanian identity. Where state repression prevents domestic discussion of identity, public contestation is often displaced into international outlets that cannot easily be repressed or controlled. When the state finds itself forced

[13] For discussion of this point in the Jordanian case, see Quintin Wiktorowicz, "Civil Society as Social Control: State Power in Jordan," *Comparative Politics* 33, no. 1 (October 2000): 43–61; Malik Mufti, "Elite Bargains and the Onset of Political Liberalization in Jordan," *Comparative Political Studies* 32, no. 1 (1999): 100–129.

[14] Marc Lynch, in "The Dialogue of Civilizations and International Public Spheres," *Millennium* 29, no. 2 (2000): 307–30, discusses the development of international public sphere theory.

[15] Lynch, *State Interests and Public Spheres*, and Barnett, *Dialogues in Arab Politics*.

to defend itself in international public spheres, it often first turns to increased repression and denial of the existence of the issue; over time, however, persistent international challenges and tactical state concessions can empower domestic actors and force the issue into the domestic public sphere.[16]

Given the repression and absence of democratic participation in the Arab world, it is important to qualify the argument being made here for the public sphere. Often collective identity formation in Arab states is understood to be primarily unidirectional, as state control of the media imposes official identities from above. Because of the extent of state power, many observers argue that public spheres do not exist in Arab states. This, of course, does not mean that questions about identity do not exist—often, as in the case of the Kurds in Iraq and Turkey, these are the most existential questions of national identity—but rather that state power prevents them from being openly contested. Even a high level of state control does not prevent citizens from subverting official discourse through irony, humor, or noncompliance.[17] My argument is more direct than this ironic subversion, however: An open public sphere offers the structural possibility for public deliberation that might change conceptions of identity and interest. Conditions of uncertainty create demand for communicative action to establish shared norms and expectations. For example, the Palestinian-Israeli agreement in Oslo forced Jordanians and Palestinians to publicly rethink the terms of future coexistence. This does not mean that public discourse will necessarily change identity and interests; often public discourse reinforces the existing consensus rather than producing a new one. This also does not mean that public deliberation will produce change in normatively desirable directions, as supporters of the peace process discovered in the popular resistance to peace treaties with Israel in Egypt and Jordan. Under conditions of uncertainty and fear, public discussion of identity might well lead to polarization and the rise of ethnic or inter-state conflict; research should identify when each outcome is expected.[18]

The need for public justifications and winning arguments means that even private, selfish interests must be presented and defended in generalizable terms

[16] Thomas Risse, Stephen Ropp, and Kathryn Sikkink eds., *The Power of Human Rights* (New York: Cambridge University Press, 1999); and Risse, "Let's Argue! Communicative Action in World Politics," *International Organization* 54, no. 1 (winter 2000): 1–40.

[17] Lisa Wedeen, *Ambiguities of Domination: Power, Rhetoric and Symbols in Contemporary Syria* (Chicago: University of Chicago Press, 1999). For an interesting discussion of public opinion formation in contemporary Syria, see Sadek al-Azm, "The View from Damascus," *New York Review of Books*, June 15, 2000, pp. 70–78.

[18] Jack Snyder and Karen Ballantine, "Nationalism and the Marketplace of Ideas," *International Security* 21, no. 2 (1996): 5–40. For a discussion of why this has not been the case in Jordan, see Lynch, "Jordan's Competing Nationalisms," paper presented to Middle East Studies Association, Chicago, December 1998.

that refer to a shared identity.[19] When actions must be justified before a public, certain kinds of behavior become less likely. Actors can find themselves bound by their public discourse, and conforming to discourse over time can lead to internal adjustment. Jordan, for example, might have wanted to control the West Bank, but it also had to be able to defend its policies in terms of the Palestinian cause and Arab security. The Jordanian army could militarily crush the PLO in 1970, but at the expense of any persuasive claim to represent Palestinians in the international arena. The need for justification acts as a sanction, constraining state behavior, but also constitutes conceptions of appropriate behavior. Over time, the need to meet the demands of Arabist argumentation imposes a consistency on policy that can become internalized, forming a new conception of interests.[20]

Analyzing the relationship between identity and foreign policy requires specifying levels of analysis, the identity of actors, and the relationship between identity and interests.[21] A focus on *communal* identity suggests that ethnic, religious, tribal, or other subnational groups hold identities that embody distinctive foreign-policy interests, rendering any discussion of a single national interest untenable (see Dawisha, this volume). Jordanians of Palestinian and Transjordanian origin would therefore differ in predictable and observable ways in their foreign-policy preferences. Such communal identities are often assumed to be fixed and coherent and conferring clear and uncontested interests. In Barry Rubin's claim that "the alliance (with Israel) is in the interest of Jordan's ruling 'East Bankers'," both the communal group and its interests are ascribed as fixed and obvious.[22] Constructivist analysis of *state* identity, by contrast, orients toward the conceptions of interests held by state policy makers and embedded in state institutions. Rather than focusing exclusively on domestic sources of identity and interests, this approach includes the effects of international interactions and institutions on state identity and attendant conceptions of interests.[23] Shaped both by domestic political struggles and by international interactions, institutionalized state identity then shapes Jordan's understanding of its role in the regional and international system. *National* identity, finally, suggests a public

[19] This is a key assertion made by Jon Elster's rationalist reconstruction of the public sphere in *Deliberative Democracy* (Chicago: University of Chicago Press, 1998).

[20] Risse, "Let's Argue!"

[21] See *Security Studies* 8, no. 2/3 (winter 1998/99–spring 1999), especially Glenn Chafetz, Michael Spirtas, and Benjamin Frankel, "Tracing the Influence of Identity on Foreign Policy," vii–xxii, and Paul A. Kowert, "National Identity: Inside and Out," 1–34.

[22] Barry Rubin, "Welcome to Jordan," *Jerusalem Post* (April 9, 1998): 6.

[23] Wendt, in *Social Theory of International Politics*, argues that state identities derive from international interactions. In contrast, Peter Katzenstein, *Cultural Norms and National Security* (Ithaca: Cornell University Press, 1996), focuses on the embedding of identities in domestic institutions.

linking of collective identity and the state. At this level of analysis, societal actors and the state engage in ongoing negotiations, in which the state offers only one possible, and not necessarily authoritative, expression of the collective identity.

These distinctions among forms of collective identity stand apart from the common focus on the individual level of analysis. While the personal convictions of the king obviously shape Jordanian foreign policy, he and his advisors are embedded in a larger field of discourse and argumentation about the collective identity of Jordan.[24] When Abdullah replaced Hussein as king, Jordan's identity did not change, even if the new king held different priorities.[25] Policy choices must be explained with reference to the publicly articulated norms, identity, and interests of Jordan. These have proven to be quite resistant to arbitrary redefinition from above; Jordanian popular resistance to the regime's conception of peace with Israel demonstrates the stickiness of these publicly secured collective identities. State identity becomes embedded through public discourse, rituals, shared myths and history, and ideas about the purpose of the state. Foreign policy serves as a particularly potent symbolic battlefield for manifesting state identity, as the means by which a government demonstrates in practice its conception of state identity. Jordanian nationalists, therefore, may meaningfully assert that Jordan holds interests in Arab cooperation and confrontation with Israel that sharply contradict King Hussein and the Jordanian government's official conceptions of the state identity.

The Case of Jordan

Jordan has often lent itself to unreflective assumptions about communal identity. Analysts who would never accept primordialist or essentialist arguments about identity in other contexts are surprisingly tolerant of bloodline conceptions of "Palestinian" or "Jordanian" identity. The assumption that Jordan has a "Palestinian" majority, which has deeply shaped most political analysis of the kingdom, obscures the significant differences among 1948 and 1967 refugees and 1990–91 returnees from the Gulf; refugee camp residents and property owners; rich and poor; intermarriage and family networks. Common debates over whether "Palestinians" make up 30 percent, 50 percent, or 80 percent of

[24] For a comparable approach to Israeli politics, see Michael Barnett, "Culture, Strategy, and Foreign Policy Change: Israel's Road to Oslo," *European Journal of International Relations* 5, no. 1 (1999): 5–36.

[25] For an intriguing discussion of this continuity, see Lamis Andoni, "King Abdallah: In His Father's Footsteps?" *Journal of Palestine Studies* 32, no. 3 (spring 2000): 77–89.

Jordan rely on these unproblematic identity assumptions. Amid profound socio-economic and political differences, as well as differential exposure to Jordanian state institutions, how can we assume a common Palestinian identity in Jordan with a single set of interests? This is not to deny the existence of a Palestinian national identity, but rather to rethink its political implications. Similarly unexamined beliefs about "Bedouin" loyalty to the throne dangerously mislead most attempts at drawing inferences about "Jordanian" foreign-policy preferences, obscuring differences among Bedouin and settled, state employed and private sector, rich and poor, northern and southern tribes. The common focus on the person of the king further obscures attempts to construct arguments about state identity and foreign policy, in that Hussein's personal convictions often demonstrably clashed with the preferences expressed by majorities of the Jordanian political public. Jordan's identity can be seen most clearly in its domestic and international contestation, with definitions emerging from a continuous process of claim and counter-claim, challenge and response.[26] "Jordanian" and "Palestinian" identities have evolved in the course of political interaction, as have conceptions of Jordan's national and state identity. I do not mean to suggest that political identities are constructed solely through discourse; public debates reflect underlying processes of state formation, the emergence of new public sphere forms, state-tribe relations, and the integration of Palestinians.[27]

Although the translation of identity into outcomes depends on the institutional status of the public sphere, different public spheres have emerged as primary in different periods of Jordanian history. Prior to the annexation of the West Bank, the Jordanian press was limited in circulation and vibrancy, commensurate with limited urbanization and low levels of education. After the unification, the West Bank press introduced a significant foundation for public sphere, but this media generally oriented its concerns toward the Arabist public arena. After opposition politics—which drew heavily on this press—led to an abortive coup in 1957, the Jordanian state controlled the media and public debate relatively tightly. Martial law governed public freedoms for a period after 1967, with particularly strong repression in the 1980s.[28] At some points, notably in the mid-1980s, Jordan's public sphere opened up to limited public debate, though the king's intervention to shut down discussion of tribalism in 1985 demonstrates the state's sensitivity.[29] For most of this period, serious questions

[26] For an innovative discussion of the formation of Jordanian identity, see Joseph Massad, "Identifying the Nation: The Juridical and Military Bases of Jordanian National Identity" (Ph.D. dissertation, Columbia University, 1998).

[27] Laurie Brand, "In the Beginning Was the State: The Quest for Civil Society in Jordan," in *Civil Society in the Middle East* 1, ed. A. R. Norton (New York: EJ Brill, 1995): 148–85.

[28] "A Policeman on My Chest, A Scissor in My Brain: Political Rights and Censorship in Jordan." *Middle East Report* (November-December 1987): 30–34.

[29] Linda Layne, in *Home and Homeland: The Dialogics of Tribal and National Identities in Jordan* (Princeton, N.J.: Princeton University Press, 1993), discusses this episode; also see Andrew

about Jordanian identity dominated international discourse, most prominently in the Israeli assertion that Jordan was really Palestine, but were suppressed in the public sphere at home.

The liberalization of 1989 produced not only the freest and most vibrant public sphere since the 1950s, but also arguably the first Jordanian public sphere specifically defined in terms of a Jordanian national identity. The emergence of this Jordanian public sphere enabled the public discourse that shaped and gave content to a new conception of Jordan's identity. The Jordanian press (though not the electronic media) flourished in the early 1990s, building on a relatively liberal law governing press and publications and a remarkable willingness of writers to push boundaries and to place virtually all issues into the public arena. Identity concerns dominated this public debate, with Jordanian-Palestinian relations in particular becoming something of an obsession. After the peace treaty with Israel in 1994, the government began to reassert control over the public sphere, silencing critics and discouraging public debates of "sensitive" topics. The Jordanian public sphere resisted this state incursion, fighting for the recently established right to publicity and criticism, but steadily lost ground in the face of state power. In 1997 the government passed a rather repressive temporary press law, which resulted in the closure of most of the independent weekly press and marked a clear break with the open public sphere of the earlier 1990s.[30] After coming to power, King Abdullah tentatively reopened the public sphere, easing the state-society tension that marked the last years of Hussein's reign. While the application of the press law subsided, the weekly press failed to recapture its central place in the political arena and the daily press regressed, most notably with the reorganization under pressure of the most critical independent Arabic language daily newspaper, al-Arab al-Yom.[31] To the frustration of liberal reformers, who hoped the new king would prove more liberal in his approach to the public sphere, the government of Abd al-Raouf Rawabdeh inclined toward more repressive policies.

Jordan in the Arab Order

Especially in the 1950s and 1960s, contestation of Jordan's identity revolved around the Arab identity of the state. While this has often been understood in

---

Shryock, *Nationalism and the Genealogical Imagination: Oral History and Textual Authority in Tribal Jordan* (Berkeley, Calif.: University of California Press, 1996).

[30] "Clamping Down on Critics," *Human Rights Watch/Middle East* 9, no. 12 (October 1997); Joel Campagna, "Press Freedom in Jordan," *Middle East Report* (spring 1998): 44–48.

[31] Andoni, "King Abdallah"; personal interviews, Samih al-Mayateh, political editor of *al-Arab al-Yawm*, and Nidal Mansour, chief editor of *al-Hadath*, Amman (January 2000).

terms of power politics, Arab identity that was manifested in a vibrant Arab public sphere shaped the interests of state and societal actors across permeable state borders. From its creation, Transjordan faced a conflicted identity, between British visions of an allied buffer state and Abdullah's conception of a minimally acceptable base for the creation of a larger Arab kingdom. Transjordan presented itself as the inheritor of the Great Arab Revolt, with Abdullah's calls for a Greater Syria under Hashemite rule occupying a central place in the politics of Arabism. With the rise of Nasser in the 1950s, the political content of Arabism shifted dramatically toward norms of independence from colonial powers, support for the Palestinian cause, and integrative unity—all of which posed special challenges to Jordan, given its close ties to Britain, its designs on the West Bank, its ongoing contacts with Israel, and its jealous defense of its monarchical regime and its sovereignty.

Arabist challenges to the Jordanian state to demonstrate its Arab identity rendered foreign policy a dramatic symbolic battleground. During the mid-1950s, the Arabist public sphere questioned the legitimacy of the existence of the state of Jordan and urged it to take costly foreign-policy actions to demonstrate its Arabist credentials. Since Jordan identified itself as an Arab state, and significant portions of the political public agreed, this challenge could not be easily denied. Most sectors of the politically aware public, and by no means only the newly naturalized Palestinian citizens, held powerful Arabist convictions. The underdeveloped Jordanian public sphere offered little competition for the nascent Arabist radio and newspapers. As a result, most Jordanians oriented their discourse and their attention toward the Arabist debate. Many Jordanians believed not only that "Jordan could not live long as an independent state" (in the words of the populist Jordanian Prime Minister Sulayman al-Nabulsi), but also that this conviction was congruent with Jordanian patriotism and Arab nationalism. The Jordanian state responded not with a denial of the validity of Arabism but with a counter-frame of Arabism in which its sacrifices and attempts to merge with Palestine should be valued, not condemned.

The turbulent politics of the 1950s revolved around the dual Arabist challenge to borders and domestic order.[32] King Hussein at first responded positively to the nationalist arguments, shifting state policy in response to Arabist identity claims. The Arabization of the army and the dismissal of its British commander, John Bagot Glubb, the decision to not join the Baghdad Pact, and the formation of al-Nabulsi's populist Arabist government all responded to public demands that the Jordanian state live up to its proclaimed Arab identity. While Hussein certainly felt the pressure of the street and of Jordan's Arab com-

[32] Uriel Dann, *King Hussein and the Challenge of Arab Radicalism* (New York: Oxford University Press, 1989).

petitors, the appeal of the Arabist call for independence from the colonial powers had deeply persuasive power for the young king.[33] Hussein, to some extent persuaded of the Arabist identity and the normative value of these risky steps, reached his bottom line at the point where the powers of the throne were at stake—when the challenge shifted from expressing identity through a change in *policy* to expressing identity through a change in *regime*. The defusing of the Free Officers coup attempt in April 1957 and the successful navigation of the 1958 crisis allowed the king to re-establish royal power, close the Arabist-oriented Jordanian public sphere, and assert personal sovereignty over the definition of Jordan's identity and interests.[34] For the rest of the Nasser period, Jordan engaged with Arabist debate over its identity defensively, while forbidding discussion of identity inside the country. This closure of the public sphere to discussion of identity seriously undermined attempts to construct a publicly shared identity binding Palestinian-origin citizens to Jordan.

Jordan clearly preferred the state-centric, private bargaining style of Arab politics in the 1970s and 1980s to the radio wars of the preceding decades. In an Arab order governed by private interactions among leaders that produced public consensus around a lowest-common-denominator policy, Jordan could much better exploit its strategic position based on its relations with the United States and Israel. Because Jordan's positions toward Israel and the Palestinians so often conflicted with the Arabist frame, less public arguing and more private bargaining suited its needs. When Jordan found itself on the losing side of Arab consensus formation, however, it accepted its defeat in order to remain inside the consensus. The most significant example of this preference for consensus over immediate gain is the acceptance of the Rabat summit resolutions in favor of the PLO in 1974. The decision not to join Egypt in the Camp David process also demonstrates this basic preference for remaining within the Arab consensus. Jordan's position in the Gulf War paradoxically supported this interpretation of Jordan's preferences. Because Jordanians believed that the Arab summit resolution did not express an authentic Arabist will, and that support for Iraq represented the real Arab will, rejection of the official Arab consensus was interpreted not as a violation of Jordan's Arabism but as its confirmation.[35]

The peace process and the Gulf War dramatically diminished the primacy of the Arabist public sphere, while introducing new opportunities and threats requiring interpretation. Jordan's developing relations with Turkey and Israel

[33] Massad, in "Identifying the Nation," offers an intriguing interpretation of the conflicting appeal of nationalism to Jordan and to Hussein during this period.

[34] Lawrence Tal, "Britain and the Jordan Crisis of 1958," *Middle Eastern Studies* 31, no. 1 (1995): 39–58.

[35] Lynch, "Abandoning Iraq: Jordan's Alliances and the Politics of Identity," *Security Studies* 8, no. 2/3 (winter 1999-spring 2000): 333–60.

demonstrate both the constant and the changing in the tension between strategic concerns and Arabist identity. In January 1998, Jordan's participation as an observer in Israeli-Turkish naval maneuvers brought loud criticism from Arab states and from the coalition of Jordanian opposition parties. In September 1998, Turkish Prime Minister Masoud Yilmaz visited Amman to discuss political and military relations, immediately after visiting Israel. While Jordanian officials considered its pursuit of closer military relations with Turkey to be a rational response to security threats and opportunities, domestic and regional critics interpreted the new relationship as a violation of Arabism. In the face of united opposition and harsh Syrian criticism, Prime Minister Fayz Tarawneh assured Parliament that "Jordan will never be a party to any alliance with a non-Arab actor."[36] Identity and strategic interests offered diametrically opposed foreign-policy preferences. The logic of the peace treaty with Israel and integration into the American security architecture pointed rather directly toward closer military cooperation with Israel and Turkey. But Syria, Egypt, and other Arab actors strategically deployed the power of Arab identity claims to pressure Jordan against deepening the alliance. The Jordanian opposition, and a wide swath of the public, agreed that an alliance with Turkey and Israel, tacitly or overtly directed against Syria, violated Arab identity and interests. In response to this tension, Jordan hedged its bets pending the fate of the peace process, holding out the prospect of further cooperation while abstaining from formal alliance.

Jordanian-Palestinian Relations

While Arabism questioned the relationship between the Jordanian state and the Arabist regional order, the internal component of state identity represented an even more deeply contested issue.[37] The annexation of the West Bank left Jordan with two distinct national communities with potentially divergent understandings of state identity and interests.[38] The integration of Palestinians into Jordan required an Arabist, non-communal state identity, but the survival of

[36] Tarawneh statement in Parliamentary debate quoted in *al-Arab al-Yawm* (Sept. 27, 1998).

[37] Brand, "Palestinians and Jordanians: A Crisis of Identity," *Journal of Palestine Studies* 24, no. 4 (summer 1995): 46–61; and Brand, *Palestinians in the Arab World* (New York: Columbia University Press, 1988), especially chapter 9. Mustafa Hamarneh et al., *Jordanian-Palestinian Relations: The Internal Dimension* (Amman: Center for Strategic Studies, 1995), offers important survey data on public attitudes. For an inside account of government policies, see Adnan Abu Odeh, *Jordanians, Palestinians, and the Hashemite Kingdom in the Middle East Peace Process* (Washington, D.C.: United States Institute of Peace, 1999).

[38] On the pre-1967 period, see Shaul Mishal, *West Bank/East Bank* (New Haven, Conn.: Yale University Press, 1978).

Jordan as an independent state increasingly required articulation of a unique, nationalized identity. While the Jordanian-Palestinian cleavage was not reinforced by ethnic or religious differences, as in Lebanon or Iraq, the national identity of the communal groups was reinforced both by domestic practices of discrimination and by socioeconomic distinctions. The demands of international argumentation, including the drive for Palestinian national identity and Jordan's need to defend against Arab critics, weighed heavily on these domestic questions. Justifying Palestinian membership in Jordan's identity required Jordan's public engagement in the pursuit of Palestinian interests against Israel, even when these conflicted with Hashemite private interests in cooperation with Israel. Arab and Palestinian efforts to establish a distinctive Palestinian identity embodied in the PLO in the 1960s greatly complicated this conception of Jordan's identity. Jordan found it far more difficult to control these international debates than its domestic political arena, where the often-intense private discussions in political salons rarely filtered into the public sphere. Arab and international actors regularly debated Jordan's identity, despite all Jordanian efforts to remove its internal identity politics from the realm of legitimate international debate.

The 1988 severing of ties with the West Bank, combined with liberalization in 1989, unleashed the first serious public discussion of Jordan's national identity in the Jordanian arena. By the early 1990s, this public deliberation had produced a formal consensus on Jordan's external identity based on the formula of "Jordan is Jordan and Palestine is Palestine," with Jordan defined within East Bank borders. Conceptions of interests shifted in response to this change in identity: Jordan shifted from opposing to supporting a Palestinian state. Palestinian-origin citizens accepted the Jordanization of politics in exchange for the Jordanian state's support for the Palestinian National Authority. The Jordanian state embarked on what Rogers Brubaker terms a "nationalizing project," establishing the discursive and institutional foundations for a new state identity.[39] This changed sense of identity and interests best explains Jordanian positions on a wide range of Palestinian-Israeli final-status issues, including cooperation between Jordan and the PNA and Jordan's outspoken support for a Palestinian state, both contrasting sharply with traditional Jordanian competition with the PLO and opposition to a Palestinian state.

The changing meaning of the idea that "Jordan is Palestine" in international discourse helps to illuminate the complex relationship between struggles over state identity and international strategic interaction. Prior to 1967, Hashemite discourse claimed that "Jordan is Palestine" to justify the assimilation of the

---

[39] Rogers Brubaker, *Nationalism Reframed: Nationhood and the National Question in the New Europe* (New York: Cambridge University Press, 1996).

West Bank. In a classic example of rhetorical self-entrapment, the Hashemites found this slogan turned against them by Palestinian leftist groups: If Jordan was Palestine, then why should they not contest political power in Jordan? Israelis, building on old Revisionist themes, appropriated these inter-Arab arguments after the occupation of the West Bank to suggest that creating a Palestinian state in the East Bank might solve Israel's problems.[40] By the early 1980s, the equivalence between Jordan and Palestine, which had been such an important part of Jordanian argumentation a decade earlier, had become a threat to be fiercely rejected in every setting. Between the 1960s and the 1980s, then, the identity claim that "Jordan is Palestine" changed from a weapon in the hands of the Hashemites against "separatists," to a weapon in the hands of Palestinian leftists against the Hashemites, to a weapon in the hands of the Israelis against the PLO. In response, Jordan's position shifted from an embrace of this international identity to a fierce public repudiation.

The "Jordan is Palestine" controversy demonstrates how Jordan's identity has been deeply interwoven with international debates about Palestinian identity. Prior to 1948, the struggle over the Palestine mandate framed a relatively clear distinction between the Palestinian and Transjordanian entities. While Abdullah looked to Palestine as an outlet for his Greater Syria ambitions, he did not consider Jordan and Palestine to be a single entity, or Jordanians and Palestinians to be a single people.[41] Transjordan lacked a strong nationalist movement during this time, primarily because it lacked the urban centers with the notable classes that tended to produce these movements.[42] The resolutions of the small nationalist conferences of the 1920s demonstrate that Transjordanian actors supported the Palestinian struggle but recognized the distinctiveness of the two arenas.

The annexation of the West Bank reconfigured Transjordan into the Hashemite Kingdom of Jordan. Shared institutions under a unitary constitutional framework were meant to produce a single Jordanian identity. While all citizens were to be considered Jordanian by virtue of citizenship, the repression of expressions of Palestinian identity cast doubt on the voluntarism of this choice. The unitary project was both enhanced and complicated by the Arabist public sphere. The merger could be normatively defended as a successful

[40] Robert J. Bookmiller, "Likud's Jordan Policy," *Middle East Policy* 5, no. 3 (September 1997): 90–104.

[41] Mary Wilson, *Abdullah and the Making of Jordan* (New York: Cambridge University Press, 1987); Joseph Nevo, *King Abdullah and Palestine* (New York: St. Martin's Press, 1996).

[42] Wilson, *Abdullah and the Making of Jordan.* Jordanian nationalist historians contest this description, pointing to National Congresses of the 1920s as evidence of Jordan's national consciousness. Also see Nahid Hattar, *On the Jordanian Arab Issue* (Amman: Dar al-Arabiyya, 1986, in Arabic).

example of Arabist unification, while calls to end it could be dismissed as illegitimate separatism. As Palestinian identity submerged into Arabism in the 1950s and 1960s, this project of merger could be plausibly justified in Arabist terms. Political opposition tended to be cast in Arabist, class or ideological, rather than communal, terms. On the one hand, the dominant conceptions of Arabism discouraged the assertion of any distinctive Palestinian identity, providing Jordan with a powerful justification for incorporating Palestinians on a unitary basis. On the other hand, the perceived illegitimacy of the Hashemite version of Arabism found Jordan always on the defensive in the Arabist public sphere and provided a potent weapon for opponents in their calls for political change.

After discussions of a Palestinian entity in the West Bank and Gaza (that is, at Jordan's expense) in the early 1960s, the formation of the PLO put Jordan's identity directly in play in inter-Arab public discourse. In its early stages, the PLO generally adopted a policy oriented toward Palestinian self-determination in Israel and maintained an uneasy modus vivendi with regard to Jordan's Palestinian population. Jordan would support the PLO as long as the PLO did not challenge the Jordanian identity of its Palestinian citizens. This compromise did not survive the 1967 war. The removal of the West Bank from Jordan's effective sovereignty created a new arena of struggle for the representation of the Palestinian people. As the *feday'in* captured the PLO, they asserted a clear challenge to Jordan's right to represent any Palestinians. As Jordan fought against this PLO claim in the international and Arab arenas, its arguments foundered against the growing popularity of the PLO but were strengthened by the Israeli and American refusal to accept the PLO as a partner in negotiations.

As its international recognition, power, and ambitions grew, the PLO (or at least some of its factions) began to look to the Palestinian citizens of Jordan as a natural constituency. Jordan then emerged as the location for PLO institutions and armed forces. In September 1970, however, the Jordanian state violently reasserted its authority over the East Bank, expelling the PLO and ending the *fida'yi* period of Jordanian history. The communalist interpretation of these events as Black September, a Jordanian-Palestinian civil war, has shaped all subsequent interactions between the two national groups. In reality, considerable cross-communal participation occurred, as significant numbers of Transjordanians participated in the Resistance, while important parts of the Palestinian elite at least tacitly supported the state's reassertion of control.[43] Black September drove *iqlimiyya* (communal chauvinism) in both the Palestinian and Jordanian

[43] Yezid Sayigh, *Armed Struggle and the Search for State* (New York: Oxford University Press, 1997); Abu Odeh, *Jordanians, Palestinians, and the Hashemite Kingdom*. Massad, "Identifying the Nation," discusses this discursive construction of Black September. For the traditional view, see Lawrence Axelrod, "Tribesmen in Uniform: The Demise of the *Fida'iyyun* in Jordan, 1970–71," *The Muslim World* 68 (1978): 25–45.

communities, as ethnic conflict so often will. Such chauvinism has also been invoked tacitly and overtly over the last thirty years to justify state repression and limits on Palestinian self-expression. Black September ended the PLO challenge to the internal power structure, decisively rejected the assertion of a distinctive Palestinian identity inside Jordan, and allowed a "Jordanian" consolidation of internal identity. In subsequent years, the "Jordanization" of the state apparatus gave institutional substance to the new political identity. This nationalizing project strengthened the domination of the Jordanian community over the state but weakened Jordan's external claim to the clearly non-Jordanian West Bank. The use of military force also demonstrated the absence of any uncoerced Jordanian identity inclusive of Palestinians, and thus increased the persuasiveness of the PLO claim to represent a distinctive Palestinian identity.

King Hussein's subsequent proposal of a United Arab Kingdom, which defined Jordan's official identity from 1972 until 1988, reflected these new realities without abandoning a claim to the West Bank. The UAK offered a federal constitutional structure, with self-governing Palestinian and Jordanian regions and a central federal government based in Amman under the Hashemite monarchy. Despite the assertion of federal unity, the UAK clearly recognized a distinction between the West and East Banks that earlier Jordanian discourse had rejected. Palestinian factions and key Arab states almost unanimously denounced the proposal. Black September was repeatedly invoked in the Palestinian and Arabist debates as evidence of Hussein's hostile intentions. Although King Hussein consulted members of the Jordanian political elite, the proposal did not become a topic of public debate in an open Jordanian public sphere.[44]

The 1974 Rabat summit, which confirmed Arab support for the PLO as the sole legitimate representative of the Palestinian people, also primarily involved argumentation at the Arabist level. The Jordanian public remained an audience, not a participant, in these debates about their identity. Jordan accepted the Rabat decisions more through power rather than persuasion; unpersuaded by Arab argumentation, Jordan nevertheless feared Arab sanctions and preferred to remain inside an undesirable consensus than to be outside the Arab order. While adhering to the letter of the Rabat resolutions, Jordan continued to compete with the PLO wherever possible. In other words, Jordan's strategies changed, but its identity did not. Since the Rabat discourse took place at the international level, and was not embedded in Jordanian institutions, discourse, or practice, it failed to bring about any significant change in Jordanian identity or interests. In the fourteen years after Rabat, relations between Jordan and the PLO continued to be governed by this identity framework. In the most notable period of cooperation, PLO weakness and Arafat's reconsolidation of power in the Palestinian National Council (PNC) led the 1985 Jordanian-Palestinian agreement on negotiations to-

[44] Sa'id al-Tal, *Political Writings* (Amman: Dar al-Fikr, 1994, in Arabic).

ward a confederation between two independent states.[45] The proposed confederation recognized a much greater degree of difference between two distinct political units than did the UAK, reflecting the international balance of power between the PLO and Jordan, but it did not signify a shift in Jordan's conception of state identity. When King Hussein grew frustrated with Arafat and ended cooperation in 1986, Jordan easily returned to its claims on the West Bank.

Analysis that does not incorporate conceptions of collective identity and the public sphere fails to explain why the 1988 decision to sever ties with the West Bank differed so profoundly from policies in all earlier periods. Unlike the earlier changes in Jordanian policy, the severing of ties produced a major change in Jordan's preferences over outcomes, not only its strategies. The transformative impact of the severing of ties was largely unintended, deriving from the unanticipated conjunction of shifts in Jordanian and Palestinian identity, power, and domestic liberalization. The key group of Jordanian decision makers were focused on the Arabist and international arenas, and expected the severing of ties to be another gambit in the ongoing struggle with the PLO.[46] The severing of ties responded to the Arab consensus expressed at the Algiers Summit, which made Arab preference for the PLO claim to representation excruciatingly clear. The Intifada (the Palestinian uprising in the Israeli occupied territories), which broke out in December 1987, dramatically undermined Jordanian claims on the West Bank. While many observers have suggested that Jordanians felt a regime threat from the possibility of the Intifada spreading to the East Bank, this is overstated; security services had the Jordanian arena under control, although the repression necessary to achieve this contributed to pressures for liberalization, which followed in 1989.[47] Israeli "Jordan is Palestine" discourse, which threatened Jordanian security through a claim about identity, became increasingly worrisome as Israeli politics became polarized over the Intifada, and more extreme possibilities entered Israeli discourse; however, few observers really expected Israel to act on its threats.[48]

[45] Khalid al-Hassan, The Jordanian-Palestinian Agreement (Amman: Dar al-Jalil, 1985, in Arabic).

[46] Lynch, "Right-Sizing over the Jordan," in Right-Sizing the State, ed. Thomas Callaghy, Ian Lustick, and Brendan O'Leary (New York: Oxford University Press, forthcoming). Personal interview, Adnan Abu Odeh, Washington, D.C., December 1995.

[47] Rex Brynen, "Palestine and the Arab State System: Permeability, State Consolidation and the Intifada," Canadian Journal of Political Science 24, no. 3 (1991): 595–621; Andoni, "Jordan," in Echoes of the Intifada, ed. R. Brynen (Boulder, Colo.: Westview Press, 1991); Brand, "The Intifadah and the Arab World," International Journal 45 (1991): 501–28; Asher Susser, In Through the Out Door (Washington Institute for Near East Policy, Policy Paper 19, 1990).

[48] Ian Lustick, Unsettled States, Disputed Lands (Ithaca: Cornell University Press, 1994). Jordanian Prime Minister Zayd Rifa'i responded that Israel could not afford to carry out transfer and that Jordan did not really fear it; quoted in al-Ra'i (Feb. 6, 1989).

The crucial difference from earlier efforts to restructure the Jordanian relationship with the West Bank was that the severing of ties became a major topic of public debate inside an open Jordanian public sphere. Jordan initially contested the severing of ties as an international rather than domestic issue and argued it primarily in the Arabist public sphere. Faced with understandable skepticism, the Jordanian state took increasingly costly steps to prove its sincerity, culminating in the dissolution of Parliament, the drawing of new electoral districts, and the recognition of the Independent State of Palestine. Eventually, the PLO and key Arab states agreed on the value of the severing of ties for the Palestinian cause. The political benefits derived from this positive Arab and PLO reaction, and the concrete measures taken by Jordan in order to achieve it, stabilized the new policy in the short term. The liberalization of 1989, forced upon the regime by uprisings among Jordanian-origin citizens in the south, opened the Jordanian public sphere to contentious debate of the implications of the severing of ties. It was this debate that allowed the fundamental change in the domestic consensus concerning Jordan's identity and interests.

This debate over Jordan's identity had two related but distinct components: borders (Jordan's claim on the West Bank) and order (the status of Jordanians of Palestinian origin in the Jordanian political system). The debate on borders quickly arrived at a consensus in favor of an East Bank-only Jordan, but no consensus could be found on the political identity and role of the Palestinian-origin citizenry. As Jordanian and Palestinian nationalists converged on the idea that this conception of borders best served the interests of both Jordan and Palestine, the 1991 Jordanian National Charter (*al-mithaq al-watani*) formalized the consensus that "Jordan is Jordan and Palestine is Palestine."[49] Jordanian state and societal institutions adjusted to this new identity, as political parties, cultural associations, and state bureaucracies alike were reconstituted along lines congruent with East Bank Jordan. The election of a new Parliament in November 1989, with East Bank only electoral districts, graphically demonstrated the new conception of Jordanian borders. The legal political parties that contested elections in 1993 and 1997 had to demonstrate full independence from foreign—understood as "Palestinian"—groups. While the Islamist movement and the professional associations held out longer against the new identity, they have in practice accepted the new reality. The contention by Islamists that the Muslim Brotherhood "does not recognize the decision to disengage from the West Bank" must be placed within the context of the internal struggles of the Muslim Brotherhood between a Jordan-oriented faction and a Hamas-oriented faction.[50] Abdullah's crackdown on Hamas in 1999 should be understood not sim-

[49] Hani Hourani, ed., *The National Charter* (Amman: Al-Urdun al-Jadid, 1996).
[50] Muslim Brotherhood Secretary General Abd al-Majid Thunaybat, quoted in *al-Quds al-Arabi* (Middle East Mirror), (Sept. 27, 1999). Mohammed Nazzal, member of Hamas political

ply as an attempt to appease Israel and the United States, but also as a gambit to encourage the Jordanization of the Muslim Brotherhood and thus to reinforce the Jordanian identity of the state.

The official vision of a Jordanian-Palestinian final status continued to be a confederation between two sovereign states, but only after Palestine had achieved independence. As this two-state consensus became increasingly institutionalized, Jordan dropped more and more of its residual claims on Jerusalem and the West Bank. While Jordan provided an "umbrella" for the Palestinians at the Madrid and Washington peace talks, the joint delegation pointedly divided itself into two distinct delegations with minimal consultation. By 1993, Jordanians across the political spectrum publicly viewed confederation as unacceptable; Jordanian nationalists argued that any relationship with the West Bank posed an unacceptable threat to the survival of Jordan.[51] King Hussein demanded that the concept of confederation be "struck from the Jordanian political vocabulary," with two independent sovereign states bound by common interests and treaty agreements emerging as the preferred formula. Oslo shocked and angered the Jordanians, sparking serious concerns about Jordan's future, but the Oslo process reinforced the East Bank conception of Jordan by decisively moving toward the creation of a distinct Palestinian entity on the West Bank.[52] After a period of uncertainty, Jordan consistently emphasized support for an independent Palestinian state, refused to negotiate for the Palestinians, and attempted to maintain coordination and consultation with the PNA. Jordan's peace treaty with Israel emphasized purely Jordanian interests and again sharply delineated this Jordan from Palestine. This new conception of Jordan's interests has often clashed with entrenched external beliefs about Jordan's presumably unchanging identity and interests. For example, when Benjamin Netanyahu in December 1997 invoked Jordanian fears of a Palestinian state to justify Israeli policies, King Hussein furiously reaffirmed Jordan's support for a Palestinian state, assuring the Israeli prime minister that Jordan was capable of defending its own interests.[53]

Jordan's policy since the passing of Hussein confirms the priority of collective identity and interests. Despite initial speculation that Abdullah's Palestinian-born wife might lead him to rethink the severing of ties, he has decisively rejected a Jordanian role in the West Bank. Whatever residual interest in the West Bank Hussein might have held, Abdullah has embraced the institu-

---

bureau, also strongly defended the legitimacy of the Hamas presence in Amman by questioning the legality of the severing of ties.

[51] Fahd al-Fanik, Jordan's leading columnist and a key figure in the Jordanian nationalist spectrum, has argued that "Confederation is suicide for Jordan"—but his assertion was a far cry from the official line that confederation would be open for future discussion.

[52] Lawrence Tal, "Is Jordan Doomed?" *Foreign Affairs* 72, no. 5 (1993): 45–58.

[53] Zeev Schiff, "King Hussein's Letter," *Ha'aretz* (Dec. 17, 1997); King Hussein's letter to Prime Minister Majali and Majali's response published in *al-Dustur* (Dec. 15, 1997): 1.

tionalized identity of an East Bank Jordan. In every forum, Abdullah asserts that "there is no such word as confederation in my vocabulary" and that Jordan "supports without reservation the creation of a Palestinian state."[54] The new regime has gone farther than Hussein in Jerusalem, renouncing a Jordanian role in the administration of the Islamic sites. As Adnan Abu Odeh put it, "Jerusalem is no longer an internal Jordanian affair."[55]

The resolution of the question of borders therefore produced a fundamental change in the identity and interests of Jordan. Instead of being viewed as a primary interest, a role in the West Bank is now viewed as a threat. Most Jordanians now argue that the creation of a Palestinian state will solve Jordan's most pressing problems, rather than complicate them. Conflicts with the PNA now involve distributional rather than existential issues: trade, banks, currency. Jordan has supported the PNA in its negotiations with Israel and has regularly intervened to facilitate Palestinian-Israeli compromise. Failure to recognize this change, or its significance, has led many observers to misunderstand and to misrepresent the current dynamics of the Jordanian role. Attributing the constant interest in contesting the PLO's position in the West Bank to a unitary Jordan with stable identity and interests, these observers interpret distributional conflicts as existential ones, constantly looking for evidence of Jordan's ambitions to "get back in." The analysis presented here suggests that Jordan has no such ambitions; because of the change in its identity, it no longer conceives of its interests in such a way. Jordan's interests are now understood in terms of resolving the peace process, which is possible only by establishing a stable Palestinian state. This consensus appears to be more deeply rooted in the political elite than in the population as a whole, however; a 1997 poll showed that 63 percent of Jordanians still supported unity between Jordan and Palestine, compared with only 37 percent of the elite sample.[56] Abdullah meets regularly with Arafat and his advisors and has sought to coordinate negotiating positions; meanwhile, PLO officials in Jordan carefully avoid intervening in Jordanian politics.[57] Abdullah's

---

[54] Quoted by William Orme, "Jordan's King Assuming Key Role in Mideast Talks," *New York Times* (Oct. 7, 1999).

[55] Abu Odeh quoted by *al-Ittihad* (Abu Dhabi, Sept. 24, 1999), translation by BBC Summary of World Broadcasts (Sept. 27, 1999). Marwan Dudin explained Jordan's position at a conference on Jerusalem attended by the author in Amman, January 2000.

[56] Opinion survey by Center for Strategic Studies, University of Jordan, 1997; by comparison, a 1995 CSS survey found that 34 percent of a national sample and 30 percent of an elite sample supported unity.

[57] Personal interviews with Asa'd Abd al-Rahman, director of the PLO Refugee Department (Ramallah, June 22, 1999, and Amman, Jan. 8, 2000), and Marwan Dudin, a longtime Jordanian official concerned with Palestinian affairs (Amman, July 1997). See Ali Jarbawi, "The Triangle of Conflict," *Foreign Policy* 100 (1995): 92–108, for a less optimistic view; and Mustafa

wide-ranging crackdown on Hamas closed one of the primary holes in Jordan's new identity.

Despite this consensus on international identity ("Jordan is Jordan"), the national identity of Jordanians of Palestinian origin remains the most disruptive question in Jordanian politics. Among the many issues that have been explicitly cast in communal terms are the privatization of the state; electoral districts and the election law; press reporting; the professional associations; economic reform; university admissions; military spending; and public spending on refugee camps. All of these issues are overshadowed by the fear of *tawtin* (resettlement). If the peace process were to end with the final resettling of the Palestinian refugees in Jordan, there would no longer be any justification for their exclusion from the center of Jordanian political life, and the current distribution of power would become indefensible. The failure of the multilateral negotiations on refugees to make significant progress led many Jordanians to assume that Jordan would eventually accept such resettlement, despite the public denials by government officials.[58] Rejection of resettlement encompasses both Transjordanians who fear for their domestic power and Palestinians who fear for their right of return. This does not mean that all Palestinians in Jordan would return, but rather that they all demand the right to choose return. Sharp disagreements involve the citizenship rights of Palestinians who remain in Jordan. Abdullah has stated forcefully that even as Jordan strongly demanded the right of return, no Jordanian citizen would be stripped of citizenship because of the peace process. Nationalists, however, view this scenario as threatening the Jordanian identity of the state.[59] The establishment of a Palestinian state is seen as removing many uncertainties about the status of Palestinian-origin citizens.

Most identity-based approaches to the Middle East assume that increased participation of Palestinians in the Jordanian political system would have important foreign-policy implications. The peace process, structural economic adjustments, and the bypassing of Prince Hassan in favor of Abdullah in the succession suggest a possible shift in the ruling coalition. Privatization and the slashing of state subsidies disproportionately hurt the "Jordanian" areas, while

---

Hamarneh, Khalil Shikaki, and Rosemary Hollis, *The Jordanian-Palestinian Relationship: Four Scenarios* (London: Royal Institute for International Affairs, 1998), for possible future scenarios.

[58] Dudin, statement in *al-Dustur* (March 11, 1997): 1; personal interviews with Dudin (Amman, June 1997), Salim Tamari (Jerusalem, June 1997), and Abd al-Rahman (Ramallah, June 1999). For a widely discussed proposed solution of the refugee issue, see Donna Arzt, *Refugees into Citizens* (New York: Council on Foreign Relations, 1995).

[59] While Abd al-Hadi al-Majali, chairman of the National Constitutional Party and Speaker of the House of Representatives, denied a report in *al-Quds al-Arabi* (Aug. 4, 1999) that he advocated stripping Palestinian-origin citizens of their citizenship rights in a final-status arrangement, few Jordanians doubted that such a report could be true. See Majali's denial, published in *al-Ra'i* (Aug. 5, 1999).

strengthening the hand of the Palestinian-dominated private sector. The economic orientation of the peace process—toward trade with Israel and the West Bank—favors the Palestinian elite over the Transjordanians, whose trade networks are oriented more toward Iraq and the Gulf. The peace process seems to suggest the permanent integration of substantial numbers of Palestinian refugees in Jordan. All of these factors point to an increased role for the Palestinian elite in the ruling coalition and a decreasing reliance on the Transjordanian tribes. Riots in the southern cities in 1996 and 1998 served notice of the growing discontent among these Jordanian-origin citizens. Such direct inferences from communal identity to foreign-policy preferences should be treated with caution, however. Even leading Jordanian nationalists often have significant economic interests in the West Bank, and the general concern with Jordan's massive economic problems often overrides communal interests. In fact, the strongest supporters of relations with Israel include Jordanian nationalists such as those associated with the National Constitutional Party, the country's second largest political party, strongly identified with Jordanian nationalism. Still, impediments to such interdependencies might please Jordanian nationalists more than their public positions would suggest. As the West Bank market becomes more important to the Jordanian political economy, these trade networks might reconstruct Jordanian identity and interests in much the same way that Jordan's trade relations with Iraq reconstructed Jordan's Arab relations in the 1980s.

The future of Jordan's identity with regard to its Palestinian-origin citizens remains the subject of rather intense political conflict. Hashemite discourse on identity in the 1990s repeatedly called for full citizenship and participation for all citizens, which would imply a greater role for the Palestinian elite. This inclusionary vision threatened both the position of Jordanian nationalists, consolidated since the severing of ties, and Palestinian insistence on the right of return. While Abdullah has endorsed greater inclusion of Palestinians, key individuals identified with this position in his first government and the Royal Court, such as Abd al-Karim al-Kabariti and Rima Khalaf, resigned after losing political skirmishes with Jordanian nationalists such as Prime Minister Abd al-Raouf Rawabdeh and House Speaker Abd al-Hadi al-Majali.[60]

Jordanians across the identity spectrum therefore reject confederation but are divided on the best future relationship with the West Bank. Palestinian-origin citizens tend to support closer economic ties, but their support for "softer" borders does not significantly differ from the interests of Jordanian-origin businessmen; indeed, many Palestinian-origin citizens agree with Jordanian nationalists about the need for a sharp distinction between Jordan and Pales-

[60] Andoni, "King Abdallah"; *Al-Quds al-Arabi* (Aug. 4, 1999).

tine, to resolve doubts about their identity and loyalty. This change in identity and interest conceptions and its fundamental importance to the Jordanian state should establish the empirical significance of identity for foreign policy. This case offers little support for post-structuralists who consider identity and interests to be constantly in flux, however. Jordan clung to its West Bank-inclusive identity and interests in the face of Arabist consensus, public denunciation, Palestinian diplomatic efforts, civil war, and the growing realities on the ground. Only the conjunction of the Intifada, the severing of ties, and the domestic liberalization of 1989 produced the necessary conditions for production of a new identity consensus.

Jordanian-Israeli Relations

Because of its transnational and internally contested nature, the Jordanian-Palestinian issue represents a somewhat easy case for establishing the importance of identity for interests and behavior. Jordanian-Israeli relations represent a harder case of state behavior under conditions of high security and political pressures. It has been widely assumed that Jordan and Israel share important strategic interests, which serve as the foundation for interstate cooperation.[61] On the other hand, Israel has been the constitutively excluded Other in Arabist discourse, and the long-standing covert (but widely known) Jordanian-Israeli relations compromised its avowed identity. The sharp contradiction between the demands of identity (Israel as enemy) and of interest (Israel as necessary partner) has long been of central concern. The Hashemite kings have traditionally not shared the Arabist view of Israel held by much of the Jordanian public.

Few relationships more clearly demonstrate the importance of public-sphere considerations for international strategic interaction than the Jordanian-Israeli relationship. Indeed, the primary significance of the Jordanian-Israeli peace treaty has been to "make public" relations that had been private. Since at least the 1930s, Jordanian and Zionist leaders have recognized important shared strategic interests.[62] These interests could not be publicly avowed, however, since such a public admission would have clashed with the central norms of Arabism and have carried serious sanctions. Furthermore, most Jordanians did not

[61] For example, see Ephraim Kam, "The Future of Strategic Relations between Jordan and Israel," *Jaffee Center for Strategic Studies Strategic Assessment* 2, no. 1 (June 1999).

[62] On the history of Jordanian-Israeli cooperation, see Avi Shlaim, *Collusion across the Jordan* (New York: Oxford University Press, 1987); for competing views, Avraham Sela, "Transjordan, Israel and the 1948 War," *Middle Eastern Studies* 28, no. 4 (1992): 623–88, and Efraim Karsh, "The Collusion That Never Was," *Journal of Contemporary History* 34, no. 4 (1999): 569–85.

share this conception of state interests, opening a key divergence between regime and public foreign policy preferences. In order to achieve these common interests, Jordan and Israel engaged in "functional cooperation" on a wide range of technical and practical issues, but avoided open coordination.[63] Israel and the Hashemites (though not necessarily "Jordan") have generally recognized a common interest in maintaining quiet along their shared border and preventing the emergence of Palestinian nationalism and a Palestinian state.

The demands of Arabist identity clearly constrained Jordan from engaging in public—though not private—relations with Israel. Despite many shared interests and functional cooperation, Jordanian-Israeli relations remained tacit until 1994. King Hussein met with Israeli leaders dozens of times, but always in secret. The need for secrecy followed directly from the conception of Arab identity embedded in the Arabist public sphere, which identified Israel as the enemy and as a threat to Arab security, identity, and interests. A public meeting would have exposed Hussein to denunciation, subversion, and even expulsion from the Arab order. While Hussein went to the brink several times, most notably in his London meetings with Shimon Peres in 1987, he did not make the final leap into a peace agreement until after the other Arab states and the PLO went first. After he did decide to openly pursue peace, he attempted to link this peace agreement to the wider regional peace process to avoid being singled out as in violation of Arab norms. The theoretical implications seem clear: Arabist norms ruled out Israel as a viable alliance partner, even when such an alliance might be the most rational as dictated by either power or threat.

Open collaboration with Israel would have exposed Jordan as outside the Arab consensus and in violation of its own norms and identity, and therefore had to be kept out of the public sphere. The divergence between Arabist and Hashemite conceptions of Jordanian interests remained excluded from public discussion inside Jordan but could not be controlled in the Arabist public sphere. Jordanians generally tried to avoid confronting a choice between Arabist and Israeli-oriented identities. For the vast majority of Jordanians, of both Transjordanian and Palestinian origin, Israel represented the enemy described in Arabist discourse, not a partner for functional cooperation. Jordanians would tolerate Jordan's strategic cooperation with Israel only to the extent to which it was not made public and thus did not compromise Jordan's position in the Arab order. Hussein's invocation of the Great Arab Revolt, of Jordan's Arab identity,

---

[63] Yehuda Lukacs, *Israel, Jordan and the Peace Process* (Albany: State University of New York Press, 1997); Adam Garfinkle, *Jordan and Israel in the Shadow of War* (New York: St. Martin's Press, 1992); Aharon Klieman, "Israel's 'Jordan Option': A Post-Oslo Reassessment," in *The Middle East Peace Process*, ed. I. Peleg (Albany: State University of New York Press, 1998): 178–224. Israeli journalist Moshe Zak claims that Jordan and Israel concluded 38 agreements prior to 1994 in "The Israel-Jordan Summit," *Jerusalem Post* (July 22, 1994).

and of Jordan's profound sacrifices for the Arab cause were well understood to diverge from the reality of effective non-hostility with Israel. But as long as the public facade was maintained, Jordanians could reconcile the state's strategic needs with their normative beliefs.

The peace treaty signed in 1994 forced a direct engagement with these contradictions. As long as the peace process moved forward on all tracks, the Jordanian government could argue that the changes in Jordan coincided with changes in Arab norms. While opposition to the treaty did refer to interests, a surprising amount of its public argumentation focused on Jordan's Arab identity. Opponents argued, with considerable success, that the formal treaty with Israel would cause Jordan to lose its Arab and Islamic identity. Cut off from its Arab roots, Jordan would stand alone and weak against Israeli domination, and in turn the sacrifice of values would provide no real corresponding increase in security. As opposition leader Layth Shubaylat put it, "what was Arab and Islamic in Jordan's strategic decisions is now Zionist and American. . . . Official Jordan has taken a strategic choice to distance itself from the Arabs and make itself their enemy."[64] While the government emphasized the Jordanian state interests achieved in the treaty, the opposition denied the priority of these interests in relation to wider Arab interests and identity. Israeli arguments that the Israeli deterrent would protect Jordan against threats from its Arab neighbors might have reflected private discussions with Jordanian military officials, but could not be usefully advanced in the Jordanian public sphere; the substitution of Israeli for Arab "friends" simply could not be reconciled with the existing Jordanian identity discourse. In this vein, Toujan Faisal, an outspoken opposition deputy, responded to a government campaign against "foreign" (that is, Ba'thi and Palestinian) funding of political parties with the angry question "Does the state now consider Israel to be domestic and Arabs to be foreign enemies?"[65]

The regime responded with a comprehensive frame linking Jordan's interests to regional transformation, which would again forestall a direct confrontation between the two incompatible identities. King Hussein tapped into a discourse of "peace," in which forces on both the Arab and the Israeli sides who wanted peace were challenged by extremists. With the treaty, Jordan stood not with Israel against the Arabs but with the Peace Camp against the Extremists. As with Arabism, the debates over the Jordanian treaty involved identity claims that could be redeemed only at the regional level, with the establishment of the institutional foundations of a "New Middle East." To this end, Jordan enthusiastically supported the process of regional economic cooperation, hosting the sec-

[64] Layth Shubaylat interviewed in *Shihan* (Jan. 26, 1998).
[65] Toujan Faisal, "Confusion in Our House," *Shihan* (May 13, 1995).

ond Middle East North Africa (MENA) economic summit in Amman and participating in all available multilateral forums.[66] Even after many Arab states had distanced themselves, Jordan continued participating in regional projects, such as the MENA economic summit in Doha, not only because of Israeli and American pressure, but also because of Jordan's need for regional identity and institutional transformation.

The regime demonstrated the link between identity and interests by justifying the peace treaty with Israel on the basis of specifically Jordanian interests, without reference to Arab or Palestinian interests. The government emphasized the return of Jordanian occupied territories and some of its rights to water, along with the potential for economic gains through joint investments and trade. Overall, official discourse held up the decisive response to the Israeli "Jordan is Palestine" claim as the single most important achievement: "the fundamental benefit of peace is to confirm the Jordanian entity" (Fahd al-Fanik); "Jordan is not Palestine!" (lead editorial, al-Ra'i).[67] The only interests invoked were Jordanian interests, defined to exclude all conceptions of Jordan that included either Palestinian or Arab identity.

Shut out of the formal foreign-policy process, the opposition focused on controlling the public sphere by preventing "normalization" with Israel. The professional associations passed binding resolutions forbidding their members from engaging in normalization with Israel, framing the struggle in terms of maintaining an Arabist Jordanian identity against state pressures to change. Leftist, Arabist, and some centrist political parties joined forces with the Islamists in a coalition opposed to normalization. Accepting that they could not force the regime to abolish the treaty, they looked to deprive it of social meaning, along the Egyptian model. Understanding that identity transformation would require public consent, the opposition used a wide variety of means, from blacklists to intimidation to principled appeals to rational debate, to prevent the entrance of Israelis into normal Jordanian public life. Even as Jordanian workers sought visas to work in Israel, and Jordanian companies quietly pursued Israeli capital, the opposition fairly successfully prevented these private actions from changing public discourse. A boycott of an Israeli trade show in January 1997 demonstrated a wide popular consensus about the dangers of relations with Israel, as virtually every political and civil society organization joined in.

In this context of a struggle between the government and the organized opposition to establish a dominant public frame, popular opposition to the treaty was not foreordained, or inherent in Palestinian communal identity, Islamic beliefs, or Arab culture. Identity does not directly produce interests, but rather in-

[66] Dalia Dassa Kaye, *Beyond the Handshake: Multilateral Cooperation in the Arab-Israeli Peace Process, 1991–1996* (New York: Columbia University Press, 2001).
[67] Fanik in *al-Ra'i* (June 8, 1995); *al-Ra'i* editorial (Oct. 24, 1994).

forms the articulation of interests in public political struggles. The initial response to the treaty was very much one of "wait and see" among Jordanians of all origins; one public opinion poll showed that 80 percent of Jordanians supported the July 1994 Washington Declaration, but that support was "soft," conditional on rapid economic improvement and progress on the Palestinian and Syrian tracks.[68]

The communal divide between Transjordanians and Palestinians did not translate into distinctive preferences regarding Jordan's relations with Israel, however. Jordanian-origin citizens could take comfort in the heavy emphasis on Jordan's identity and self-interest, while Palestinian-origin citizens supportive of the wider peace process could embrace the congruence between Arafat and Hussein's positions—but those opposed to the wider peace process could oppose this treaty for the same reason. Despite heavy-handed regime efforts to claim that "the opposition wears a Palestinian face," little evidence indicates that communal origin directly correlated with positions on the treaty.

After the treaty, the regime, the opposition, and the undecided engaged in spirited, open debate about Israeli behavior, economic trends, and public freedoms. The shift toward the opposition followed from competitive framing along each of these indicators and led the government to sharply repress a public sphere it could not persuade. First, the opposition argued that Israeli behavior did not justify Jordanian friendship, because Israel was failing to honor its signed agreements, especially with regard to water and access to West Bank markets. As Israeli-Palestinian relations deteriorated and Israel attacked Lebanon, many undecided Jordanians came to believe that Israel had not changed. With the election of Netanyahu, this belief deepened immensely. The demands of the novel "peace camp" identity claim could be met only by an Israel committed to peace with the Palestinians and Arab states. From the narrow perspective of strategic interests, regime officials could see the potential for cooperation with the new right-wing Likud government; from the perspective of identity and publicly avowed interests, the Jordanian public could not. Israel's failed attempt to assassinate Hamas leader Khalid Misha'al in Amman in October 1997 outraged even the most enthusiastic advocates of peace, leading to a near freeze of security cooperation.

Economic conditions fed the debates about the value of the new identity. Since the "peace camp" identity had partly been sold with the promise of regional economic prosperity, the failure of prosperity to materialize undermined more than just economic indicators. The continuing deterioration of the Jordanian economy was exacerbated by International Monetary Fund (IMF) demands for reductions in bread subsidies, continued closure of West Bank mar-

[68] Center for Strategic Studies (July 1994).

kets, and a relatively small American assistance package. Joint ventures with Israel and the free-trade areas in Irbid produced only marginal benefits to the Jordanian economy. In June 1996 and again in February 1998, major riots broke out in protest over economic conditions and government repression. At the level of regional integration, the first MENA economic conferences in Casablanca and Amman held out the prospects of developing economic ties. After Netanyahu's election, however, the 1996 conference in Cairo was deeply politicized, while the 1997 conference in Doha was boycotted by almost all Arab states (Jordan attended). Hussein's anger with Netanyahu should be interpreted in light of Israel's abandonment of the idea of transforming regional structures, which undermined the new regional identity frame. In a series of increasingly bitter open letters, speeches, and interviews, Hussein asserted that Netanyahu was neither interested in nor capable of making peace with the Arabs; in other words, Israel had abandoned the peace camp.

As opposition to the peace treaty escalated, the regime responded with increasingly harsh repression, in a destabilizing and dangerous cycle.[69] Increasing repression convinced many Jordanians that the price of the treaty was democracy, which helped to consolidate the belief that the regime had pursued "regime" interests at the expense of "the nation." While Jordan adhered to the peace treaty, a profound split between the interpretations and discourse of state and society could be observed. For example, a December 1997 opinion survey found that 59 percent of the members of Parliament believed that the peace treaty had ended the Israeli "alternative homeland" threat, while 73 percent of political party leaders and 72 percent of newspaper columnists believed that it had not.[70] Opposition figures, particularly those from the Islamist movement, regularly swept elections in professional associations, university student councils, and other civil institutions; in fact, opposition leader Layth Shubaylat was re-elected head of the professional associations in 1997 while in prison, with over 90 percent of the vote.

While repression enhanced the regime's autonomy and its freedom of maneuver, it also signaled the failure of its attempt to establish a new state identity. Security cooperation with Israel was not perceived by most Jordanians as involving anything beyond state interests, which public commentators pointedly contrasted with "national" interests. The labeling of the treaty as "the King's peace" demonstrated the increasing willingness of Jordanians to make this distinction. Furthermore, the regional failure of identity transformation after Netanyahu's election affected the domestic Jordanian debate. I have argued that transformation of collective identity requires public sphere interaction; by clos-

[69] Campagna, "Press Freedoms in Jordan."
[70] Center for Strategic Studies (December 1997).

ing the public sphere, the regime implicitly accepted that Jordan's identity would not change. Having lost the argument, the government could use only repressive power to maintain its position. The treaty would remain in place, and the coercive power of the state would prevent effective opposition, but the larger project of embedding a new identity into Jordanian institutions was largely abandoned. While Hussein (and Abdullah) emphasized that Jordan's decision for peace was strategic and not subject to change, the failure to embed this "strategic" decision in Jordanian identity or institutions made it vulnerable to strategically motivated reconsideration.

In contrast to the failure to institutionalize new identities in Jordan, the peace treaty has clearly transformed Israel's conception of Jordan's identity. The argument that "Jordan is Palestine" has disappeared from the political landscape in Israel, as even its most powerful proponent, Ariel Sharon, has become a leading advocate of close relations with the Hashemite kingdom.[71] The special relationship with Jordan has been embraced across Israel's political spectrum. Israel treated the death of King Hussein in a manner more consistent with the death of an Israeli elder statesman than with the head of a longtime "enemy" state; the decision to issue a King Hussein stamp angered rather than honored many Jordanians, who resented the appropriation of their king by the Israeli state. When Netanyahu ventured in a public forum that Jordan might again pose a threat to Israel—whether through revolution or an alliance with Iraq—the outrage, ridicule, and condemnation that flooded the public sphere indicated a remarkable change in Israeli perceptions of Jordan's identity.[72] The treaty changed Jordan's attributed identity in Israel, therefore, even if it failed to transform internal Jordanian conceptions of identity.

After Hussein's death, Israelis expressed concern that Abdullah would not continue Hussein's peace policies. Abdullah carefully preserved the strategic relationship and reassured both Israel and the United States of his commitment to the peace process, taking risky and unpopular steps such as an the expulsion of Hamas in September 1999. On the other hand, he did not openly prioritize relations with Israel over relations with neighboring Arab states. He worked assiduously, albeit with mixed success, to rebuild ties with Syria and Iraq and to coordinate with the PNA; during his first, short state visit to Israel, on April 23, 2000, he avoided Jerusalem and focused on economic development rather than on politics.[73] Israeli commentators noted that "Abdullah does not feel that Israel

[71] Klieman, "Israel's Jordanian Option: A Post-Oslo Reassessment."

[72] "Netanyahu Worries Aloud about Possible Jordan-Iraq Alliance," *Agence France-Presse* (Feb. 26, 1999); "Officials Reject Netanyahu's Statement on Jordan-Iraq Ties," *Jordan Times* (Feb. 28, 1999).

[73] Zvi Barel, "Why Won't Abdullah Visit?" *Ha'aretz Internet Edition* (Jan. 28, 2000); Barel, "Israel Courts Jordan's King," *Ha'aretz Internet Edition* (April 23, 2000); "Abdullah Envisions an Open Jerusalem," *Ha'aretz Internet Edition* (April 24, 2000).

is the most important or unique relationship, and is willing to trade it off against other possible alliances."[74] In other words, Abdullah, like most Jordanians, has not invested identity in the Israeli relationship and is more willing to treat it strategically and to balance interests and opportunities.

Conclusion

As Barnett and Telhami suggest, simply claiming that "identity matters" is no longer sufficient. This chapter suggests a broadly constructivist causal theory linking institutional change, identity, interests, and foreign-policy behavior. This chapter offers little support for approaches to identity that attempt to explain behavior directly as a product of ascribed ethnic, religious, cultural, or national identities. Instead, the experience of Jordan demonstrates that struggles over identity in national and international public spheres produce the conceptions of interest that strategic actors attempt to realize. Jordan's identity has changed in the course of these struggles, and these shifts have led to very different conceptions of Jordan's interests. Competing interpretations of the Arab component of Jordan's state identity constrained its ability to publicly align with Israel. Even those Jordanians most invested in the pursuit of state interests tried to demonstrate adherence to Arab identity. Relations with Israel involved both strategic interests in cooperation and challenges to this Arab identity. Finally, the transformation of Jordan's conception of its interests in the West Bank after the severing of ties offers a powerful demonstration of the relationship between identity and interests. The opening of Jordan's public sphere and the intensification of a nationalizing project in the 1990s had observable and significant implications for its foreign-policy behavior, even in the most sensitive and strategically important issue areas.

The impact of shifts in the structure of the Jordanian public sphere on the political significance of identity raises interesting possibilities for comparative research. Syria's foreign policy has not been contested in the public sphere as in Jordan, but Asad pays great attention to the Arab public sphere and arguably to privately articulated Syrian opinion. Syria's contested identity, between Syrian nationalism and Arabism, over the integrity of Syrian territory in the Golan Heights and over Lebanon, has been at the forefront of its behavior; how does it matter that these issues are kept out of public debates? Would an Arab state with an open public sphere have been able to side with Iran against Iraq, as Syria did in the 1980s? Egypt's move to peace with Israel, which began during a period of relatively open public debate, did not seem to be caused by identity, but certainly posed a major challenge to state identity. Sadat's failure to persuade the

[74] Barel, "Abdullah Unites Jerusalem," *Ha'aretz Internet Edition* (Sept. 19, 1999).

Egyptian public sphere led first to his turn to repression, then to his assassination, and finally to Mubarak's policy of a "cold peace" of strategic stability but popular hostility. Israel's open public sphere, by contrast, has allowed sharp divergence between religious and secular, hawk and dove, Ashkenazi and Mizrahi to deeply influence the possibilities for Israeli negotiations with the Palestinians and Syria. In each case, the structure of the public sphere affects the extent to which state identity constrains leaders and constitutes official conceptions of interests.

3. The Israeli Identity and the Peace Process

Re/creating the Un/thinkable

MICHAEL BARNETT

Israel might be excused had it used the occasion of its half-century anniversary in 1998 to indulge in hubris, chest-thumping, and gauche congratulations paying tribute to the miracle of Israel's birth and continued existence. Instead, the Israeli public seemed in no mood to celebrate and more ready to talk themselves into a state of despair and self-recrimination.[1] Two heated debates caused this national dysthymia. The first concerned the tremendous fear that the ever-present divisions in Israeli society were a prelude to a domestic clash of civilizations. Israel has always been a multicultural society, even one that has demonstrated strong divergencies, most famously between the Ashkenazim and the Sephardim. But such tensions, even at their worst moments, have not threatened the foundational belief among Israelis in a common identity, fate, and faith in a national project. During the past several years, there was growing concern over the widening divisions between different identity-based groups that lacked a core identity or unifying national project. The 1996 elections dramatically telescoped those divisions. The unexpected electoral successes of the Russian, haredim (ultra-Orthodox Jews), Arab Israeli, and Sephardim parties triggered a growing concern that the core Israeli identity was being eclipsed by subnational groups whose loyalties resided below and above the state.[2] In the view of *Ha'aretz* columnist Gideon Samet, what had occurred was the "collapse of the common denominator. . . . [T]he Israeli identity is becoming increasingly blurred."[3] How can Israelis agree now that all of the grand narratives have collapsed?

---

[1] Lee Hockstader, "A Sour Mood Grips Israel As It Prepares to Turn 50," *Washington Post* (Feb. 9, 1998): A1; Serge Schmemann, "Israelis, Proud and Worried, Now Ask: What Is Our State?" *New York Times* (April 30, 1998): A1, A16.

[2] On the changes in loyalties among Israelis, see Gabriel Sheffer, "Individualism vs. National Coherence: The Current Discourse on Sovereignty, Citizenship, and Loyalty," *Israel Studies* 2, no. 2 (fall 1997): 137–38.

[3] Gideon Samet, "The Collapse of the Common Denominator," *Ha'aretz* (English edition, April 10, 1998).

The second debate concerned the peace process, or, more specifically, the emaciating body of the Oslo Accords, which held out the promise of a mutually negotiated settlement to the Israel-Palestinian conflict. The November 1995 assassination of Israeli Prime Minister Yitzhak Rabin, an architect of Oslo, followed by the election of Benjamin Netanyahu, a foe of Oslo, predictably led to an abrupt brake on negotiations. Accordingly, many observers cited the change in Israeli domestic politics to explain the peace process's reversal of fortunes. Exactly how Israeli domestic politics produced this outcome was a matter of dispute, with various critics blaming Netanyahu the person, the makeup of the coalition government, or the structure of electoral politics.

These debates over the peace process and the Israeli national identity are not simply coterminous—they are causally linked. The peace process is not simply a territorial issue; it fundamentally concerns the Israeli national identity. To a vocal segment of religious Israelis, Judea and Samaria are part of Israel and are connected to its Jewish soul; these lands are no less a part of Israel than is Tel-Aviv. To revisionist Zionists, the peace process threatens the very idea of Zionism; withdrawal or "redeployment," according to Yoram Hazony, "is the destruction of the Jewish state in the mind of the Jewish people. It is a return to exile. It is retreat into a void."[4] To centrist, secular, and leftist constituencies, Israel must rid itself of these territories if it is to maintain a Zionist and liberal identity; to absorb these territories would mean extinguishing either its liberal or its Zionist character, depending on whether the Palestinian population was denied or granted full citizenship. [5]

To move forward or to complete the peace process requires that Israel address some fundamental issues regarding who it is and what it is to become. Israeli politicians are aware of this and have spent considerable energy balancing, negotiating, and ultimately trying to fix an Israeli identity that facilitates—or rejects—a two-state solution. But the increasingly contentious debate about the national identity, with its melange of religious-secular and ethnic-civic rifts, hampers Israeli politicians in building the consensus required for the peace process. Breaking out of the current impasse requires the mobilization of individuals along a common cultural space. This cultural space is not given but rather is

[4] Yoram Hazony, *The Jewish State: The Struggle for Israel's Soul* (New York: Basic Books, 2000): 73.

[5] For related claims that the peace process is tied to identity, see Lilly Weissbrod, "Israeli Identity in Transition," in *From Rabin to Netanyahu: Israel's Troubled Agenda*, ed. Efraim Karsh (Portland, Ore.: Frank Cass, 1997): 47–65; Yaron Ezrahi, *Rubber Bullets: Power and Conscience in Modern Israel* (Berkeley: University of California Press, 1997): 290; and Ilan Peleg, "The Peace Process and Israel's Political Cultures: The Intensification of a KulturKampf," in A. Dowty et al., *The Role of Domestic Politics in Israeli Peacemaking* (Jerusalem: Leonard Davis Institute, Hebrew University of Jerusalem, September 1997): 13–24.

constructed by leaders who can imaginatively and strategically frame issues in ways that are connected to widely accepted narratives. In an age of ethnic and post-Zionist politics, however, these narratives are increasingly elusive. This is strategic social construction at its typified and common best.

Four issues in particular pertain to my argument regarding the relationship between identity politics and the peace process. First, I am not making a narrow, positivist claim that a particular cultural fabric narrowly causes a particular foreign-policy orientation. But, as the editors note in their introduction, the constitutive argument I am making attempts to identify the conditions that make certain action possible.[6] What Israelis view as possible and desirable regarding the peace process depends on the cultural foundations and the institutional context that favor certain actors and their voices and visions; whether these visions are ever activated depends on a host of other triggering and contextual variables. Second, while I elevate these cultural features, I acknowledge that other actors often play an important role in shaping Israeli domestic politics, including the Palestinian Authority, Hamas, other Arab states, and the United States. Third, whether a peace treaty is ever finalized will depend on a host of other variables—from third-party mediation to a calculation of the strategic balance, to a more narrowly defined coalition that supports the peace treaty. Still, any Israeli government that aspires to sell a peace treaty to the Israeli public will be forced to address not only its security implications but also its impact on national identity.

Fourth, this argument acknowledges the relevance of systemic—that is, material—forces. Some scholars compellingly argue that mighty shifts in the international and regional environment created the conditions for a major foreign-policy change. The end of the Cold War and the Gulf War represented seismic shocks to the region; for Israel it both reduced the risks for peace and increased the incentives to take such risks. While the changing correlation of forces stirred Israeli elites to recalculate their strategies, these changing security parameters appeared insufficient to push Israel toward peace. This could be readily seen on two counts. One, how Israeli military and political elites evaluated the strategic balance depended not only on the material capabilities of their enemies but also on the enemies' intentions, which depended in part on whether these countries could ever reconcile themselves to Israel's existence. This question caused heated debates in Israeli circles.[7] Two, even if the environment turned rosy, some Israelis fundamentally objected to the idea of a territorial compromise because of its implications for the identity of the Zionist state. This position became more promi-

[6] Alexander Wendt, "Constitution and Causation in International Relations," *Review of International Studies* 24, no. 5 (1998): 101–18.

[7] Efraim Inbar, "Israel's Predicament in a New Strategic Environment," in *The National Security of Small States in a Changing World*, ed. E. Inbar and G. Sheffer (London: Frank Cass, 1997).

nent after 1990, when many Israeli analysts began to see the environment as more conducive to a peace settlement, bringing those who believed in Greater Israel for mystical and redemptive reasons in sharper focus. Israelis ultimately have to be convinced that reasonable risks could be taken for peace, but they wanted to know how this compromise would affect not only their physical security but also their national identity. For some, an Israel behind more circumscribed, though securer, borders, was only a faux Jewish state; for others, this Israel would be more secure and would fix a proper identity.

Section I examines the concepts of identity, narratives, and frames, the conceptual apparatus that informs my approach to the impasse in the peace process. The peace process has triggered a debate over the Israeli national identity, an identity within a historical narrative that provides lessons for the future. These cultural foundations make possible and desirable certain actions. Yet what is possible and legitimate also is shaped by political institutions that influence strategic actors and provide the incentives and disincentives for collective action. Surveying the ideational and institutional context of Israeli politics permits me to forward several propositions regarding the differential fortunes of the peace process under Rabin and Netanyahu.

Sections II and III, then, are a tale of the 1992 and 1996 elections. A defining feature of Rabin's path was the attempt to instantiate an Israeli national identity that was Zionist and liberal, tied to a frame that promised peace and prosperity; this was a critical factor in generating the cultural foundations for a withdrawal from the territories. The assassination of Rabin, the election of Netanyahu, the emergence of narrowly-defined political parties that have more contentious understandings of the past and the future, and the subsequent impasse in the peace process provide the basis for the provisional claim that the identity conflict that Rabin attempted to address grew more severe, in no small measure due to his secular and liberal response. Although Netanyahu was a disciple of the ultranationalists, his ambiguous stances accepted in principle the idea of territorial withdrawal without accepting the idea of devolving control to the Palestinian National Authority; this ambiguity left his closest aides angry and confused over his true intentions. In the end, Netanyahu's enigmatic properties became seen as character blemishes that left him unfit to rule and left those who had made their peace with the Oslo Accords and those who had not equally hostile to his leadership. I conclude by briefly extending this analysis to the 1999 election of Ehud Barak and the ever-so-close but ever-so-far final peace treaty.

Section I: The Identity of the Possible

I forward four concepts—identity, narrative, frames, and institutions—to consider the relationship between the contestation of national identity; how that contestation is tied to a historical narrative linking past, present, and future; and how frames that link historical narratives and discrete interests affect societal mobilization in favor of a particular project or policy. In the following passages I briefly discuss each concept.

IDENTITY

An identity is the understanding of oneself in relationship to others.[8] Identities, in short, are not personal or psychological; they are social and relational, defined by the actor's interaction with, and relationship to, others; therefore, all political identities depend on the actor's interaction with others and the actor's place within an institutional context. Thus, national and state identities are partly formed in relationship to other nations and states; the identities of the political actors are tied to their relationship to those outside the community and the larger territory.[9]

Although national and state identities are always in negotiation, these negotiations can be particularly intense when rapid changes occur in international and domestic politics. At the international level, a change in systemic patterns, caused either by transnational, economic, or military politics, can trigger wide-scale domestic change and debates concerning national identity and the state's relationship to the wider community. Such a possibility was evident in the years after the Cold War as many states began debating their national identities and their relationship to other international communities. At the domestic level, changes in territorial boundaries, political economy, and demography can also enliven the debate over national identity.

Particularly divisive debates over national identity can be characterized as moments of "identity conflict." Identity conflict is likely to emerge under two conditions.[10] The first is whenever competing definitions of the identity call for contradictory behaviors. Although the following refers explicitly to the notion of role conflict, identity conflict might be seen to exist:

[8] Henry Tajfel defines a social identity as "that part of an individual's self-concept which derives from his knowledge of his membership in a social group (or groups) together with the value and emotional significance attached to that membership." Tajfel, *Differentiation Between Social Groups: Studies in the Social Psychology of Intergroup Relations* (London: Academic Press, 1978): 63. Wendt, in turn, distinguishes between "corporate identities," including identities of political actors, and "social identities," identities that political actors generate through interactions with other actors. See Wendt, "Collective Identity Formation and the International State," *American Political Science Review* 88 (June 1994): 385.

[9] For discussions of national and state identities that build on this definition, see Lowell Dittmer and Samuel Kim, "In Search of a Theory of National Identity," in *China's Quest for National Identity*, ed. Kim and Dittmer (Ithaca: Cornell University Press, 1993): 1–31; Anthony Smith, *National Identity* (Reno: University of Nevada Press, 1991); and Wendt, "Collective Identity Formation."

[10] Dittmer and Kim, "In Search of a Theory," 6–7.

when there are contradictory expectations that attach to some position in a social relationship. Such expectations may call for incompatible performances; they may require that one hold two norms or values which logically call for opposing behaviors; or they may demand that one [identity] necessitates the expenditure of time and energy such that it is difficult or impossible to carry out the obligations of another [identity].[11]

Identity conflict can also exist whenever definitions of the "collective self are no longer acceptable under new historical conditions."[12] In this view, identity conflict arises when the state's identity calls for behavior that is at odds with the demands and defining characteristics of the current challenge.

In general, as we think about the relationship between state identity and foreign-policy behavior, we should remain attentive to two issues. First, national identity is a source of interests. Identity, however, does not cause action but rather makes some action legitimate and intelligible and others not so. Second, political actors are likely to have competing interpretations of a specific identity; the actors compete to fix a particular national identity because of their convictions and interests. Although these competing visions are an ongoing feature of political life, periods of "identity conflict" emerge as domestic groups compete to establish how a particular identity is functional or dysfunctional for current circumstances.

The debate about Israel's identity has concerned the articulation of four constitutive strands: religion, nationalism, the Holocaust, and liberalism.[13] First, Israel has a Jewish identity; it is, after all, a Jewish state.[14] While opinions differ on the specific meaning and practices associated with being a Jewish state, little debate exists that religion should have some role in guiding everyday life in Israel.[15] Zionism, the Jewish people's version of nationalism, emerged as a response to the Jewish community's exclusion from and persecution in European

---

[11] Sheldon Stryker, *Symbolic Interactionism: A Social Structural Perspective* (Reading, Mass.: The Benjamin/Cummings Publishing Co., 1980): 73.

[12] Ibid., 7.

[13] Amos Elon, "The Politics of Memory," *New York Review of Books* (Oct. 7, 1993): 4. Elon features the first three elements in his essay; I have added the fourth. In recent years a flood of writing has addressed the Israeli collective identity. See, for instance, *The Shaping of the Israeli Identity: Myth, Memory, and Trauma,* ed. Robert Wistrich and David Ohana (New York: Frank Cass, 1995); and Yael Zerubavel, *Recovered Roots: Collective Memory and the Making of Israeli National Tradition* (Chicago: University of Chicago Press, 1995).

[14] S. N. Eisenstadt, *Change and Continuity in Israeli Society* (New York: Humanities Press, 1974).

[15] The debate over Israel's Jewish identity is perhaps best illustrated in the continuing controversy over "Who is a Jew?" This has been a feature of Israeli politics since the establishment of the state, but the attempt by religious parties to enact a conversion law has brought such debates hotly to the surface.

Christian society and is an obvious component of the national identity.[16] The Holocaust is the third component of Israel's identity; memorials such as Yad Vashem, Holocaust Remembrance Day, and a host of other symbols deeply embed the Holocaust in Israel's national identity.[17]

These three features of Israel's identity are linked to a view that Israel is existentially isolated, its existence is always in jeopardy, and it faces a series of threats from various quarters that vary only in the level of overt intensity.[18] While all national identities differentiate "us" from "them," arguably the centrality of religion, nationalism, and the Holocaust in Israel's identity make these affective and cognitive boundaries more severe and austere.[19] In *Security Threatened*, Asher Arian provides attitudinal evidence and labels this attitude the "People Apart Syndrome," distinguishing between religious and historical roots of that "syndrome."[20] Regardless of the specific pathogen, most Jewish Israelis have this syndrome and reject a "geopolitical explanation of international conflict and persist in analyzing the Israel-Arab conflict in the spirit . . . of persecution suffered by Jews." Arguably, then, a cultural basis exists for a foreign policy that is quintessentially realist if not hyperrealist, as observers have linked culture to practices that include a defiant and strident foreign policy, a reluctance to take risks for peace, and a "Masada complex."[21]

A fourth element—liberalism—has become more widely featured in debates about Israel's identity in recent years. Although Israel's status as a liberal democracy generally goes unchallenged, four potential problems exist. The first is the Arab minority in the Israeli state, a minority that Israeli authorities view as having dual loyalties, and, therefore, unable to be trusted with the full benefits, obligations, and markings of citizenship that are available to Jewish Israelis.[22] The second is Israel's record regarding the territories captured in the 1967 war. Palestinians live in tremendous insecurity, without the same civil rights and protections available to Israeli citizens. These issues became more pressing when the extension of Israeli sovereignty over these territories became a realistic op-

[16] Shlomo Avineri, *The Making of Modern Zionism* (New York: Basic Books, 1981).

[17] Elon, "Politics of Memory"; Tom Segev, *The Seventh Million* (New York: Hill and Wang, 1993).

[18] David Grossman, "Fifty is a Dangerous Age," *New Yorker* (April 20, 1998): 55.

[19] Zerubavel, *Recovered Roots*, chap. 6.

[20] Asher Arian, *Security Threatened* (New York: Cambridge University Press, 1995): 27.

[21] On Israel as a realist state, see Shibley Telhami, "Israeli Foreign Policy: A Realist Ideal Type or a Breed of Its Own," in *Israel in Comparative Perspective*, ed. Michael Barnett (Albany: State University of New York Press, 1996): 29–52. For illustrations of how the legacy of the Holocaust translates into specific foreign-policy action, see Segev, *The Seventh Million*. For the cultural basis of Israel's realist foreign policy, see Yehoshafat Harkabi, *Israel's Fateful Decisions* (London: I. B. Taurus, 1988).

[22] Yoav Peled, "Ethnic Democracy and the Legal Construction of Citizenship: Arab Citizens of the Jewish State," *American Political Science Review* 86 (June 1992).

tion. The third is the relationship between liberalism and Judaism and whether law emanates from the citizenry or from God. Although during the first decades of the state's existence this tension was temporarily resolved, the decline of Labor Zionism and the rising power of Orthodox Jewry have created a divergence that many Israelis believe is more threatening to the state's existence than that posed by the Arab states or the Palestinians. Fourth, the communal narrative that defines the religious and nationalist ethos of Israeli identity makes an individualistic liberalism difficult to sustain.[23]

Since the beginnings of Zionism, Jews and Israelis have debated how the constituent threads of religion, nationalism, the Holocaust, and liberalism would and should shape Israeli identity. For the first three decades of the state's existence, however, little debate occurred about that identity because of the territorial status quo and the hegemony of Labor Zionism, which produced a nationalist, Zionist personality. After 1967, however, that debate returned, first like a lamb and then like a lion because of demographic shifts, the decline of Labor Zionism, the capture of the occupied territories, and the collapse of the Cold War.[24] These cascading developments are responsible for Israel's widely observed identity crisis.

NARRATIVES

National identities are typically situated within a broader historical narrative. The establishment of a narrative, argues Yael Zerubavel, "constitutes one of the most important mechanisms by which a nation constructs a collective identity."[25] Quite simply, a narrative is a story with a plot.[26] As applied to national

[23] Ezrahi, *Rubber Bullets.*

[24] For various statements on how the basic values of Zionism and the Israeli political culture increasingly conflict, see Ezrahi, *Rubber Bullets;* Erik Cohen, "Citizenship, Nationality, and Religion in Israel and Thailand," in *The Israeli State and Society: Boundaries and Frontiers,* ed. Baruch Kimmerling(Albany: State University of New York Press, 1989): 66–92; Arian, *Security Threatened,* chap. 8; Sammy Smooha, "Minority Status in an Ethnic Democracy: The Status of the Arab Minority in Israel," *Ethnic and Racial Studies* 13, 389–413; Kimmerling, *Zionism and Territory* (Berkeley: University of California Press, 1983); and Dan Horowitz and Moshe Lissak, *Trouble in Utopia: The Overburdened Polity of Israel* (Albany: State University of New York Press, 1987).

[25] Zerubavel, *Recovered Roots,* 214.

[26] For narrative analysis, see Lawrence Stone, "The Revival of the Narrative," *Past and Present,* in Stone, *The Past and the Present Revisited* (London: Routledge and Keegan Paul, 1981): chap. 3; Hayden White, *Metahistory* (Baltimore: Johns Hopkins University Press, 1973); William Sewell, "Introduction: Narratives and Social Identities," *Social Science History* 16, no. 4 (winter 1991): 479–88; Jerome Bruner, "The Narrative Construction of Reality," *Critical Inquiry* 18, no. 1 (1991): 1–21; Alex Callinicos, *Theories and Narratives* (Durham, N.C.: Duke University Press, 1995): chap. 2; Dcnald Polkinghorne, *Narrative Knowing and the Human Sciences* (Albany: State University of New York Press, 1986); Paul Riceour, *Time and Narrative,* 3 vols. (Chicago: University of Chicago Press, 1984, 1985, 1988); and *On Narrative,* ed. W. J. T. Mitchell (Chicago: University of Chicago Press, 1980).

identity, the claim is that nations typically construct a story line concerning their origins, the critical events that define them as a people, and broad agreement over where they should be headed. This claim raises several critical issues concerning how the nation constructs an understanding of its history and how that interpretation provides a map for the future.[27]

First, narratives are not simply imposed by the outside observer but rather are constructed by the participants themselves.[28] Because actors locate themselves within a story line, an actor's identity continues a story line from the past through the present and some imagined future. Early Zionists told a story about the Jewish people that had a concrete beginning, the expulsion of the Jews from ancient Israel by the Romans; a middle, in which Jews resided in fear and insecurity in alien lands; and a hopeful ending, in which Jews were resurrected and transformed as a result of their relationship to the land. The story also depicted the Jews as ultimately being treated as a "normal" people among the community of nations.[29] This narrative was constructed, lived, and acted on by all of those who defined themselves as Zionists.

Second, to the extent that actors locate themselves within a shared story line, they can be said to have a collective identity.[30] Part of what makes a nation an "imagined community" is its ability to imagine itself within a shared historical space distinct from the story line that defines other nations and political communities. Zionism, as it shapes the Israeli "nation," explicitly defines the period of Jewish life in exile as a wholly negative reference point, characterizing non-Zionist religious Jews as having lived a life of "cultural stagnation, political inaction, and victimization that was characteristic of the Exile." This characterization stands in sharp contrast to the perceived vitality of Jewish life in antiquity and in modern Israel.[31]

[27] For forays into the nationalism literature that inform this discussion, see Benedict Anderson, *Imagined Communities*, 2nd ed. (New York: Verso Press, 1991); and Eric Hobsbawm, *Nations and Nationalism Since 1780: Programme, Myth, Reality*, 2nd ed. (New York: Cambridge University Press, 1992).

[28] Brian Fay, *Contemporary Philosophy of Social Science* (Boston: Basil Blackwell, 1996), chap. 9. Also see Renato Rosaldo, *Culture and Truth* (Boston: Beacon Press, 1993), chap. 6; and Karl Schiebe, "Self-Narratives and Adventure," in *Narrative Psychology: The Storied Nature of Human Conduct*, ed. Theodore Sabine (New York: Praeger Press, 1986): 131.

[29] Zerubavel, *Recovered Roots*; Ezrahi, *Rubber Bullets*, 6; and Don Handelman, *Models and Mirrors: Toward an Anthropology of Public Events* (New York: Cambridge University Press, 1990): 227.

[30] David Carr, *Time, Narrative, History* (Bloomington: Indiana University Press, 1986): 163.

[31] Zerubavel, *Recovered Roots*, 215. Yitzhak Rabin, for instance, stated that in childhood he learned an image of the Diaspora Jew who was a "bent-over Jew possessed of meager bodily strength and immense mental powers." Rabin proceeded not to disavow that image but to describe how the Israeli Jew matched powers to strength. See Yitzhak Rabin, *The Rabin Memoirs* (Berkeley: University of California Press, 1996): 396–97.

Third, events play a central role in a historical narrative; in fact, it is virtually impossible for a narrative to exist without a series of events that are cognitively connected. The connection of the present to the past is a fundamental feature of historical time; temporality is organized around turning points that are made meaningful by their placement within the context of a community that understands its origins and its history.[32] In this fundamental way, events do not have an objective meaning but rather are made politically meaningful by actors who locate them within an overarching narrative that links an interpretation of the past and an image of the future.[33] As Zerubavel notes, Masada and Tel Hai were not simply events that occurred nearly two thousand years apart but rather were similarly situated and became symbols that defined the collective identity because they were invested with political and cultural meaning.[34]

National societies debate what is the dominant narrative. Different narratives connect different events in different ways with different emphases and with different implications for collective identity. Consider the case of Masada, a mountain fortress overlooking the Dead Sea that was the site of the last Jewish resistance to the Roman empire in 73 C.E. According to Zerubavel, in the Zionist narrative Masada connected the present-day Israel to ancient Israel, became a symbol of willingness to fight nearly insurmountable odds for the national homeland, and generated a symbol to distinguish Zionists from Diaspora Jews who had a "defeatist" and "passive" mentality.[35] But by the early 1970s an alternative narrative had challenged the historical foundations and interpretations of Masada. According to this alternative narrative, Masada distorted the nature of the Jewish resistance and generated a "complex" that led Israel to take uncompromising positions and to perceive itself to be much weaker than it was. According to one revisionist study, Masada's centrality has receded in recent years, suggesting the shift from a Zionist to a post-Zionist narrative.[36]

The debate over how to understand the past implicates the understanding of the present and an orientation toward the future. Conflict over how to understand the past as well as the past's implications for the future has been exacerbated by many factors, including the diversification and political polarization of Israeli society, revisionist historians, controversy over the television program *Tekumah*, and new editions of Israeli textbooks that de-emphasize the Jewish experience. As actors fix a narrative of the past, they imagine, in Jerome Bruner's

[32] Carr, *Time, Narrative, History*, 166; also see A. P. Cohen, *Symbolic Construction of Community* (New York: Tavistock, 1985).

[33] Murray Edelman, *Constructing the Political Spectacle* (Chicago: University of Chicago Press, 1988).

[34] Zerubavel, *Recovered Roots*.

[35] Zerubavel, *Recovered Roots*.

[36] Nachman Ben-Yehuda, *The Masada Myth* (Madison: University of Wisconsin Press, 1995).

words, "possible maps and possible worlds."[37] In order for actors to have a sense of how they should proceed, they must have some understanding of where they have been, and they use those narrative understandings to reason, calculate probabilities, and estimate the consequences of their actions.[38]

As long as actors are aware of the influence of such narratives on guiding the future, they can be expected to appropriate a narrative for ulterior purposes and to try to alter that narrative so that it better connects to their vision of the future. In other words, the underlying structure that both constitutes and constrains actors also provides the wellspring for social practices and allows for strategic behavior. Several important social theories refuse to reduce action to either preordained interests or social rules, but rather recognize how actors combine the models, symbols, and scripts that compose the normative structure in their strategies of action. This feature of social life is captured by Ann Swidler's famous metaphor that culture provides a "tool kit," Mary Douglas's concept of bricolage, and Pierre Bourdieu's logic of practice.[39] However we do it, we must recognize the "self-conscious capacity of actors to engage in deliberate and creative transposition . . . to inject agency into structural explanations and develop a more refined and dynamic theory of action."[40]

In general, the narrative of national identity provides an understanding of the past, present, and future; events are subjectively linked to that identity; and a particular construction of the past provides a link to the present and the future. This narrative of the national identity is a social construct, and actors will reconstruct the past as they debate the future. But they do so not simply for principled reasons but also for pragmatic and strategic ones. These are politicians whose actions we study, after all.

FRAMES

Frames "are specific metaphors, symbolic representations, and cognitive cues used to render or cast behavior and events in an evaluative mode and to suggest

[37] *Actual Minds, Possible Worlds* (Cambridge, Mass.: Harvard University Press, 1986): 49–50.

[38] See, for instance, Emery Roe, *Narrative Policy Analysis: Theory and Practice* (Durham: Duke University Press, 1994); Bruner, *Acts of Meaning* (Cambridge: Harvard University Press, 1990); James March, *Decisions and Organization* (Boston: Basil Blackwell, 1988); March and Johan P. Olsen, *Rediscovering Institutions: The Organizational Basis of Politics* (New York: Free Press, 1989); and March, "Understanding How Decisions Happen in Organizations," in *Organizational Decision Making*, ed. Z. Shapira (New York: Cambridge University Press, 1997): 9–33.

[39] Ann Swidler, "Culture in Action: Symbols in Strategies," *American Sociological Review* 51, no. 2 (1986): 273–86; Mary Douglas, *How Institutions Think* (Syracuse University Press, 1986); and Pierre Bourdieu, *Logic of Practice* (Stanford, Calif.: Stanford University Press, 1980).

[40] John Campbell, "Institutional Analysis and the Role of Ideas in Political Economy," *Theory and Society* 27 (1998): 383. Leading scholars of foreign-policy analysis have made comparable pleas. See Walter Carlsneas, "The Agency-Structure Problem in Foreign Policy Analysis," *International Studies Quarterly* 36, 245–70.

alternative modes of action."[41] Actors strategically deploy frames to situate events, to interpret problems, to fashion a shared understanding of the world, to galvanize sentiments as a way to mobilize and guide social action, and to suggest possible solutions to problems. Frames have two key characteristics that are particularly relevant for my purposes. First, actors compete to frame the event because how the event is understood has important consequences for mobilizing action and furthering their interests. This competition can be regarded as the "conscious strategic efforts by groups of people to fashion shared understandings of the world and of themselves that legitimate collective action."[42] Toward that end, political elites draw on "cultural symbols that are selectively chosen from a cultural toolchest and creatively converted" into frames for action.[43] This cultural toolchest includes symbols that can be used to mobilize sentiment and to guide action.

Second, although frames are always important for collective mobilization, their importance is amplified at historical moments defined by cultural contradictions and competing visions of the future. As Mayer Zald notes:

> Political and mobilization opportunities are often created by cultural breaks and the surfacing of long dormant contradictions that reframe grievances and injustices and the possibilities for action. Sometimes these breaks are behavioral events that recast or challenge the prevailing definitions of the situation, thus changing perceptions of costs and benefits of policies and programs and the perception of injustice of the status quo.[44]

At such moments political entrepreneurs must construct frames that can do one of the following: reconcile these contradictions, situate these events in ways that

[41] Mayer N. Zald, "Culture, Ideology, and Strategic Framing," in *Comparative Perspectives on Social Movements: Political Opportunities, Mobilizing Structures, and Cultural Framing*, ed. D. McAdam, J. McCarthy, and M. Zald (New York: Cambridge University Press, 1996): 5, 262. Also see Erving Goffman, *Frame Analysis* (Cambridge: Harvard University Press, 1974): 21; Johnathan Turner, *The Theory of Social Interaction* (Palo Alto, Calif.: Stanford University Press, 1988): 108–13; David Snow and Robert Benford, "Master Frames and Cycles of Protest," in *Frontiers in Social Movement Theory*, ed. Aldon Morris and Carol Mueller (New Haven, Conn.: Yale University Press, 1992): 138; Snow, E. Rochford, S. Worden, and Benford, "Frame Alignment Processes, Micromobilization, and Movement Participation," *American Sociological Review* 51 (August 1986): 464; Zdzislaw Mach, *Symbols, Conflict, and Identity* (Albany: State University of New York Press): 36; and Benford and David Snow, "Dramaturgy and Social Movements: The Social Construction and Communication of Power," *Sociological Inquiry* 62 (February 1992): 36–55.

[42] McAdam, McCarthy, and Zald, *Comparative Perspectives*, 6.

[43] Sidney Tarrow, *Power in Movements* (New York: Cambridge University Press, 1994): 119; also see Swidler, "Culture in Action," and Cohen, *Symbolic Construction of Community*.

[44] Zald, "Culture, Ideology, and Strategic Framing," 268.

mesh with the cultural terrain, or recast the relationship between the cultural foundations, the costs and benefits of particular policies, and the circumstances at hand. For an Israel in the midst of an identity crisis caused by conflicting visions of the future, a successful frame is one that accomplishes this seemingly herculean task.

Thus far I have contended that connecting the Israeli identity to the peace process requires consideration of the debate over Israeli identity, how that identity is situated within a larger historical narrative, and how that narrative itself provides important elements of the "cultural tool kit" that is available to Israeli leaders as they vie to frame the peace process in various ways. Political elites are keenly aware that legitimating their policies requires demonstrating how they are consistent with the cultural terrain—and sometimes that requires revising the cultural terrain.

INSTITUTIONS

These debates over national identity, construction of national interests, and policy orientations also have to be situated within an institutional context. Identity shapes policy by drawing together and shaping societal interests into a national interest,[45] the formal institutional context represents the political space in which that occurs and suggests whose interests are incorporated. This point is generally accepted by students of social movements and collective action, who recognize that the mobilizing capacity of a frame also depends on a "political opportunity structure," broadly understood as the institutional context that gives incentives and disincentives for individual and group action.[46] This point is also generally accepted by students of historical institutionalism, who recognize how institutions not only determine which groups are mobilized but also reconfigure societal constellations.[47] To concentrate on the ideational to the neglect of the institutional is to ignore the political context in which actors strategize and can be organized toward a policy outcome.

In Israel the relevant institutional contexts are electoral, coalition, and party politics. Briefly, Israel's proportional representative system makes it relatively easy for smaller parties to get elected to the Knesset, the Israeli parliament. One result of this electoral system is that no party has ever gained an outright majority, forcing the largest vote-getting party to assemble a coalition with

[45] Mlada Bukovansky, "American Identity and Neutral Rights from Independence to the War of 1812," *International Organization* 51, no. 2 (spring 1997): 209–43.

[46] John McCarthy, "Constraints and Opportunities in Adopting, Adapting, and Inventing," in *Comparative Perspectives*, ed. McAdam, McCarthy, and Zald, 141–50.

[47] Kathleen Thelen and Sven Steinmo, "Historical Institutionalism in Comparative Politics," in *Structuring Politics: Historical Institutionalism in Comparative Analysis*, ed. Steinmo, Thelen, and Longstreth (New York: Cambridge University Press, 1992): 1–32.

smaller parties, handing the latter greater clout than is arguably warranted by their electoral tally. Electoral reforms that took effect in the 1996 elections only encouraged this splintering tendency. The result was an increase in the ever-present politics of coalition formation that carry over into the politics of coalition maintenance, with smaller parties extracting economic and political dividends in return for their pledge to stay in the coalition.

Israeli political parties play a central role in mobilizing group action, defining policy options, and articulating alternative paths. In articulating these alternatives, different parties interpolate different elements of the Israeli national identity in different ways. Public-opinion data suggest that the Jewish Israeli population ranks the following four values in descending order: maintaining Israel as Jewish state; securing peace; and, running neck and neck, maintaining Israel as a democracy and preserving Greater Israel. Although the Jewish Israeli public agrees on the necessity of maintaining Israel as a Jewish state, the parties on the left and the right differ dramatically in terms of the value they place on democracy and Greater Israel, with leftist parties preferring liberalism and democracy over Greater Israel, and rightist parties reversing this order.[48] Labor and Likud are somewhat hazier on these fundamental issues, but Labor articulates a narrative that can be sustained without the territories and offers a more hopeful appraisal of progress and coexistence. Likud's narrative is based on the saga and unceasing nature of Jewish persecution, the redemption and protection provided by Jewish military power, and a mission to settle the whole of Israel and the occupied territories.[49] In sum, the nature of party and coalition politics profoundly shapes the articulation of Israeli national identity and how that identity relates to a national interest and the possibility of peace.

These ideational and institutional considerations provide the basis for some propositions concerning the evolution of the Oslo Accords. Israel's identity conflict is partly shaped by its control over the territories. A peace process that explicitly involves a withdrawal from the territories will exacerbate that identity conflict, suggesting that any movement in the peace process is predicated on the establishment of an Israeli national identity, narrative, and frame tied to a withdrawal.[50] But because a significant percentage of Israelis—those in the "political middle"—articulate values that are consistent with a withdrawal given the proper conditions, shrewd political elites strategically frame the peace process by rearticulating core values and immediate interests toward that end.

[48] Arian, *Security Threatened*, 230.

[49] Ezrahi, *Rubber Bullets*, 12, 14; on their haziness, see Arian, *Security Threatened*, 230.

[50] "The dilemma facing Israel," Arian writes, "is to order the values of a Jewish state, democracy, and equality for all, peace and the land of Israel, in a manner which will preserve consensus in the polity." *Security Threatened*, 230.

Whether these cultural resources are re-articulated and aligned in a way that makes a withdrawal legitimate and desirable depends on the institutional context in which political elites calculate their interests, and even cause actors to discover their preferences. Because of the political and symbolic resources at his disposal, the prime minister plays a commanding, though not exclusive, role.[51] The prime minister's willingness and ability to create the cultural conditions for a change in the peace process, however, are affected by the ruling party's dependence on smaller, extreme parties for coalition maintenance. Consequently, a left-center coalition is likely to articulate a view of national identity that is tied to withdrawal from the territories, a centrist coalition is less likely to do so, and a center-right coalition is least likely to do so. In fact, a center-right coalition will articulate a national identity that depends on control over these territories. Blending ideational and institutional politics enhances one's ability to identify the conditions under which a peace process defined in terms of withdrawal from the territories becomes possible, legitimate, and even desirable. In other words, if the Israeli identity is defined by an explicit preference of democracy and Zionism over Greater Israel (defined in both religious and security terms) and a coalition ranks these values in a similar way, then the cultural foundations exist for a peace process that allows for the withdrawal from the occupied territories. These possibilities are not always present and readily available to the first willing politician. Instead, actors create these possibilities by appropriating cultural and symbolic resources.

Section II: The 1992 Elections, the Two Yizthaks, and the Two Israels

Three developments in the late 1980s and early 1990s provoked a crisis about the Israeli identity. One was the Israeli state's relationship to the territories, a hotly contested issue from the moment Israel captured the lands in the 1967 war. Friction escalated when settlement expansion was scrutinized more intensely, during the Intifada, and whenever a land-for-peace deal was discussed. But until Israel entered into direct negotiations with the Arab states and the PLO, the debate over whether and how Israel should dispose of the territories was largely academic.

The second event was a growing and grudging acceptance by Arab states of Israel's legitimacy and existence. The Arabs' readiness to negotiate directly with Israel was the result of various factors—decades of frustration with a conflict that clearly had no military solution, the end of the Cold War, the decline of Arabism and the rise of statism, and the aftermath of the Iraqi invasion of

[51] See McAdam, McCarthy, and Zald, *Comparative Perspectives*, 17, for the general point, and Gadi Wolfsfeld, *Media and Political Conflict: News from the Middle East* (New York: Cambridge University Press, 1997), for the case of Israel.

Kuwait. During that aftermath, the Arab states determined that they had had enough of conflicts in the name of pan-Arabism and of the PLO, which had provided emotional support to Saddam Hussein. Most important, the Arab states signaled their readiness to negotiate directly with Israel.[52] It was well understood, however, that any solution would require Israel's withdrawal from the territories and the real possibility of a Palestinian state.

The third event was the end of the Cold War. The United States and Israel supposedly had a "special relationship" that presumably was forged not by shared interests but rather by a shared bond. The end of the Cold War, however, tested that hypothesis. Since 1967 Israel had been a strategic ally of the United States in the fight against communism and Soviet interests in the Middle East, but the end of the Cold War stripped Israel of that role and, some feared, the true basis of its alliance with the United States. In the context of the aftermath of the Gulf War and possible momentum for the peace process, the Bush administration argued that the U.S.-Israeli bond was unshakable—but that the United States expected Israel to capitalize on this rare opportunity for peace. In response to a fall 1991 request by the Shamir government that the United States provide $10 billion in loan guarantees, the Bush administration announced that such guarantees were contingent on the Shamir government's pledge not to use these loans for West Bank activities. Shamir balked, Bush and Secretary of State James Baker refused to renege on this demand, and for the next several months the United States and Israel were at loggerheads. In Israel, this crisis in U.S.-Israeli relations unleashed a debate over whether this episode opened a new chapter in U.S.-Israeli relations, whether Shamir was unnecessarily provoking a crisis, and whether Israel's economic fortunes were being sacrificed for the ideology of Greater Israel.

These three developments placed tremendous pressure on Israel to reconsider its relationship to the territories and to determine what were acceptable risks for peace. Israeli Prime Minister Yitzhak Shamir made quite clear that he could never envision an Israel that did not include the West Bank. Although he agreed to meet in Madrid with his Arab neighbors and a PLO-sponsored delegation, his reluctance to do so, he proclaimed, sprung from am unwavering belief that Israel must retain Judea and Samaria. His views were supported by an array of domestic groups. Settlers and the religious right argued that Israel had a God-given right to the land, and Israeli hawks insisted that the West Bank was an important buffer between itself and Jordan; a Palestinian entity, they said, would represent a military threat to Israel's existence. The Israeli Labor Party and others on the left assailed these pre-negotiation conditions as sacrificing a

[52] Barnett, *Dialogues in Arab Politics: Negotiations in Regional Order* (New York: Columbia University Press, 1998): chap 7.

rare opportunity for peace and Israel's prosperity. The subtext to this debate was: What was Israel to be?

The 1992 Israeli election transformed subtext into text. Israel's identity crisis was played out in the election, pitting the "two Yitzhaks"—Shamir and Rabin—with two alternatives visions of Israel's identity in relationship to the territories. Shamir campaigned in defense of his policies, on his handling of the United States, and, fundamentally, on his belief in Greater Israel.[53] Rabin countered with a campaign that deftly framed Shamir's policies as costing Israel a chance for peace and causing Israel to divert scarce resources from high-priority domestic items—that is, from Israel proper—to superfluous ideological settlement expansion and to undeserving yeshivot and religious institutions.[54] At a campaign rally in the Likud stronghold of Beer-Sheva, he sent the crowd wild with enthusiasm when he stated: "The Likud took your money, the money you paid in taxes, and threw it away in the territories."[55] Rabin, in short, consistently framed the settlements as holding hostage Israel's future peace and prosperity and as depriving Israel of its Zionist and liberal identity; in doing so he won over constituencies who were historically hostile to Labor.[56]

The contrast between Rabin and former Prime Minister Shamir could not have been more stark. Shamir, the Likud, and those on the right who continued to embed Israel's past in a religious and ultranationalist story line rarely acknowledged that the end of the Cold War—that is, a rupture of a narrative—might have political relevance for Israel. Meanwhile, Rabin and others on the left constantly elevated this event as an unprecedented break in the narrative of international politics that provided Israel with a rare moment to join the other Western nations in a common story. Whereas Shamir articulated a characteristically collectivist position that Israel is an "ideological country" that must retain the territories, Rabin exclaimed at his swearing-in ceremony that "we are determined to put the citizen at the top of our concerns," and then proceeded to connect the citizen who is interested in security and welfare to a withdrawal from the territories.[57] An Israel that was consumed by the legion of injustices that were committed against the Jews and believed that such injustices were always part of Israel's future would have difficulty recognizing the values that bound it

[53] Yitzhak Shamir, *Summing Up: An Autobiography* (New York: Little, Brown, 1994): 251–56.

[54] Arian, *Security Threatened*, 157.

[55] Quoted from David Horowitz, ed., *Shalom, Friend: The Life and Legacy of Yitzhak Rabin* (New York: Newmarket Press, 1996): 131.

[56] *In Security Threatened*, 156–57, Arian contends that settlements and spending on religious institutions were the critical "wedge" issues of the 1992 elections. Also see Arian and Michal Shamir, *The Elections in Israel, 1992*, ed. Arian and Shamir (Albany: State University of New York Press, 1995): 6–7.

[57] Ezrahi, *Rubber Bullets*, 71.

to other states and even more difficulty relinquishing the territories that would be expected in a peace agreement.

Although interpreting electoral results is always tricky, Rabin's victory was widely read as a mandate for a vision of a "State of Israel" and a blow to those championing "Greater Israel."[58] Called the *mahapach*—the reversal or turnabout—the election gave Labor 44 seats, Likud 32, Meretz 12, Tsomet 8, the religious parties 14, and the Arab parties 5. Marking the first governmental change since 1977 and the second in Israel's history, Yitzhak Rabin's Labor Party returned to power and entered into a coalition with the leftist Meretz and several smaller parties. The election was more than a defeat for Likud; it also signaled a dramatic drubbing of the parties on the political right.[59] Not only did the rightist parties fare quite badly; the extreme right Moledet Party, which advocated the forcible expulsion of the West Bank Palestinians, failed to capture a single seat.[60] The nationalist and religious compact that had largely ruled Israel since 1977 was now in the opposition, and the Labor-left coalition basked in this widely interpreted mandate for change.

Rabin's onslaught continued after the campaign.[61] The moment he was sworn into office, Rabin voiced his views on the Israeli collective identity, attempting to redefine the dominant narrative that informed that identity and to frame the peace process in a way that was consistent with that identity and narrative. In a series of highly visible speeches and interviews, he articulated a view of the Israeli identity defined by Zionism and democracy, reserving a marginal space for religion.[62] In an address at the commencement exercises at National Security College, Rabin answered his own question of "What kind of Israel do we want?" by offering an "all-encompassing one: We want a state of Jews, a Zionist state, a progressive democratic state, and a strong state."[63] He omitted a Jewish state. In these and other moments he stressed Israel's secular and human-

---

[58] Arian, *Security Threatened*, 151.

[59] For an analysis of the 1992 elections, see Arian and Shamir, "Introduction," and Daniel Elazar and Shmuel Sandler, eds., *Israel at the Polls, 1992* (Lanham, Md.: Rowman and Littlefield, 1995).

[60] See Ehud Sprinzak, *The Ascendance of Israel's Radical Right* (New York: Oxford University Press, 1991), on the rise of the radical right.

[61] The focus on Rabin both is deliberate and is not intended to downplay the complex relationship between him and Shimon Peres. I focus on Rabin precisely because he was viewed as unsentimental, coldly calculating, and as a soldier first and foremost. Peres, on the other hand, had a well-earned reputation for being philosophical and prone toward grand speculation. The conventional wisdom at the time was that their different traits and long-standing political rivalry meant that they formed a formidable team, each holding in check the extremes of the other and providing a grounded base from which to take the various political and security risks required to sustain the peace process.

[62] Peleg, "The Peace Process," 15.

[63] Rabin, *The Rabin Memoirs*, 398.

istic tradition, which, he argued, could thrive only in a democratic Israel connected to the West. In the same spirit, he ridiculed the religious right and the settlers who he believed were a threat to that tradition. In his memoirs he wrote that "in Gush Enumim, I see an extremely grave phenomenon, a cancer in the body of Israeli democracy"; during the 1992 campaign he called the settlers "parasites"; and as prime minister he referred to the Bible as an "antiquated land registry." Rabin's assault on the settlers and the religious right paled in comparison to that leveled by Meretz, his coalition partner. The minister of education suggested that references to religion be eliminated in war memorial services, that Jewish dietary laws were unnecessary, and that the Israel Defense Forces needed a new code of ethics that should highlight the defense of democracy and downplay references to Judaism.

This identity was situated within a historical narrative that slightly but consequentially altered Israel's relationship to other states and political communities. By attempting to expunge ideology and religion from the Israeli collective identity, he challenged the alternative narratives that were being offered by the religious right, the settlers, and the security hawks. All of these groups believed that Israel stood as a people apart because of either historical or religious reasons, that past events clearly demonstrated that narrative, and that the future could be deterministically spun from the past. By forwarding Israel's secular and liberal tradition, Rabin was situating Israel in the West's historical narrative of progress, development, democracy, and modernity, and was encouraging Israelis to reconsider the extent to which they were truly isolated in the international community. He introduced his government to the Knesset by challenging the nation "to set aside the notion that Israel stands alone, that the whole world is against us."[64] Although Rabin and his allies constantly acknowledged the Holocaust, past persecution of the Jews, and Israel's existence as a testimony to its own efforts and not to the assistance of non-Jews, they also imagined Israel's future as contained in a new story line that it shared with others and thus represented a break from its existential isolation.

Rabin's moves toward a new historical narrative did not occur in a political or intellectual vacuum. Broader currents within society made his message resonate and politically conceivable. Rabin followed a decade of intellectual and cultural developments within Israel that challenged many of the most cherished interpretations of the past, symbols, and taboos of Israeli society and history. The "New Historians" forced open many of the "myths" of Israel's beginnings. In doing so, they made Israeli history less unique and suggested that Zionism was not a divinely inspired revival; it was a typical product of modern nationalism.

---

[64] "Address to the Knesset by Prime Minister Yitzhak Rabin Introducing His Government," Jerusalem, July 13, 1993; cited from Rabin, *The Rabin Memoirs*, 386.

Thus, the challenge of creating a liberal society based on a universal concept of citizenship in an ethnically divided society was not unique either.[65] Authors, playwrights, and literary critics likewise questioned the foundational under-standings of what made Israel Israel, and the Intifada stimulated development of nongovernmental organizations and social movements that attempted to "pro-tect" Israel's liberal and humanistic values.[66]

Rabin offered a vision of Israel's national identity and its historical narrative that were explicitly tied to a frame for the peace process.[67] The frame that he used depicted a withdrawal from the territories as furthering Israel's long-term security and development; the withdrawal also would generate peace dividends that included budget reallocations from defense to social welfare, plus a climate conducive to foreign investments and Israel's integration into the world economy. The frame delivered by this warrior-politician assembled a somewhat diverse coalition, including nationalists who worried that Israel was endanger-ing its security, "liberalizing" economic elites who believed that their economic futures depended on becoming linked to the world economy, and many Sephardim and Russians who believed that they would economically benefit from any peace dividend and reduction in governments subsidies to religious and settler communities.[68] The frame that he employed, in short, organized ex-perience, alerted individuals how their interests were at stake, and directed those interests to a particular outcome.

The relationships between Israel's national identity, historical narrative, and frame on peace and security converged in Israel's decision to recognize the PLO and to sign the Declaration of Principles in fall 1993. This milestone provided a framework for proceeding with negotiations to end the decades-long conflict between Israel and the Palestinians.[69] The two most important features of Oslo were mutual acknowledgment of the legitimacy of each side's national aspira-tions and Israel's readiness to hand over the territories to a Palestinian authority. Both the PLO and Israel were asked to redefine their national missions and

[65] This argument is made by Zeev Sternhell, *The Founding Myths of Israel* (Princeton, N.J.: Princeton University Press, 1995). For a sampling of the scholarship of the New Historians, see *New Perspectives on Israeli History: The Early Years of the State*, ed. Laurence Silberstein (New York: New York University Press, 1991). For a particularly stinging rebuttal, see Efraim Karsh, *Fabricating Israeli History: The 'New Historians'* (Portland, Ore.: Cass, 1997).

[66] Peleg, "The Peace Process and Israel's Political Cultures," 15.

[67] Ben-Yehuda, "Attitude Change and Policy Transformation: Yitzhak Rabin and the Pales-tinian Question, 1967–1995," in *From Rabin to Netanyahu*, 201–24.

[68] On coalitions that have an internationalist outlook, see Etel Solingen, *Regional Orders at Century's Dawn: Global and Domestic Influences on Grand Strategy* (Princeton, N.J.: Princeton University Press, 1998).

[69] For descriptions and analyses of Oslo, see David Makovsky, *Making Peace with the PLO: The Rabin Government's Road to the Oslo Accord* (Boulder, Colo.: Westview Press, 1996).

aspirations through this compromise, expunging the extremist voices from their midst. For the PLO this meant disavowing the desire for a Palestinian homeland in all of Israel and being ready to live within a smaller entity in the West Bank and Gaza. For Israel it meant ridding itself of the religious and nationalist tenets that were constitutively tied to the territories.

Rabin legitimated and framed the accords in a way that articulated a direct relationship between the Israeli collective identity, its national interests, and the peace process. In an interview the night of the historic handshake between himself and Yasir Arafat, Rabin explained:

> I believe . . . annexation will bring . . . racism to Israel, [and] that racism and Judaism are in contradiction by their very essence. Israel that will preach racism will not be a Jewish state by my understanding. . . . Otherwise [Israel will have to give the Palestinians] full civilian rights as we give to every individual who is an Israeli citizen. . . . Every one of them, once inside, can be a full Israeli citizen . . . [and will constitute] 35 percent of the voters to the Knesset. . . . They'll dictate if Israel will be a Jewish state with a destiny to serve the Jewish people all over the world, or we will become another small Jewish country . . . because 35 percent of the voters will be non-Jewish. . . . I don't expect [the Palestinians] to be Zionists. And if Israel will lose the Zionists from its very existence, Israel will be an entirely different country. . . . Therefore, whoever speaks now about the whole land of Israel speaks either of a racist Jewish state which will not be a Jewish or a binational state. I prefer Israel to be a Jewish state, not all over the land of Israel.[70]

Acknowledging a direct link between a continuation of certain practices and Israel's collective identity, Rabin was responding to a 25-year-old identity crisis caused by Israel's capture of the territories in the 1967 war. The only way to resolve that crisis in favor of a Western, Democratic, and Jewish Israel was to relinquish Israel's control over the territories.[71]

[70] Interview with Yitzhak Rabin on the *MacNeil-Lehrer NewsHour* (Sept. 13, 1993). Also see Ben Lynfield, "Rabin Tries to Make Less of 'Greater Israel,'" *Christian Science Monitor* (Jan. 25, 1994): 22.

[71] The Israeli government's decision to label Kach and Kahana Hay as terrorist organizations after the terrorist attack in Hebron in February 1994 was also read through the image of the Western "self" in general and the belief that Israel's democratic and liberal identity was being challenged from within. See, for instance, "Rabin Addresses Knesset on Hebron Massacre," *FBIS-NES* (March 1, 1994): 31–33; and Clyde Haberman, "Israel Votes Ban on Jewish Groups Linked to Kahane," *New York Times* (March 14, 1994): 1.

Although a Zionist and liberal identity made the Oslo Accords possible and meaningful, a necessary and critical shift occurred in the security calculations of Rabin and many other Israelis. In fact, Rabin's security views changed dramatically. For most of his life he had staunchly opposed direct negotiations with the PLO and anything resembling a Palestinian state. But because of a series of important events, including the Intifada, the end of the Cold War, and the Gulf War, he resigned himself to the idea of direct negotiations with the PLO, and came to believe that Israel could preserve its physical and existential security only by ridding itself of these poisonous territories.[72] The evolution of Rabin's political and military thinking mirrored a significant percentage of Israeli society. Moreover, indirect evidence indicates that his own changing public position contributed to the growing belief among the Israeli public that Israeli security could benefit from a territorial settlement. Since 1967 the percentage of Israelis who believe that Israel should withdraw from the territories given the proper conditions and security guarantees has increased significantly, with a notable increase occurring after Oslo. In a 1994 survey asking Israelis why they were willing to give back the territories, 39 percent said to lower the risk of war, 27 percent said that there was no alternative, 17 percent wanted to preserve Israel as a Jewish state, and 17 percent argued that both Israelis and Palestinians have a right to live there. And, as significantly, the percentage of people who thought that Israel should hold on to the territories because of a "right" declined from 1986 to 1994 (the last year of the survey).[73] In general, an articulation of a particular Israeli identity converged with a shift in security to make the idea of territorial withdrawal possible and desirable.

The surest indication that Rabin's statements and policies on the peace process contributed to the debate about Israel's national identity was the response he received from opponents. The settlers and the religious community were up in arms, frantic and angered by his assault on their positions and core values.[74] The tragic conclusion to this debate between Rabin and his opponents came in an assassin's bullet, delivered by the person of Yagil Amir but arguably by the corporate body of the extreme right. Rabin's assassination provoked a national and collective soul-searching, causing all to question the direction in which Israeli society was headed, whether democracy was under assault, and whether a civil war would soon erupt between religious and secular Israelis, a war whose first shot was generated by the peace process. The identity crisis that ensued with the debate over the territories had taken a murderous turn.

[72] For a discussion of the metamorphosis in Rabin's views, see Yoram Peri, "Afterword," in Y. Rabin, *The Rabin Memoirs*, 341–79.

[73] Arian, *Security Threatened*, 30–32.

[74] Horowitz, *Shalom, Friend*, chaps. 13 and 14.

In an attempt to hold elections when he was strongest and thus most likely to receive a mandate for his stewardship and his peace policies, Prime Minister Shimon Peres scheduled elections for May 1996. Confounding all pundits and the pre-election polls, however, Netanyahu squeaked by Peres by the narrowest of margins. His stunning, come-from-behind victory was attributed to many factors, from Peres's poorly run campaign to Netanyahu's televangelism. But the mortal blows probably were delivered by a string of Hamas-sponsored terrorist attacks during the election windup. Accordingly, many interpret the elections as a referendum on the Oslo Accords in practice though not in principle. Over the years Israelis had become more dovish on the territories but more hawkish on short-term security issues.[75] The ever-present danger contained in the Oslo process was that a move toward the former would incite an increase in the latter. This is exactly what happened. Netanyahu tried to assure Israeli voters that he would guard Israeli security as he struck a better deal on Oslo, in contrast to Peres, who was willing to sacrifice Israeli security for a peace treaty at any price. Peres learned that in a situation of cultural contestation and identity conflict, "Israeli leaders who seem to go too far, or too fast . . . without taking the other [side] into account, tend to pay dearly."[76]

The elections also demonstrated that Israel had become increasingly divided and fragmented. Although Labor and Likud remained the two largest parties, they lost power to smaller parties that represented more specialized interests and identity-based groups. Specifically, Labor dropped from 44 to 34 seats; the Likud-Gesher-Tsomet alliance fell from a combined total of 40 seats to 32 seats; the religious parties now had 23 seats (Shas went from 6 to 10 seats, the National Religious Party now had 9 seats, the Ahdut Ha'Torah Party remained steady at 4 seats); Natan Sharansky's Yisrael b'Aliya Party stunningly won 7 seats; and the two Arab parties, Hadash and the United Arab List, did better than ever, winning 5 and 4 seats, respectively. Netanyahu formed a government with 68 seats, 36 of which belonged to five small parties. Israel's first "American president" was now prime minister in a "coalition of outsiders and minorities," Sephardim, Russian immigrants, and ultra-Orthodox Jews who were unified in their belief that the traditional elite's time had passed.[77]

Identity-based politics and institutional reforms played key roles in this major political development. The decline of Labor Party hegemony alongside demographic changes meant that subnational groups were becoming better organized politically, increasingly mobilized, and more assertive of their views and protective of their identities. The Sephardim now had two political parties, David Levy's

[75] Arian, *Security Threatened*, 92.

[76] Ezrahi, *Rubber Bullets*, 15.

[77] Schmemann, "Outside In," *New York Times Magazine* (Nov. 23, 1997): 56.

Gesher Party and Arieh Deri's Shas, and the religious Jews had several parties to choose from, including Shas. Added to the mix was a Russian immigrant party, a possibility unleashed by a recent surge in Russian immigration. From 1989, when Soviet Premier Gorbachev first opened the gates, to 1996 more than 700,000 Russians immigrated to Israel, motivated largely for sectarian and nonideological reasons. By 1996 Russian immigrants constituted roughly 20 percent of the Israeli population, potentially wielding considerable political clout.[78]

In large measure this accretion of identity-based parties was made possible by a change in Israel's electoral laws that gave voters incentive to express more localized interests and identities. A long-standing complaint of the Israeli political system was that because no party had ever won an outright majority and smaller parties got elected to the Knesset fairly easily, larger political parties had to form coalitions with smaller, fringe parties, which then gained disproportionate power. Rabin's government, with necessary assistance from Likud, pushed through an important change in the electoral law that was intended to shrink the power of the smaller parties. In past elections Israelis had voted for a single party list, with the person occupying the top position designated to become prime minister if that party formed the next government. Beginning with the 1996 elections, however, voters voted twice—once for prime minister and once for a party list for the Knesset. The result of this electoral reform was exactly opposite of what the authors of the electoral law had presumably intended: Israelis now engaged in split-ticket voting, voting for either Labor or Likud for prime minister and then for a smaller party that represented their narrower interests for the Knesset. These electoral reforms not only enabled individuals to express their more localized identities and interests but arguably also encouraged the individuals to discover these identities and interests.[79]

In general, the success of these smaller parties, along with the existing debate over national identity, led to tremendous speculation that the Israeli polity was

[78] Schmemann, "Outside In," 76; Grossman, "Fifty is a Dangerous Age," 57.

[79] Israeli politicians have proposed various ways to suture the divisions between Ashkenazim and Sephardim, and between religious and secular Israelis. Education and Culture Minister Yitzhak Levy proposed "an ethnic revolution to promote Sephardic Jewish culture." Ehud Barak traveled to Netivot, a development town populated by Sephardim. Barak apparently hoped that his act of contrition would solve Labor's Sephardim woes, but his apology fell short of concrete measures that many Sephardim sought and angered many of the Labor faithful, who felt that the sacrifices of the founding fathers had been denigrated. See, for instance, Sarah Honig, "Barak Apologizes to Sephardim," *Jerusalem Post* (Sept. 26, 1997): 4; Abraham Rabinovich, "Barak Has No Right to Beg Forgiveness," *Jerusalem Post* (Oct. 1, 1997): 9; "The Hunt for the Minorities," *Ha'aretz* (Sept. 29, 1998). Several initiatives and proposals have tried to stem the conflict between religious and secular Jews. Yossi Beilin (Labor), Alex Lubotzky (Third Way), rabbis from the Meimad movement, and Derachim, a group promoting religious-secular dialogue, hammered out a document called "New Covenant on Religion and State" that was intended to assure the other side that their values would be honored; cited from "Editorial: A New Status Quo," *Ha'aretz* (English edition, Feb. 23, 1998).

collapsing into a "cultural tribalism" where a shared Jewish heritage barely masked the antagonism among distinct identity-based groups.[80] Although the causes of this identity crisis could be traced to long-standing cultural cleavages in Israeli society, two recent ideational and institutional developments amplified these trends. The first was the debate over Oslo and the secular, liberal, and pro-Oslo response to that identity crisis. Ultranationalists and orthodox Jews took issue with Rabin's answer to the crisis and sharpened their own positions, becoming more fully and politically mobilized.[81] In addition, the new institutional environment enabled these voices and made them politically consequential. The simultaneous injection of the Oslo Accords and the new electoral laws arguably provided the stimulus and the opportunity for these divisions to present themselves and to take on a more ominous and fragmenting character.[82]

The Netanyahu years are infamous for a paralysis in the peace process. A host of viable explanations address this condition, most of them focusing on the character and enigmatic attitude of Netanyahu toward Oslo: He was sympathetic to Oslo but was determined to bargain hard to extract the best deal; he was a foe of Oslo but was masquerading as a tough bargainer to kill it through asphyxiation; he was sympathetic but hamstrung by his coalition partners; or, he was, as former Likud Prime Minister Yitzhak Shamir claimed, a man without principles who cared only about the survival of his regime.[83] While these are viable possibilities, I want to consider two alternative explanations that focus less on Netanyahu the person and more on Netanyahu as an agent of the ultranationalist narrative and as a transmitter of the cultural fragmentation of the society he represented.

Although many claim that Netanyahu was devoid of principle and thus was ideologically promiscuous, he was, in almost all respects, a child of ultranationalism. To begin, the Likud Party in general and Netanyahu in particular consistently articulated an Israeli identity that is Jewish, nationalist, and liberal and retains control over the territories, suggesting that all of these values can be reconciled.[84] The 1996 Likud Party platform, Netanyahu's various statements

---

[80] For another interpretation of the elections as representing a fragmenting moment, see the editorial in the Israeli newspaper *Ma'ariv* (June 18, 1996): 73–74, in which it claimed that "the 1996 elections will be seen as a crossroad, in which different population groups went their separate ways." Stunningly, twice as many Israelis believe that internal conflicts are more serious than the conflict with the Palestinians, and 62 percent of Israelis believe that the religious-secular conflict is the most serious one confronting Israel. Poll conducted by the Steinmetz Center at Tel-Aviv University and cited in "Editorial: A New Status Quo."

[81] See Danny Ben-Moshe, "Elections 1996: The de-Zionization of Israeli Politics," in *From Rabin to Netanyahu*, ed. E. Karsh (Frank Cass, 1997): 66–76.

[82] For a pre-1996 assessment of these identity-based parties, see Hanna Herzog, "Penetrating the System: The Politics of Collective Identities," in *From Rabin to Netanyahu*, 81–102.

[83] Interview with Leslie Susser, "Living Legends," *Jerusalem Report* 9, no. 1 (Independence Day, 1998): 121.

[84] Also on this point see Weissbrod, "Israeli Identity in Transition," 54.

on the Oslo Accords, and even his speeches surrounding the January 1997 Hebron redeployment insisted that control over the territories could be maintained without compromising these values.[85] Even so, compelling evidence indicated that his value hierarchies were closer to the ultranationalist wing of the Likud Party, which attitudinal survey data suggested ranked Greater Israel more highly than democracy. This ranking was partly informed by the view that the Arab states and the Palestinians are culturally and politically unable of making peace with Israel and of respecting anything but a show of force.[86]

Moreover, Netanyahu's coalition depended on politicians whose constituencies were existentially threatened by the Oslo Accords, who valued Greater Israel and religion over democracy, and, therefore, who opposed policies that they believed gave the peace process greater legitimacy and momentum.[87] During the campaign Netanyahu played to those groups, including settlers, Orthodox Jews, and ultranationalists, who felt assaulted and alienated by Rabin and his coalition partners. During his reign Netanyahu attempted to guard that base of support, occasionally flirting with the idea of a national unity coalition with the Labor Party that would free him from the smaller parties' demands, but ultimately returning to his home territory. During his reelection campaign he desperately tried to court those elements and to represent himself as a guardian of their interests against the "liberals."

In addition, the historical narratives that he drew from and the way he telescoped past events to consider the present and to draw lessons for the future suggest someone who has an affinity for the nationalist narrative. Before going to London in May 1998 to confront the Americans over their proposals for breaking the impasse, Netanyahu traveled to Poland to visit the concentration camps. While at the negotiations he stated that he would never forget what he saw or that the allies refused to help the Jews of Europe, implying his determination to resist the American demands.[88] Recognizing that events are transformed into symbols and become guides for future behavior, one Israeli observer noted that "to really deal with the issue of peace, we must change the whole nature of the discourse which has been central to Israeli society for the past 50 years. The Holocaust, Masada and Tel Hai cannot continue to be the single unifying raison

[85] See, for instance, his Knesset address when he presented his government (June 18, 1996); his address to the annual meeting of the Israeli Editors Association (Nov. 27, 1997); and Herb Keinon and Saul Singer, "True Visions: An Interview with the Prime Minister," *Jerusalem Post* (April 30, 1998).

[86] See David Remnick, "Netanyahu," *New Yorker* (May 25, 1998): 42–58.

[87] See the poll published in Tamar Hermann and Ephraim Yuchtman-Yaer, "The Peace Process and the Secular-Religious Cleavage," Tame Steinmatz Center for Peace Research, Tel-Aviv University (January 1998).

[88] Uri Dan and Dennis Eisenberg, "US Pressure," *Jerusalem Post* (May 7, 1998).

d'etre of the state for another 50 years. We must move from defining the state in negative terms, of threat and security, to the positive elements—social, moral, and welfare—with which we imbue the state with meaning."[89] But this observation was offered in a context in which ultranationalist and religious meanings were ascribed to past episodes of injustice, episodes that arguably received greater attention under Netanyahu than they did under Rabin. In general, although Netanyahu might not have been an ideological zealot and certainly demonstrated a pragmatist's touch, he consistently articulated an ultranationalist narrative.

A second explanation notes that this identity crisis proceeded alongside a paralysis in the peace process, suggesting a link between the two; that is, an ambivalent posture toward Oslo reflected a fractured Israeli identity or one that was then more clearly opposed to the identity implications of Oslo. Assuming for the moment a foolish willingness to, first, accept a deterministic link between culture and behavior and, second, deny to Netanyahu the agency that I previously insisted we accord to all actors, we might posit that Netanyahu was caught between the crosswinds of the two archetypical camps in Israel. He clearly had reservations about Oslo, but he also was forced to deal with the only game in town and eventually to accept the principle of territorial withdrawal. Although suspicious of Oslo for security and ideological reasons, he determined that the material cost of jettisoning the Accords would be too great. But every move he made that legitimated the Accords, however cosmetic they might have appeared to outsiders, only served to alienate him from his ultranationalist base. It was his ambivalence that proved to be his undoing. The consummate politician proved unable to satisfy the core concerns of either camp.

The Wye Accords proved to be the proverbial straw that broke his coalition. By accepting Wye and the principle of territorial withdrawal, his moderate and rightist partners were alienated and found that their own ideological commitments had moderated or been reinforced, respectively. Specifically, his moderate allies, including Defense Minister Yitzhak Mordechai, became so disgusted with Netanyahu's leadership style and tepid approach to Oslo that Mordechai finally defected and offered himself as an alternative to the prime minister in the 1999 elections. A similar result occurred on the Right, though for the opposite reasons. Netanyahu's conservative allies, including Benny Begin, were so angered by Netanyahu's acceptance of the idea of territorial withdrawal that they withdrew from the coalition and formed a more purist political party—a resurrected Herut—to represent core ultranationalist principles. Netanyahu ultimately stumbled into the widening crevice of cultural divisions, finding that he not only had alienated his coalition partners but also was alienated from the central tenets of any major ideational camp.

[89] David Newman, "An Independence Wish," *Jerusalem Post* (April 29, 1998).

Conclusion

Israel is in the midst of a collective-identity crisis produced in large measure by various domestic and international changes and by an ongoing consideration of the relationship between the Israeli identity and what are occupied territories to some and sacred lands to others. These different understandings of the Israeli identity are tied to different historical narratives that provide a cognitive link between the past, present, and future. As Israelis situate the Israeli identity in relationship to a past, they also situate that identity in relationship to an imagined future. Some of those futures make possible and desirable an Israel within constricted borders; other futures make such an Israel an incomplete project. The map of possible and desirable worlds is generated by an ongoing debate about the present and the past.

The contrast between Rabin and Netanyahu is striking and illustrative of this argument. Rabin doggedly attempted to forward an understanding of the Israeli national identity and a set of narratives that were directly tied to a withdrawal from the territories. As he did so, he offered a frame that helped to organize experience, appealed to diverse interests, and contained a solution. The institutional context made that voice politically powerful and consequential, as he was in league with other political parties that ranked their values in a way that was generally consistent with a constricted Israel. In contrast, Netanyahu came to power with an ambiguous pledge on Oslo and a solemn pledge to maintain a "strong" Israel that responded severely to any short-term threats to its security. On those rare occasions when Netanyahu presented his idea of what Israel was to be, it was an Israel that retained strong nationalist residues. Unlike Rabin, Netanyahu did not address the trade-offs that maintaining a grip over the territories entailed. The institutional context certainly gave Netanyahu every reason to be vague on such matters, for his coalition was maintained by political parties that generally preferred a Greater Israel for nationalist and religious reasons— even if that meant sacrificing Israel's liberal and democratic personality.

The contrasts between Rabin and Netanyahu are plentiful, though for our purposes it is important to highlight how they adapted and attempted to mold the cultural landscape to legitimate their stance toward the Palestinian-Israeli conflict. Both recognized that different story lines led to different conclusions and orientations. For Rabin, altering that narrative was important in order to provide the cultural glue for a compromise. Although Rabin's policies led some to accept, however grudgingly, a smaller Israel that would be more secure, the same policies generated nothing but fear for others, causing them to lash out against Rabin and Peres and to sweep Netanyahu to power. Although Netanyahu entered office offering consoling words to a shattered and divided Israel, his policies and statements over the next several years only replicated the fissures in Israeli society and unintentionally caused others to make their peace with peace.

Important differences existed between the cultural landscapes that Rabin and Netanyahu confronted, in part because of events that occurred and processes that deepened during Rabin's stewardship. The debate over Oslo, which polarized Israeli society, and the electoral reforms, which furthered that fragmentation, contributed to a more culturally contentious Israeli society. Netanyahu's policies and rhetoric were not aimed at erasing these cultural fault lines, though his three years in office did sharpen the divisions and clarify what was at stake in the debates over Israel's future.

These widening divisions were evident in the May 1999 elections, which gave Israelis another opportunity to voice their views on the peace process and Israel's identity.[90] Again confounding the pundits, Israelis handed the Labor challenger, Ehud Barak, a stunning and commanding victory over a visibly crushed Netanyahu. The elections delivered responses to the twin debates over peace and identity: a fairly strong voice in favor of the peace process and a cacophony of voices for Israel's identity. Barak's victory was undoubtedly connected to Netanyahu's handling of the peace process, though how central is unclear given the series of charges that were leveled at Netanyahu daily. Indeed, Netanyahu appeared to be the loneliest man in Israel as his closest friends made the most uncharitable observations about his character and his top cabinet officers resigned, declaring him unfit to rule. But Barak's strong endorsement of Oslo and his attempt to forward himself as cut from the same cloth as his mentor, Yitzhak Rabin, certainly made it clear that those voting for Barak were voting for a rejuvenated peace process. Not to be missed was the basic acceptance of the vast majority of Israelis—including Jewish Israelis—of the principles underlying the Oslo Accords.[91] Certainly the accolades and expressions of relief from around the region and the world suggested that Barak's victory was expected to breathe new life into a dying Oslo.

But the vote for the Knesset revealed ongoing fragmentation, with several important outcomes. First, following an electoral trend, the two major parties continued to lose popularity and the smaller parties gained seats and electoral power. Labor's share slid from 44 seats in 1992 to 34 in 1996 to 26 in 1999, while Likud's share dropped from 32 in 1996 to 19 in 1999, leaving it just two seats more than the third most popular party, Shas. Second, the right-wing parties fared poorly while the moderate and liberal-secular parties picked up seats, leav-

[90] As one headline before the election summarized: "Israelis Will Shape Their Identity in Monday's Vote." Tracy Wilkinson, *Los Angeles Times* (May 16, 1999): A1.

[91] Barry Rubin, "Special Report: Israel's Election and New Government Coalition," www.biu.ac.il/SOC/besa/meria.html; Don Peretz and Gideon Doron, *Middle East Journal* 54, no. 2 (spring 2000).

ing the clear impression that the election represented a shift toward a secular Israel and away from a hardened religious Israel. Third, Shas, a party that is moderate on foreign policy and represents both religious Jews and Sephardim, did incredibly well, going from 10 seats in 1996 to 17 in 1999. The unmistakable outcome was that the real identity divisions revolved around the religious-secular debate.

Barak, aware of the difficulties involved in jump-starting the peace process and addressing Israel's identity wars, also was concerned that he could not fight two battles at once; he thus assembled a coalition that would allow him to address the peace process first and Israel's identity woes second. While he toyed with the idea of inviting Likud into his coalition, in the end he opted for a Shas party despised by his left-wing partners because it was more flexible on the peace process. His hope at the time was that after bringing closure to the peace process, he then would be in a position to turn to Israel's identity crisis, its secular-religious split, and the debate over a constitution. At that point, he reasoned, he would no longer need a Shas that would probably bolt in any event and could count on Likud to support Labor's broad cultural directions. That was the plan. Barak was never able to compartmentalize in his intended way, and instead had to watch identity and coalition politics complicate and, at times, frustrate his peace strategy. Every mention of a peace process that included withdrawal from the territories stirred new imaginings of what Israel was to become. For some, the idea stirred tidings of a "normal" Israel that was at peace with itself and its neighbors, as Barak himself prophesied on the eve of his departure for the Camp David summit. For others, such as Yoram Hazony, the very essence of the Jewish national identity would be extinguished with the completion of the Oslo process, a death made all the more tragic because it would be delivered by Jewish hands.

The shape of peace, if it ever comes, is unknown, but what is known is that even its discussion unleashes a cauldron of fears and clouds of hope regarding what Israel will become.

4. Identity and Change in Iran's Foreign Policy

SUZANNE MALONEY

An imposing concrete structure looms above the traffic-choked freeways that run through western Tehran. Built by Mohammad Reza Shah Pahlavi in 1971 to commemorate 2,500 years of Iranian monarchy, this futuristic monument was stripped of his name only eight years later in the aftermath of the revolution that swept the shah from power and abrogated Iran's long tradition of dynastic rule. The symbolic expression of the successor regime can be read south of the capital city, in the enormous, gilded shrine that serves as the final resting place of Ayatollah Ruhollah Khomeini, and in the vast cemetery called *Behesht-e Zahra* just beyond it, where acres of stone slabs and cases of childhood mementos mark a generation lost to war. In the contrast between the shah's cement modernism and the Islamic Republic's ostentatious religiosity, we can see the trajectory of the transformation in the identity and agenda of the Iranian government as a result of the 1979 revolution.

The twin processes of recasting the *institutions* and the *identity* of the state represent the fruition of revolution, and few countries have experienced a more radical reinvention than Iran over the past twenty years. The establishment of an Islamic Republic in Iran dramatically transformed the nation's internal politics, economy, and society, and reconfigured the regional landscape, the geostrategic balance in the Middle East, and the discourse of political and economic development. The leaders of the diverse movement that toppled the shah recognized the historic implications of this transformation. From the start, they seized the opportunity to assert a new vision for the country, announcing the new government in a radio broadcast that began: "This is the voice of Tehran, *the voice of the true Iran*, the voice of the revolution."[1]

The voice of this "true Iran" spoke in very different terms and in very different tones than its predecessor; the assumption of a new, professedly more au-

---

[1] Emphasis added. Ervand Abrahamian, *Iran between Two Revolutions* (Princeton, N.J.: Princeton University Press, 1982): 529.

thentic identity paralleled an overhaul in the framework of the state and its relationship with its citizenry and its neighbors. The impact of this new identity was especially clear in Iran's post-revolutionary foreign policy, which crystallized even before the new government took its place. The Islamic Republic quickly spurned Iran's previously intimate relationship with the United States and the West, renouncing the shah's aspirations in favor of the Ayatollah's pan-Islamic vision. To its former allies, Iran was suddenly transformed from "an island of stability in one of the more troubled areas of the world" to one of the leading threats to the regional status quo and to the stability of the international system.[2] At the same time, divisions within the post-revolutionary coalition set the stage for a bitter power struggle in the aftermath of the coup. As a result, Iran's revolutionary identity has served as the focal point for intense and protracted political contention that continues, albeit in a different form. This internal wrangling over the nature of the new state has had a formative impact on Iran's politics, with foreign policy as one of the key battlegrounds. In turn, the evolution in the country's institutions and international relationships has helped to shape conceptions of national identity that resonate and find expression in its politics.

For these reasons, the Islamic Republic of Iran presents a challenging test case for theories of identity and foreign policy. As one of the world's only modern theocracies, Iran helps clarify the impact of the spiritual aspect of identity in general, and Islamist ideology in particular, upon the state's security dilemmas. The literature on Iran typically adopts divergent explanations of this dynamic, either dismissing religion as merely a cynical tool for legitimating state interests or, alternatively, interpreting Islamic evangelism and doctrine as the primary determinants of Iran's international agenda. The more nuanced view advanced here suggests the hazards of exaggerating or ignoring the religious component of Iranian identity. In addition, the case of Iran provides an opportunity to consider the implications of identity in the aftermath of revolutionary change, which is a critical juncture for the state and a decisive opportunity "to set and control the agenda of the nation."[3] Given the constructivist supposition that identity is chosen, rather than innate, any revolutionary transition offers a uniquely opportune interval and a forceful political imperative through which to reconfigure assumptions and institutions that underlay national interest.

[2] President Jimmy Carter made this oft-repeated reference to Iran's stability at a gala in Tehran on New Year's Eve 1977—only weeks before the initial salvos of the revolution were heard. James A. Bill, *The Eagle and the Lion: The Tragedy of American-Iranian Relations* (New Haven, Conn.: Yale University Press, 1988): 233.

[3] John Erik Fossum, *Oil, the State, and Federalism: the Rise and Demise of Petro-Canada as a Statist Impulse* (Toronto: University of Toronto, 1997): 12.

A careful assessment of the interplay between Iranian identity and foreign policy since 1979 demonstrates the complexity of the dynamics between the two. For instance, the post-revolutionary regime embraced and, in some ways, invented a conspicuously altered national identity that has corresponded to stark changes in Iran's foreign policy. This correlation suggests the efficacy of regimes and institutions in identity politics and the salience of both in framing the roles that a state adopts in the international arena. And yet Iran also serves as a cautionary tale about assuming too causal a link between identity, ideology, and policy. Underlying the Islamic government's often bombastic rhetoric, a striking continuity is evident in the broad themes of Iranian foreign policy, and these patterns argue for a deeper conception of national interests and identity. Such a conception transcends the instrumental deployment of religious and revolutionary rhetoric on behalf of elite interests. Moreover, the institutional dynamics of revolutionary change—the debates among the various factions of the anti-shah coalition, and their deployment of the organs of foreign policy— have had an equally powerful impact on the tenure and conduct of Iran's foreign policy since 1979.

These qualifications are not intended to suggest that identity was not an important variable in the new state's international policies. Like other societies in the aftermath of regime transition,[4] the Islamic Republic found great significance in the issue of national identity, as its leaders evoked the ideal of legitimacy—a prominent theme of all modern revolutions—and modified the new government's position in the international system. The shift toward an Islamic conceptualization of the state and the use of an ostensibly religious rationale in institution building informed Iran's approach to its neighbors and its interpretation of particular threats and opportunities. However, Iran's experience also reveals that identity is not infinitely malleable, especially when survival of the nation itself is at stake. The official articulation of state identity found itself in competition with other dimensions of Iran's post-revolutionary self-conceptualization. These alternatives also found expression in the institutional overhaul that accompanied the clerical transition to power, and they have remained equally salient in shaping the new regime's foreign policy.

The case of post-revolutionary Iran demonstrates the powerful, but paradoxical, instrumentality of identity in foreign affairs. The course charted by the Is-

---

[4] A wide-ranging and conceptually challenging discussion has addressed national identity in countries of the former Soviet Union, particularly Russia, where this concept and its relationship to the government's foreign policy have a long and important legacy. For example, see Glenn Chafetz, "The Struggle for a National Identity in Post-Soviet Russia," *Political Science Quarterly* III, no. 4 (winter 1996/97): 661–88, and Ilya Prizel, *National Identity and Foreign Policy: Nationalism and Leadership in Poland, Russia and Ukraine* (Cambridge: Cambridge University Press, 1998).

lamic Republic illustrates that the revolutionary convulsion—particularly when it is the product of a mass movement and a messianic leadership—can profoundly reconfigure the prevailing conceptualization of the nation's norms and values. In turn, those norms and values can empower a different role in the international arena. Both the invocations of identity and the institutions established to advance them create path dependencies that are often exceedingly slow to adjust to the realities of holding power. In the Islamic Republic, identity politics has consistently represented a central component in the struggle for ultimate political authority, shaping the options available to political leaders, their frame of reference for the world, and the ways in which their actions and rhetoric have been perceived by other actors.

In contrast to studies of other regions, the study of the Middle East has always emphasized identity as an explanatory variable, often at the expense of rigorous analysis. Ironically, however, debates over identity and its construction, and the balance between identity and interests, have occupied the forefront of political contestation in the Islamic Republic, and have in fact remained oversimplified and under-explored by Western scholarship on Iran. The simplistic view of Iranian foreign policy since the revolution has tended to juxtapose religion and rationality, when in reality the trade-off entails more variables and a more complex interrelationship. Iranian political identity embodies different and often divergent identities, which are variously invoked as domestic political competition and international circumstances demand. An analysis of the different layers of self-reference advanced since the revolution will enable us to develop a more refined representation of Iran's domestic power struggle and dueling international agendas. This inquiry will also help illuminate the institutional durability of national identity and its influence in structuring foreign-policy choices beyond the specificities of post-revolutionary Iran.

Iranian National Identity: A Prism of Competing Influences

An appropriate starting point is an exploration of the concept of identity and its utility, and the appropriation and inculcation of various models over the course of Iran's history. Insofar as we understand national identity to be a direct product of the primordial nature of the environment itself,[5] the shared conceptualization of Iranians appears on the surface far less problematic than that of its neighbors. Iran is largely unencumbered by "the original sin of state creation" and the legacy of colonial artificiality that has so compromised the legitimacy of

---

[5] For an example of this perspective applied to the Middle East as a whole, see Bernard Lewis, *The Multiple Identities of the Middle East* (New York: Schocken Books, 1998).

other states in the developing world;[6] nor is the modern state seriously fractured by communal divergencies, unincorporated irredentist populations, or the lingering effects of tribal segmentation. In contrast to nation building in several Middle Eastern states, nation building in Iran claims long ideational roots, as evoked by the eleventh-century national epic, Ferdowsi's *Shahnameh*, which glorifies an ideal monarchy in the reconstructed vernacular. The country boasts a legacy of territorial integrity stretching back several millennia, borders that have been essentially fixed and stable for five hundred years, and a relatively cohesive shared political culture and religious heritage. As one strategic analyst concluded, Iran is "blessed" by "a strong sense of identity, a notable culture and ancient civilization from which it takes inspiration."[7]

However, the historic profundity of Iranian national identity is vulnerable to overstatement[8] and the essentialism that is the traditional weakness of Middle Eastern studies. In fact, the modern history of Iran, including the continuing struggle to redefine the basis of Iranian nationalism, reveals the inadequacies of inferring a direct relationship between political identity and race, religion, or language. Understanding identity and its impact on a country's foreign policy demands contextual interpretation that extends beyond simple ascriptive classification. As political scientists have begun to explore the salience of identity, the discipline has enhanced our understanding of identity as a concept, the foundations of its formation and evolution, and its utility in framing social and political developments.

One of the primary contributions of this valuable and growing body of literture is the focus on identity as "invented" rather than innate. This has decisively shifted scholarly analysis from ethnic and religious affinities to the roles of elites and institutions in the social construction of identity and to the factors that structure individual and group preferences. "Today . . . few students of ethnicity would quarrel with the notion that individuals possess multiple identities, that different identities become salient in different settings, and that the salience of one identity vis-à-vis another is often a product of the bearer's own choosing."[9] This is pointedly manifest in Iran, where historic political coherence belies

[6] Ghassan Salamé, in *The Foundations of the Arab State*, ed. Salamé (London: Croom Helm, 1987): 3.

[7] Shahram Chubin, "Iran's Strategic Predicament," *The Middle East Journal* 54, no. 1 (winter 2000): 15.

[8] For a discussion of the ways in which Western observers and strategists have implanted the idea of Iran among Iranians over the past two centuries, see Mostafa Vaziri, *Iran as Imagined Nation: The Construction of National Identity* (New York: Paragon House, 1993).

[9] Daniel N. Posner, "The Institutional Origins of Ethnic Voting," paper delivered at the 1998 annual meeting of the American Political Science Association, Boston (Sept. 3–6, 1998): 4, as referenced in Ian S. Lustick, "Agent-Based Modelling of Collective Identity: Testing Constructivist Theory," *Journal of Artificial Societies and Social Simulation* 3, no. 1 (2000), http://www.soc.surrey.ac.uk/JASSS/3/1/1.html.

ethnic heterogeneity; just over half its population is ethnically Persian, with Azeri Turks (approximately 25 percent), Kurds (estimated between 8 percent and 10 percent), and an assortment of Qashqais, Boir Ahmadis, Turkomans, Afshars, Bakhtiaris, Baluchis, Arabs, and Lurs composing the rest.[10] In addition, several of Iran's most powerful dynasties have emerged from its Azeri population. The country's extensive tradition of minority rule and diversity has long empowered the development of shared loyalties on bases other than pure ethnic nationalism.

Given the proposition that identities are adopted and not intrinsic, the central question becomes how and why a particular conception assumes precedence, and in what contexts various formulations are more likely to be invoked. This entails a complex set of issues beyond the scope of this chapter; at minimum, however, identity must be regarded as multi-dimensional. One of the foremost influences is, of course, the state; as many other chapters in this volume demonstrate, the institutionalization of political identity has become the defining mechanism for asserting and maintaining authority in the modern era. The propagation of a national myth represents a core element of state legitimacy, as well as a key dimension of its capacity to assert its dominance over competing polities. State leadership, policies, and institutions shape the nature of public debate on this issue, sometimes—as Yahya Sadowski notes in his study of Syria in this volume—in wholly unintended ways. Despite the relatively wide berth of the modern state's influence, identity issues are fraught with constraints that, in turn, mediate their instrumentality in shaping the national agenda. Identity is not simply a series of normative alternatives or an affirmative statement of self; it is "inherently relational" and highly contingent.[11] We are defined as much by whom and what we reject as different, as by references that resonate. In this respect, Iran's predominantly Shia Muslim and non-Arab population distinguishes it from its neighbors and its historic allies and enemies in the region. This perception of difference has long cultivated a sense of strategic vulnerability—as well as a somewhat proud dissociation—among its various regimes.

The complexities of the concept itself exacerbate the theoretical problems of exploring the relationship between identity and foreign policy. Traditional models of international relations posit systems constructed around the assumption of rationality and interests as the primary components of state behavior.[12] However, as the narrative of Iran's dramatic transformation from one of the pillars of American interests in the Persian Gulf to one of its perils demonstrates,

[10] See Ali Banuazizi and Myron Weiner, in *The State, Religion, and Ethnic Politics: Afghanistan, Iran, and Pakistan*, ed. Banuazizi and Weiner (Syracuse, N.Y.: Syracuse University Press, 1986): 3–4.

[11] Alexander Wendt, "Anarchy Is What States Make of It: The Social Construction of Power Politics," *International Organization* 46, no. 2 (spring 1992): 397.

[12] As the archetype of this field, see Kenneth N. Waltz, *Theory of International Politics* (New York: Addison Wesley, 1979).

"identity and interests intermingle."[13] Moreover, these are not mutually exclusive options for explaining state behavior; an analysis that integrates identity politics does not preclude recognition of the basic principles of systemic realism. From this perspective, the various layers of identity that impinge on foreign policy generate a variety of avenues and constraints for state action. The objective of the following discussion is to consider the alternatives of national identity that have proven particularly resonant in Iran and why, and to examine the ways in which they advanced and adjusted its post-revolutionary foreign policy.

Despite Iran's apparent cohesion, the struggle to ascertain and to advance a peculiarly Iranian national identity has dominated its domestic and international politics throughout modern history. The metaphor of the Persian carpet suffers from orientalism and overuse, particularly in the popular literature on Iran, and yet it offers an almost irresistible utility in evoking the multiplicity of influences on Iranian self-conceptions and the intricacy with which they are intertwined. Iran is "a very old country but a new modern state," one that fuses a legacy of cosmopolitan imperialism, ethnic and linguistic amalgamation, and religious innovation.[14] We have chosen to explore three predominant elements of that identity—"great power" nationalism, Islamism, and anti-imperialism. Each of these dimensions has played an important, if variable, role in shaping the international agenda of the Islamic Republic over the past twenty years, and the rivalry among them has been a central feature of the struggle among the diverse groups sparring for control of the Iranian system.

Iranian regimes are rightly renowned for their dexterous approach to identity questions, and in the modern era their constructions have tended to evoke two extremes: Persian nationalism and political Islam. The latter was first deployed by the founder of Iran's Savafid dynasty, Shah Ismail (1501–24), who successfully invoked Shia Islam as the state religion to legitimize his tribal dynasty in a mostly Sunni country. Struggling to forge control over the country, Ismail astutely gauged the dynamism and cohesion that national conversion and the promulgation of a unifying religio-political myth could generate, particularly given Iran's long reverence for kingship. More than four centuries later, another centralizing monarch, Reza Shah Pahlavi, adopted a fictitious dynastic name and changed the name of the country from Persia to Iran, to conform to the indigenous name for the country and to emphasize its "Aryan"—that is, Indo-European—heritage. These actions were features of his larger program of state-building, patterned after Kemalism in Turkey, that was largely devoid of a parallel state ideology but which had a practical agenda that descended to the

[13] Glenn Chafetz, Michael Spirtas, and Benjamin Frankel, "Tracing the Influence of Identity on Foreign Policy," *Security Studies* 8, no. 2/3 (winter 1998/99–spring 1999), xvi.

[14] Nikki Keddie, "Religion, Ethnic Minorities, and the State in Iran: An Overview," in *The State, Religion, and Ethnic Politics*.

minutia of his subjects' daily lives, including their hat styles. Unfortunately, Reza Shah misjudged the perception that this new identification would evoke among the European powers and the United States, particularly in the context of his pro-German sympathies; his reign ended with the 1941 Allied occupation of Iran and his own ignominious exile to South Africa via a British warship. When it comes to identity and foreign policy, perception is as important as reality, if not more.

PERSIAN NATIONALISM

Reza's departure advanced his Swiss-educated son to the throne. Only 22, Mohammad Reza faced a daunting inheritance: a regime "politically discredited by its failure to resist foreign armies" and a nation occupied by those armies for the purposes of supporting a global war.[15] These powerful internal and external challenges did not conclude with the end of World War II, but instead intensified as the centralization tenuously attained by his father disintegrated, especially in the Azeri and Kurdish provinces, where remaining Soviet troops encouraged the development of short-lived autonomous Marxist regimes.[16] The devolution of central authority, together with war-related economic instability, generated a vibrant political pluralism among nationalist and leftist groups, which pushed for the nationalization of the country's oil industry and set the stage for a dramatic showdown between the young monarch and his rivals, particularly Prime Minister Mohammad Mossadeq. That confrontation erupted in 1953, in a series of events that drove the shah fleetingly into an Italian exile only to be reinstated with the help of the American and British intelligence services.

The details and implications of this episode have been examined in great depth in both the English- and Persian-language literature;[17] however, for our purposes, the Mossadeq crisis can be seen as a turning point for modern Iranian international relations, one that continues to reverberate throughout the Iranian political debate. On one hand, the active intervention of Washington and London reinforced the extent to which Iran's external identity had become a captive of petroleum politics and Cold War competition. Just as consequential,

---

[15] Fred Halliday, *Iran Dictatorship and Development* (New York: Penguin Books, 1979): 24.

[16] For a full account of the dispute and Prime Minister Ahmad Sultan Qavam's bluff that created the appearance of linkage between Soviet withdrawal and an oil concession, see Abrahamian (1982), and George Lenczowski, *Russia and the West in Iran, 1918–1948* (Ithaca: Cornell University Press, 1949).

[17] Two of the many useful English-language works on the Mossadeq period are Mark J. Gasiorowski, "The 1953 Coup d'Etat in Iran," *International Journal of Middle East Studies* 19 (August 1987): 261–86, and Homa Katouzian, *Musaddiq and the Struggle for Power in Iran* (New York: St. Martin's Press, 1990). See also U.S. government documents, featured in *The New York Times*' coverage, which can be found on the Internet at <http://www.nytimes.com/library/world/mideast/041600iran-cia-index.html>.

however, was the impact of this intervention in framing Iranian foreign policy in virulently defensive terms vis-à-vis the great powers. It empowered the anti-imperialist "third rail" of Iranian national identity, infiltrating both of the traditional conceptions—which focused alternatively on Persian nationalism and Shia Islam—and upsetting the historic balance between them.

The Mossadeq crisis prompted Mohammad Reza Shah to assume direct, and often obsessive, control over the reins of power, and to undertake an even more ambitious program of nation-building oriented around his vision of an Iranian "Great Civilization." Fueled by increasing U.S. assistance and the renegotiation of the oil concession, the shah formulated a land reform and political development program dubbed his "White Revolution" (later expanded to incorporate thirteen tenets called "The Revolution of the Shah and the People.") The "Revolution" was accompanied by the assertion, with U.S. assent under the Nixon Doctrine, of an imperial mission for Iran in the region. The monarchy's domestic political domination and international posturing intensified as oil prices, and the state's revenues, skyrocketed in the early 1970s.

With the withdrawal of the British navy from the Persian Gulf in 1971, Iran emerged as the dominant regional power, courting both superpowers. (It signed a friendship treaty with the Soviet Union in 1972 even while intensifying potent economic and political links with the United States.) Iran also staked a security claim beyond the Gulf to the Indian Ocean. These actions on the world stage were mirrored by an even more aggressive regional campaign, as Iran occupied three small but strategic Gulf islands, engaged in escalating skirmishes with Iraq, funded a covert war in Iraqi Kurdistan, and sent troops to help defeat an Omani insurgency. All of these moves were designed to "put Iran into a preeminent position in the region."[18] An important component of the shah's vision of Iran was the messianic ambition involving Iran's place in the world. The shah was repelled by traditionalism; he swore to raze all of the country's *bazaars* in order to build supermarkets, and he boasted of plans to boost the Iranian economy beyond that of Germany and France by the turn of the century. In the international arena, this translated into a sense of hegemonic destiny for Iran, particularly with respect to the Persian Gulf.[19]

The shah's vision for the country was also defiantly secular and vehemently nationalist. Wherever possible, his government sought to eradicate references to Iran's Islamic heritage; for example, he altered the official calendar—heretofore a solar calculation beginning with the start of the Islamic era—to spotlight his regime's purported multimillennial lineage. (This experiment in social engineering was abandoned after two years, but it provoked lasting resentment among a population who woke to find the most meaningful gauge of their his-

---

[18] Bill, *The Eagle and the Lion*, 199.

[19] Mohammad Reza Shah Pahlavi, *Answer to History* (New York: Stein and Day, 1980): 156.

tory and their lives arbitrarily altered.) In 1971 he staged a grandiose celebration for the ostensible 2,500-year anniversary of the founding of the Achaemenian Empire at Persepolis, where, before sixty-eight heads of state and a throng of foreign dignitaries, the shah addressed the tomb of Cyrus the Great and linked himself to this legacy as *shahanshah* (king of kings). The expenses incurred for this event were estimated as high as $300 million, with everything except the carpets and the caviar imported from abroad.[20]

The celebration, like the calendar manipulations, quickly became the subject of great derision and outrage among Iranians, and yet the references evoked by these activities were in no way artificial. It would be tempting to dismiss the shah's domestic and international vision for Iran as simply extravagance or egoism; however, this conception of Iran has deep roots in the national identity and has proven remarkably enduring. The exploits of the ancient Persian empire, which eventually stretched from Central Asia to all of modern Turkey and into Egypt, remain the stuff of great popular legend and pride. Iran's pre-Islamic heritage occupies a central place in daily life, expressed through enduring allegiance to the solar calendar and the festivals around *No Ruz*, the Zoroastrian New Year, as well as through abiding reverence for Hafez, Saadi, and the poetic traditions of Persian culture. These are not simply remnants of the country's cultural pluralism, but evidence of the Iranian claim to a history, and a future, as one of the great civilizations and the leading regional power. "Iran believes it has the historical, cultural, even moral weight to powerfully shape the region where classic Persian empires have at one time held sway."[21] This "Great Power" pride infuses Iranian strategic thinking and colors its outlook, particularly along its own borders.

ISLAMISM

While the shah's guests at Persepolis were dining on cuisine prepared by Maxim's of Paris and toasting him with French champagne, another leading Iranian stood before a different tomb, and he too summoned the imagery of Iranian history to herald the country's future. At Ali's tomb in Najaf, Ayatollah Ruhollah Khomeini vilified the imperial celebration and its participants. Khomeini used this address from his Iraqi exile to assail the legitimacy of the regime itself and the system of government that had endured in Iran more or less since the time of Darius, charging that monarchy was inherently contrary to Islam and that the shah's rule was tyrannical and dominated by foreign masters.

---

[20] Details of the celebration have been widely reported. See Bill, *The Eagle and the Lion*, 183–85, and William Shawcross, *The Shah's Last Ride: The Fate of an Ally* (New York: Simon and Schuster, 1988): 38–48.

[21] Graham Fuller, *The "Center of the Universe": The Geopolitics of Iran* (Boulder, Colo.: Westview Press, 1991): 241.

At the time, despite increasing popular alienation from the shah's regime, few Iranians would have predicted that Khomeini's vision would prevail and endure. And yet the imagery that he summoned in Najaf and in the hundreds of his taped and typewritten messages furtively disseminated over the next eight years resonated deeply among Iranian citizens. In fact, it propelled masses of people into the streets of Qom in January 1978 to protest the publication of an article insulting Khomeini in a government newspaper. This demonstration gave rise to police violence and public mourning ceremonies that generated a chain reaction of political protest, rioting, and repression, all of which translated into revolutionary mobilization. In addition, the passion plays and self-flagellation of Ashura (the anniversary of Imam Hussein's martyrdom at Karbala) spawned impromptu political rallies among large, emotive crowds. The shah became the personification of Yazid, Hussein's assassin, linking the processions with modern repression and illegitimacy. Events such as these combined religious ceremony and political action, providing opportunities to organize easily and granting to political action the higher sanction of religious obligation. Coming on the heels of intensified activism among intellectuals and professionals, the rituals fueled the Islamic Revolution to a successful conclusion.

Although Iran had produced one of the most renowned advocates of pan-Islamism, the nineteenth-century modernist intellectual Jamal ad-din al-Afghani, the country had no direct historical precedent for governance by the clergy. In fact, as a social group, Iranian *ulema*, or clergy, traditionally exhibited ambivalence toward political activity, a dissociation facilitated by Shia doctrine. The basis for Khomeini's theory of Islamic governance—the guardianship of the religious jurist (*velayet-e faqih*)—rests on a novel and almost unprecedented reinterpretation[22] of religious canon that continues to be contested by senior theologians. Given the lack of an authoritative archetype for an "Islamic" state, it is hardly surprising that post-revolutionary Iranian political institutions are deliberately bifurcated by the system's inherent contradictions: populism vs. elite rule; republicanism vs. religiosity; central control vs. continuing contention. The system incorporates limited democratic elements—a popularly elected president and parliament—within a full civil bureaucracy; however, ultimate authority resides in the office of the supreme religious leader, or *faqih*. Yet despite these institutional innovations and Khomeini's assertion that scripture bequeathed an "entire system of government" in perfect form,[23] the Islamic Re-

---

[22] The concept of *velayet-e faqih* cannot be solely attributed to Khomeini, as is often suggested; the principle in fact has deep roots in classical Shia thought. Khomeini's contribution was to forcefully and explicitly transform this idea into a system of political administration. See Hamid Enayat, "Iran: Khumayni's Concept of the 'Guardianship of the Jurisconsult,'" in *Islam in the Political Process*, ed. James Piscatori (Cambridge: Cambridge University Press, 1983): 160.

[23] *Islam and Revolution Writings and Declarations of Imam Khomeini*, translated and annotated by Hamid Algar (Berkeley: Mizan Press, 1981): 137.

public has hewed in most respects rather closely to the standard nation-state model.

As a result, Iran's Islamic identity is best understood through its ideological deployment, which, due to the endorsement of clerical interpretation (*ijtihad*) of religious traditions and doctrines, has been in a process of continual evolution since al-Afghani's efforts to reconcile religion with modernism more than a century ago. Throughout this evolution, the intersection of Islamism with politics in Iran has invoked consistent themes in framing domestic and foreign policy. Priority is accorded to man's pursuit of justice, in the sense of achieving a more equitable distribution of wealth and power, and to the admonition of oppression. During the 1960s and 1970s, these principles were forcefully resurrected by young Iranian intellectuals, particularly sociologist Ali Shariati, who articulated traditional Shia themes in a sharply contemporary light influenced by Marxism. In his lectures to the *Husseiniyeh Ershad*, a religious center that became a haven for Islamist political agitation, Shariati depicted a world divided between the oppressed (*mostazafin*) and the oppressors (*mostakbarin*), and he argued that the true Islam was vested in the struggle of the oppressed. Shariati's rhetoric thus linked social and political grievances with the traditional sanctification of martyrdom and sacrifice. This worldview appealed to Iranians experiencing the profound socioeconomic transformations of the 1960s and 1970s, and it was assimilated in increasingly broad, populist fashion in the official discourse of the revolution and of the subsequent state.[24]

Another key feature of the Islamic dimension of Iranian identity is millenarian utopianism—another twist on the traditional tenets of Shia theology, which enjoins the principle of *intizar*, or anticipation of the return of the twelfth imam for establishment of a truly just society. Ironically, this principle formerly rationalized clerical apoliticism, but in the hands of Khomeini and his contemporaries, it was reinterpreted to vindicate the clergy's zealous leadership in a quest for a transformed social order.[25] Islamic utopianism entails an idealized perception of history, whether it is Islamic or more narrowly national, and a resolute

[24] Several scholars have noted that Khomeini made more frequent references to the plight of the "oppressed" and accommodated the term to suit his own purposes over the course of revolutionary mobilization. Khomeini's own idea of the oppressed expanded to embrace his diverse constituency, to broaden the appeal of Islamic discourse, and to outmaneuver his leftist rivals within the revolutionary coalition. See Abrahamian (1993), 13–38, and Asef Bayat, *Street Politics: Poor People's Movements in Iran* (New York: Columbia University Press, 1997): 43.

[25] This reinterpretation of traditional Shia Mahdism concerned some clerics that Khomeini was trying to justify his policies on the basis of the divinely guided imams. One rival, Ayatollah Kazem Shariatmadari, "warned the faithful that the long awaited twelfth Imam did not return to earth on a chartered Air France jumbo jet." Quote from Abbas Kelidar, "Ayatollah Khomeini's Concept of Islamic Government," *Islam and Power*, ed. Ali Dessouki and Alexander S. Cudsi (Baltimore: Johns Hopkins University Press, 1981): 89. For the principles of *intizar* and *velayet-e faqih*, see Enayat, "Iran: Khumayni's Concept," 174.

optimism in man's ability to achieve a more righteous society.[26] These ideas highlight the need for reform, which has been the central political, social, and cultural issue in Iran for more than a century.

In addition, Islamic self-references are intrinsically universalist, concerned with the community of believers as a whole and with the application of Islamic norms irrespective of affiliation or nationality. In many respects, universalism is not peculiarly Iranian, nor uniquely Muslim; advocacy of a particular set of values—whether it is Marxism, human rights, or the amorphous "globalization"— seldom confines its prescriptions within boundaries established by men. In practice, the transnational appeal of Iran's Islamic identity is constrained by its cultural specificities, as it comes couched in the vocabulary and imagery of Shiism and Persian ethnicity. In addition, universalism is inherently difficult to reconcile with concepts of national identity in the modern era, as the focus on the *umma*, as a transnational relationship among Muslims, negates the relevance of the nation-state. These contradictions have been dramatically evident in the foreign policy of the Islamic Republic.

REVOLUTIONARY ANTI-IMPERIALISM

Since the revolution, Iranian identity has often been depicted as a binary system that oscillates between Persian nationalism and Islam. However, a third component of identity has been equally significant in the modern period and in some ways in ascendance since 1979. Rather than originating in Iranian culture and the reflection of self, this conception derives from an enduring sense of rejection of the other, which manifests itself both in the pursuit of "true" sovereignty and authenticity as well as a passionate rejection of foreign influence. It corresponds and commingles naturally to some degree with both the nationalist and Islamist frameworks, but it is not an inevitable outgrowth of either. This conception of Iranian identity rejects the constraints of superpower hegemony and is jealously defensive of the country's independence and autonomy.

This third dimension of Iranian identity can be understood as the legacy of its history and has emerged repeatedly in the country's foreign and domestic politics: in 1892, when popular opposition forced the revocation of a tobacco concession awarded to a British conglomerate; in 1911, when British and Russian intervention prompted the dismissal of the parliament and the demise of the

---

[26] For more on the relationship between utopianism and the Islamic Revolution, see Farhang Rajaee, "Iranian Ideology and Worldview: The Cultural Export of Revolution," in *The Iranian Revolution: Its Global Impact*, ed. John L. Esposito (Miami: Florida International University Press, 1990): 63–80; James F. Rinehart, *Revolution and the Millennium: China, Mexico, and Iran* (Westport: Praeger, 1997); Ram Haggay, *Myth and Mobilization in Revolutionary Iran: The Use of the Friday Congregational Sermon* (Washington, D.C.: American University Press, 1994).

hopes of the Constitutional Revolution; in 1941, with the Allied invasion and exile of Reza Shah; and, of course, with the cataclysmic events of 1953. It remained a central element through the revolution; resentment of the 1963 decision to grant legal immunities to American citizens living in Iran prompted Ayatollah Khomeini to violate the government's strictures against his political activity, which resulted in his deportation.[27] One of the most devastating intellectual critiques of the monarchy focused on the wholesale insertion of Westerners and foreign values. Jalal al-e Ahmad diagnosed the problem as *gharbzadegi*, or Westtoxification—profound psychological dislocation produced by an internationally orchestrated economy and a bifurcated culture—which he compared to cholera infecting Iran.[28]

In the era of Cold War conflict, this resentment of foreign influence tended to manifest itself in the widespread resentment of American and "Western" interference in Iranian domestic politics. This burgeoning antipathy focused on the existing, rather than historic, threats to Iran's independence, and was intensified by the predominance of leftist opposition groups such as the communist *Tudeh Party* and two radical Marxists groups, the *Mojahedin-e Khalq* and the *Fedayin-e Khalq*, during this period of Iranian history. Ervand Abrahamian finds evidence of the conspiratorial mindset among all periods and factions of Iranian politics,[29] and these concerns about foreign plots and subversion have been inwardly directed as well. Overall, "Iran's sense of its own victimization and humiliation by others is both genuine and an essential prerequisite to understanding Iranian foreign policy."[30]

An equally important dimension of Iran's anti-imperialist identity is the pursuit of genuine sovereignty and cultural authenticity. Although the country was never explicitly colonized, a common theme of political movements and intellectual writings is the ongoing struggle for *true* freedom and independence. This theme represents not simply a rejection of the outside but also a sincere pursuit of self. Mehrzad Boroujerdi explains this characteristic as a "preoccupation with the problematic of authenticity. . . . For the prototypical Iranian intellectual, this has translated into a rejection of the apish imitation of the West on the grounds that mimicry and submission are fraudulent and counterfeit states of being. This explains why anti-Westernization and anti-imperialism have become two of the fixed hallmarks of the modern Iranian intelligentsia's identity

[27] Roy Parviz Mottahedeh, "Iran's Foreign Devils," *Foreign Policy* 38 (spring 1980): 19–34.

[28] Jalal al-e Ahmad, *Plagued by the West (Gharbzadegi)* (Delmor: Center for Iranian Studies, Columbia University, 1982).

[29] Abrahamian, *Khomeinism: Essays on the Islamic Republic* (Berkeley: University of California Press, 1993): 111–31.

[30] Jerrold D. Green, "Ideology and Pragmatism in Iranian Foreign Policy," *Journal of South Asian and Middle Eastern Studies* 17, no. 1 (fall 1993): 65.

discourse."[31] It is no coincidence, then, that independence (*esteqlal*) and liberty (*azadi*) have been the rallying cries of each of Iran's revolutions and are heard again today in the rhetoric of the movement that aims to peacefully reform the Islamic government.

Identity and the Revolution

These three components of Iranian identity—nationalism, Islamism, and anti-imperialism—have coexisted throughout its modern history, often in combination but equally often in competition. They contain certain common threads, in particular a Manichean dualism in which Iran is "always the origin of all good things and the symbol of all good deeds whereas our enemies (political currents, powers, regimes and the countries which are at odds with us) are the symbols of all evil things and blackness."[32] However, in other respects, the various layers of identity that are operational in Iran today are intensely contradictory, as in the universalism of Islamism, which conflicts with both Persian nationalism and Iran's defensive anti-imperialism. Generating and articulating a new identity for the Iranian state and its citizens proved far more complicated than the removal of the shah's government, and the divergent groups of the revolutionary coalition became mired in a struggle for the soul of the nation that continues to rage within the Iranian political elite.

These conflicts added to the already complicated challenge of consolidating power after the revolution to establish the framework and day-to-day policies of this "true Iran." The revolutionary coalition comprised a diverse assortment of liberal, leftist, and religious groups that agreed on little other than their antipathy for the shah and the institution of absolute monarchy. Their negative consensus[33] and the sheer breadth of their ideological and socioeconomic agendas set the stage for a bitter feud after their coup. On the surface, the eventual victory of the clerics would appear to endow the Islamic Republic with an aura of domination and the expectation of totalitarianism. The reality of post-

[31] Mehrzad Boroujerdi, "Iranian Islam and the Faustian Bargain of Western Modernity," *Journal of Peace Research*, 34, no. 1 (1997): 4.

[32] Sadeq Zibakalam, "Black or White, Our Problems," *Jame'ye Saalem (Healthy Society)* 33 (August 1997): 7–11, from <http://netiran.com/Htdocs/Clippings/DEconomy/970800XXDE01.html>.

[33] This dynamic has been widely noted by scholars of the revolution. As an example, one analysis compares the "utopian" slogans of the French and Russian Revolutions, promising "liberty, equality, fraternity" and "bread, peace, and land," respectively, to the "primarily negative" rallying cry of the Islamic Revolution: "Death to the shah (*marg bar shah*)." Annabelle Sreberny-Mohammadi and Ali Mohammadi, *Small Media, Big Revolution: Communication, Culture, and the Iranian Revolution* (Minneapolis: University of Minnesota Press, 1994): 118.

revolutionary Iran differs vastly, however, with enduring contention among a constantly mutating political elite. As a result, factional politics, including deployment of individual institutions of foreign policy on behalf of distinct agendas and identities, has had a significant impact on the tenor and conduct of Iran's foreign policy throughout the past twenty years.

The initial outlines of post-revolutionary Iran's international agenda were sketched in the preliminary policies of the Provisional Government, and in the new constitution, which was formalized after much infighting in December 1979. These initial lines of foreign policy pointed toward a defiantly non-aligned stance: canceling arms contracts and treaty relationships with the United States, as well as renouncing long-resented articles of Iran's 1921 treaty with the Soviet Union. The constitution appeared to be similarly neutral; the passages that deal with international affairs are general and unexceptional, but they reflect the revolutionary preoccupation with independence as the primary force shaping strategic thought in preliminary stages of the new state. The constitution states that Iran's foreign policy is based on:

> the rejection of all forms of domination, both the exertion of it and submission to it, the preservation of the independence of the country in all respects and its territorial integrity, the defence of the rights of all Muslims, nonalignment with respect to the hegemonist superpowers, and the maintenance of mutually peaceful relations with all non-belligerent States.[34]

Although the constitution satisfied the differing ideologies of the various groups within the revolutionary coalition, a duality in purpose and proscription was engrained in the mindset of the leadership. For example, Article 154 circumscribes interference in other countries' internal affairs, but also insists on support for all struggles against oppression. The constitution's paradoxical invocation of two of Iran's rival layers of identity—anti-imperialism and Islamism—was further muddled later in 1980, when the Iraqi invasion generated an appeal Persian nationalism.

The contention between the dueling conceptions of Iranian identity was reinforced by the investiture of multiple sources of authority and sovereignty in the new state. Creation of the Provisional Government accompanied the empowerment of parallel institutions with potent military, financial, and ideational assets controlled by various political factions. Khomeini and his clerical allies

---

[34] Article 152 of the Constitution of the Islamic Republic of Iran. The text can be found on the Internet at <http://www.uni-wuerzburg.de/law/ir00000.html>, or see *The Constitution of the Islamic Republic of Iran* (Tehran: Islamic Propaganda Organization).

embarked on a "phenomenal project of appropriating the monumental Revolution as an 'Islamic' event"[35]—a process undertaken not simply for the sake of satisfying a particular worldview but painstakingly programmed to legitimize the new regime and to outmaneuver its rivals. The Islamists strove to inculcate a religious identity through the comprehensive cultural revolution inaugurated alongside the political one. In this way, the struggle among competing claims to legitimacy after the shah's departure was conflated with bureaucratic rivalries; the urgency of the stakes involved, as well as the philosophical diversity within the post-revolutionary coalition, sanctioned the deployment of Iran's foreign policy within this factional competition. Indeed, the most dramatic foreign policy step of the post-revolutionary era—the seizure of the American embassy in November 1979 and the holding of fifty-two U.S. diplomats for the ensuing 14 1/2 months—was fueled by the contestation to assert institutional *and* ideational dominance over the state.[36]

As in the constitution, however, the day-to-day politics of the Islamic Republic's formative early years were marked by the persistence of competing claims to Iranian identity, producing a fusion of revolutionary and Islamic components. Although the government adopted a formal policy of non-alignment—"neither east nor west"—the embassy takeover and Khomeini's fiery rhetoric cultivated the appearance of antagonism rather than neutrality. In addition, the Islamic Republic immediately repudiated all of the *ancien régime*'s dealings with the Israeli and South African governments and assumed an insistent opposition toward both (until the change in the South African regime). Moreover, under the banner of "export of the revolution," the Islamic Republic supported terrorist organizations, subversion of its neighbors through force as well as through propaganda, plus assassinations and threats of individuals abroad deemed enemies of the Islamic Republic. What began with a sort of "demonstration effect"[37] of opposition among Shia populations in Kuwait, Bahrain, and Saudi Arabia evolved into a semi-official administration for toppling the status quo in the Persian Gulf and the larger Islamic world, conducting a proxy war in Lebanon, and sponsoring worldwide violence against a loosely-defined set of adversaries.

These policies reflected a pattern of revolutionary millenarianism characteristic of successful opposition movements, intoxicated by unexpected success and the attractiveness of "a new idea that transcends the locality and the parochial

[35] Peter Chelkowski and Hamid Dabashi, *Staging a Revolution: The Art of Persuasion in the Islamic Republic of Iran* (New York: New York University Press, 1999): 29.

[36] James Bill argues that Khomeini initially hesitated, but after several days endorsed the student takeover of the embassy because he recognized "the overwhelming popularity of the act among the Iranian masses." Bill, *The Eagle and the Lion*, 295.

[37] Fuller, *"Center of the Universe,"* 94.

circumstances that first permitted it to take root and flourish."[38] They were also cultivated by the institutional and ideational exigencies of the chaotic aftermath of the shah's ouster. In consuming the tenuous Provisional Government and any residual moderation, the hostage crisis fused the extremist dimensions of the divergent worldviews remaining within the revolutionary coalition: radical anti-Westernism and vehemently Islamist self-identification. This entailed a broad appeal to the global community of believers, the *umma*, deliberately bypassing the leaders of fellow Muslim states, whom in many cases the Islamic Republic considered illegitimate, and addressing their citizenry directly on the basis of shared faith. This worldview could be seen in the initial response to the war with Iraq, for example, when the Islamic Republican Party enjoined Iranians to undertake a defense of the country because it was the only "liberated part of the country of Islam."[39] For the most part, however, opportunity, dogma, and sociopolitical resonance conditioned a distinctly sectarian bias toward exporting the revolution to fellow Shia in the Gulf and in Lebanon.

While the religious component of the new regime's foreign policy is evident, the role of Iran's Islamic identity should not be overemphasized in determining its post-revolutionary policies. Despite his utilization of universalist rhetoric, Khomeini himself maintained a stridently nationalist agenda,[40] and even during this heady early period—when the Iranian government invoked pan-Islamic imagery frequently and with great apparent conviction—the basic outlines of its policies resonated strongly with Iran's nationalist and anti-imperialist heritage. Moreover, while competing visions of Iranian identity were foremost in framing the early foreign policy of the Islamic Republic, neither Islamism nor messianic revolutionary fervor unvaryingly superseded a less ideological interpretation of Iranian strategic interests; likewise, non-alignment did not preclude selective cooperation to promote the country's survival.

The muted reaction to the Soviet invasion of Afghanistan is an excellent case in point. Rather than leaping to the defense of a brother Muslim nation on its border, Khomeini demonstrated that he was keenly aware of the potential economic and military threat from the United States in the wake of the hostage crisis. When the Soviet ambassador informed him of the invasion, Khomeini

[38] Gary Sick, "Iran: The Adolescent Revolution," *Journal of International Affairs* 49, no. 1 (summer 1995): 147.

[39] Yann Richard, "The Relevance of 'Nationalism' in Contemporary Iran," *Middle East Review* 21, no. 4 (summer 1989): 33.

[40] The minimal political weight of the concept of *umma* in the modern era is perhaps best illustrated by Khomeini's tortured logic in his classic tome, *Hukumat-e Islami* (Islamic Government): "In order to assure the unity of the Islamic umma, in order to liberate the Islamic homeland from occupation and penetration by the imperialists and their puppet governments, it is imperative that we establish a government." See Algar, trans. (1981): 49.

sought to extract a quid pro quo from Moscow in the form of opposition to anticipated American efforts to sanction or blockade Iran in exchange for Iran's quiescence over Afghanistan.[41] The clerical government took a similarly flexible position five years later when, at the height of the war with Iraq, it chose to make a deal with the devil (to be precise, the "Great Satan") to obtain desperately needed arms for the war effort. In this respect, Khomeini's policy of "neither east nor west" can be seen less as an absolute rejection of the two superpowers, than as a pragmatic endeavor to maximize his government's options and its leverage by deploying all three of Iran's historic identities.

The Iran-Iraq War

The Iraqi invasion of Iran on September 22, 1980, was a turning point in the foreign policies and domestic positions of both belligerent nations and for the Persian Gulf region as a whole. The war that followed, which proved to be the longest and most devastating conflict in terms of casualties since World War II, had a cataclysmic impact on the tumultuous post-revolutionary state in Iran and on its national identity. The war was framed in both Islamist and, increasingly, nationalist terms, to generate popular support for the war effort and to consolidate the tenuous position of the clerical government. In addition, the institutional dimensions of Iran's competing identities continued to shape its foreign-policy agenda; President Abolhassan Bani Sadr's assiduous courting of the regular branches of the military to bolster his own tenuous position intensified the politicization of the armed forces, and to some extent subordinated the early war effort to the factional disputes that degenerated into civil war among the revolutionary coalition.[42]

Both in spite of its lack of preparedness and because of it, the regime depicted the conflict with Iraq in terms of total war; as two noted experts observed, the Islamic Republic "launched a crusade."[43] The themes that the regime employed resonated with an Islamic ethical framework, and the circumstances of the war's inception fit well within the themes of martyrdom, sacrifice, and struggle—prominent features in the discourse of the revolution and Shia history. The conflict was presented as a reenactment of the prophet's wars against unbelievers or, more

[41] Adam Tarock, "The Politics of the Pipeline: The Iran and Afghanistan Conflict," *Third World Quarterly* 20, no. 4 (August 1999): 801–20.

[42] Hossain Khomeini, the leader's grandson, has reported that leading members of the Islamic Republican Party preferred to sacrifice half the country rather than cede power to Bani Sadr. See Shaul Bakhash, *The Reign of the Ayatollahs: Iran and the Islamic Revolution* (New York: Basic Books, Inc., 1986): 136.

[43] Shahram Chubin and Charles Tripp, *Iran and Iraq at War* (Boulder, Colo.: Westview Press, 1988): 70.

pointedly, likened to the defining event in Shia history, the conflict between Hussein and Yazid.[44] By evoking the most central images and emotions of Iranians' religious identity, this rhetoric contributed immeasurably to the country's capabilities by producing a seemingly unlimited tolerance for casualties. Besides facilitating the war effort, the conceptualization of the conflict as a total war imbued with uncompromising Islamic objectives helped to solidify and sanctify Khomeini's articulation of radical Shiism as the official ideology of the regime and the only mode of political discourse permitted in Iran. Moreover, this rhetoric served as part of a broader program by the Iranian government to appeal to the presumably divided loyalties of Iraq's substantial Shia population to hamper the Iraqi war effort.

As the war continued, however, such sectarian appeals to Iraqi Shia proved ineffectual, and the national appetite for martyrdom waned. As a result, the Islamic Republic increasingly relied upon traditional imagery of Iranian nationalism to motivate both conscription and a population weary of the economic hardships engendered by the conflict. This rhetorical appeal was matched by a gradual shift in the Iranian strategy in conducting the war. Despite the rhetoric and the utilization of such extreme measures as "human wave" combat, Tehran did not wage a "total war." Instead, several analysts have argued, Iran's strategy was essentially conservative, because of the constraints in its human and financial resources as well as a recognition of the broader risks—for example, fully engaging the superpowers in Iraq's defense—that intensification of the conflict might entail. Iran rejected full mobilization, focused less on episodic attempts to seize military momentum than on attrition, reengaged somewhat with both superpowers, and—officially at least—displayed considerable restraint with its neighbors, despite their support for Iraq.[45] As Efraim Karsh has noted, the war transformed revolutionary Iran's approach to the Persian Gulf region: Iran reverted to the shah's former ambition of regional hegemony rather than embracing the "spiritual hegemony" that Khomeini had initially envisioned.[46] The vision of Iran as a great regional power was decisively reinforced.

[44] Edmund Ghareeb, "The Roots of Crisis: Iraq and Iran," in *The Persian Gulf War: Lessons for Strategy, Law and Diplomacy*, ed. Christopher C. Joyner (New York: Greenwood Press, 1990): 25. For a detailed discussion of Iran's usage of Islamic imagery and doctrine in mobilizing and sustaining the war effort, see Saskia Gieling, *Religion and War in Revolutionary Iran* (London: I. B. Tauris, 1999).

[45] Chubin and Tripp, *Iran and Iraq at War*, 247; Anthony Cordesman, "The Regional Balance," in *The Gulf War: Regional and International Dimensions*, ed. Hans W. Maull and Otto Pick (New York: St. Martin's Press, 1989): 76; Chubin, "Iran and the War: From Stalemate to Ceasefire," in *The Gulf War*, 7–9. Most interesting is Chubin and Tripp's contention that Iran exhibited "restrained" conduct, and that its escalation merely prolonged the war rather than broadening or intensifying it. Also see Philip A. G. Sabin's discussion on the war and escalation theory in "Escalation in the Iran-Iraq War," in *The Iran-Iraq War: Impact and Implications*, ed. Efraim Karsh (London: The MacMillan Press, 1989): 280–95.

[46] Karsh, "The Islamic Republic in the Gulf," in *The Iran-Iraq War*, 26–41.

Although traditional conceptions of Persian nationalism increasingly came to the fore, Iran's perpetuation of the war onto Iraqi territory was widely viewed as an unmitigated example of relentless drive to forcibly export the Islamic Revolution.[47] For example, Deepa M. Ollapally concludes that "religious identity conceptions {were} the defining elements of foreign policy-making" during the conflict.[48] This analysis errs in two crucial respects, however: First, it conflates Islamism with Iranian identity, when in fact revolutionary fervor, Persian nationalism, and the politics of a regime battling insurgency at home were at least as operative in framing the Islamic government's decision to shift from a defensive to an offensive war. More important, ascribing this tragic miscalculation to the obfuscatory powers of identity assumes that identity and system realism represent discrete explanatory alternatives, rather than coexistent and even symbiotic factors in conditioning policy choices and outcomes.

An understanding of the impact of Iranian identity on its foreign policy must also acknowledge the tendency for positions based on ideologically oriented motivations to assume a progressively more innate identification with the national interest, even as "rationally" conceptualized. In other words, identities establish path dependencies from which future policy makers may find it politically painful to stray. Having described the war with Iraq in terms of morality and survival to mobilize popular support and military zeal, Iranian leadership thus incurred a substantial cost in terms of its own legitimacy in acknowledging the futility of the war's continuation. The same dynamic has afflicted another contentious aspect of Iran's foreign policy, its unmitigated hostility toward Israel. Here too, a consciously adopted identity—the Islamic Republic as the primary champion for oppressed Muslim brethren—has framed its decision-making and has conditioned consistent rejection of both Israel's right to exist and its peace-making attempts. However, in engraining this issue so prominently and so absolutely, the Iranian leadership has gradually found itself in the awkward position of being more unyielding than the Palestinians are. One might argue that Iran's support for resistance groups in Lebanon is another case in point; Iran's present choices are governed by its past professions, despite the changing circumstances of Hezbollah's effective autonomy and the June 2000 Israeli withdrawal.

More than a decade after its conclusion, the war with Iraq continues to play a significant role in shaping Iranian identity. The invasion generated an overrid-

---

[47] This decision, which was at least in part a product of Iran's "uncompromising" insistence on the removal of Saddam Hussein, appears somewhat less peculiarly Iranian in light of the similarly enduring and personalized U.S.-led campaign against Saddam. R. K. Ramazani, "Iran's Islamic Revolution and the Persian Gulf," *Current History* (January 1985): 6.

[48] Deepa M. Ollapally, "Foreignpolicy and Identity Politics: Realist versus Culturalist Lessons," *International Studies* 35, no. 3 (July-September 1998): 255.

ing sense of vulnerability and isolation among Iranians that was never fully cast aside, even though the bulk of the war was conducted on Iraqi soil. The depiction of the war in terms of both martyrdom[49] and national survival conditioned Iranians' perceptions of the world around them, and remnant disputes over the perpetuation of the conflict still divide the country's political leadership.[50] Much as American identity and foreign policy were haunted by the ghosts of Vietnam for two decades, the war with Iraq will continue to inform the strategic outlook of the Islamic Republic for years—a fact that is vastly underappreciated by the rest of the world.[51]

Post-War, Post-Khomeini Foreign Policy

Iran's acceptance of United Nations Resolution 598 in July 1988—a decision that Khomeini likened to "drinking a bitter chalice of poison"—effectively concluded the formal hostilities with Iraq (although full implementation and a genuine political resolution remain elusive). The termination of the war laid the ground for dramatic shifts in Iranian foreign policy, and with the death of the supreme leader less than a year later, for the nation to redefine itself in the absence of its charismatic leadership. This redefinition was marked by a revival of Iran's non-revolutionary ambitions to establish itself as a great regional power; this goal was a result of both the opportunities at its disposal and the reduction in the force of revolutionary Islamism. At the same time, domestic political factors and the consistent influence of the third layer of Iranian identity, a visceral trepidation of the superpowers, maintained a distinctly conflictual orientation within its foreign policy.

The end of the war lured a bevy of European ambassadors and emissaries to Tehran, and for a fleeting period, it appeared that the ruptures caused by the Revolution and its attempted export might finally be healed. However, Iran's burgeoning reintegration in the world community was deferred as a result of Khomeini's February 1989 *fatwa* condemning Anglo-Indian author Salman

[49] See Manouchehr Dorraj, "Symbolic and Utilitarian Political Value of a Tradition: Martyrdom in the Iranian Political Culture," *The Review of Politics* 59, no. 3 (summer 1997): 489–521.

[50] This is particularly true because of limitations on public debate over national security issues in Iran. For example, Akbar Ganji's newspaper columns questioning former President Akbar Hashemi Rafsanjani about his role in continuing the war contributed to Rafsanjani's lackluster finish in the February 2000 parliamentary elections, and, no doubt, to Ganji's arrest and imprisonment on charges of libel and sedition two months later.

[51] Ambassador Abdulla Bishara, president of Kuwait's Diplomatic Center for Strategic Studies and former Gulf Cooperation Council (GCC) secretary general, recently expressed the puzzled reaction from Iran's vastly smaller neighbors. "They feel threatened—I don't know why." Washington, D.C.: public discussion at the Kuwait Information Office, May 3, 2000.

Rushdie to death for apostasy. This inflammatory action apparently stemmed from the recurrent domestic struggle between Islamic radicals and more traditionalist clergy, which intensified in the wake of the controversial cease-fire and the battle over the succession decision. Whatever its true genesis, the Rushdie *fatwa* came at great cost to the effort to attract the return of Western investment so desperately needed after the devastation of eight years of conflict. The power struggle and awareness of the fragility of the Khomeini's health instigated a fundamental realignment of the governing institutions of the Islamic Republic, beginning in 1988 with the elevation of state interest above all other principles of Islamic law. This decree was reinforced through the establishment of a state institution to mediate between the feuding legislative bodies, a bureaucratic mechanism that formalized the pragmatic role that Khomeini had played.

Khomeini's death and the need to replace the "irreplaceable" brought with it the prospects of greater uncertainty and increased factionalism.[52] Khomeini had left an ambiguous foreign-policy legacy for his successors; as his personal authority had been indisputable, his dictates had overridden competing perceptions of national interest or national identity, and his governance was marked by a tendency to mediate among the fractious interests of the divisive political elite. Upon his demise, the regime formulated a minor restructuring of the state to divide Khomeini's mandate between the new *faqih*, Ali Khamenei, who possessed relatively limited religious qualifications and charisma, and the then-parliamentary speaker, Akbar Hashemi Rafsanjani, a renowned political facilitator who assumed the newly strengthened office of the presidency.

Khamenei and Rafsanjani enjoyed a brief respite of relative stability in Iran's international agenda to focus on securing their own positions and beginning the massive reconstruction effort needed to repair damage and neglect produced by the war. Throughout the early years of their dual governance, Iran's conduct on the world stage was evocative of the fissures that dominated its political structure; no individual commanded enough authority to impose a coherent vision over the contentious ideological differences within the polycephalic political elite. This produced a foreign policy characterized by inconsistency and stagnation; for example, efforts to facilitate the release of Western hostages in Lebanon coincided with a renewed onslaught against Iranian dissidents abroad. Rapprochement with the Arab states of the Persian Gulf accompanied an aggressive rebuilding of Iran's armed forces. As a result of these erratic actions, Iran failed to receive substantial recompense or recognition for its cooperative behavior; goodwill did not, as President Bush had suggested, beget goodwill, and the Islamic Republic remained largely isolated in terms of attracting significant investment or diplomatic overtures.

[52] Mohsen M. Milani, *The Making of Iran's Islamic Revolution: From Monarchy to Islamic Republic* (Boulder, Colo.: Westview Press, 1994): 219.

Still, the overall thrust of this period reflected both new thinking and new horizons for Iranian foreign policy. The coalition war against Iraq in 1991 appeared to downgrade the urgency of the Iraqi threat—for the first time in the history of the Islamic Republic—and gave the Iranian government unwitting allies in restraining the ambitious regime of Saddam Hussein. Iran's conduct in this case demonstrated the ascendance of its historic "great power" aspirations, in willingly acceding to the Western-led suppression of Baghdad, as well as the *relative* indifference of Islamism. Those same aspirations were evident as Rafsanjani pointedly rejected an opportunity to support the Shia uprisings in southern Iraq after the conflict had ended. The Islamic Republic for the first time declared itself a status-quo power, insisting that it would "tolerate no alteration of the political geography of the region."[53] Later that year, the crumbling of the Soviet Union opened new vistas for Iranian foreign policy by reducing the Russian threat for the first time in two centuries and creating new opportunities for Iran in the newly independent states of Central Asia and the Caucasus.

And yet despite these apparent openings for the Islamic Republic in the early 1990s, this period just as definitively established new threats and concerns. The successful prosecution of the second Gulf War under U.S. leadership dramatically expanded Washington's influence over Iran's neighbors, established a vested position for the U.S. armed forces on Iran's borders, and sanctioned the growing autonomy of Iraqi Kurdistan. To the north, the breakdown of Soviet control sparked the rejuvenation of long-suppressed ethnic conflicts, such as the one between Azeris and Armenians, which posed serious concerns for Iranian territorial integrity. In addition, the collapse of the Soviet Union drew Turkey, Saudi Arabia, and even Israel into a competition for influence along Iran's northern borders, as each viewed the Central Asian states as fertile ground for expanding its own influence.

The consequence of these mixed blessings was a similarly inconsistent Iranian foreign policy over the same period. Islamism appeared at its lowest ebb in shaping Tehran's decisions, with the unity of the *umma* decisively challenged by the realities of international politics. Iran continued its support for Shia groups in Lebanon, Palestinian resistance groups, and an occasional Muslim group beyond (such as in Bosnia) and issued a relatively mild appeal to religious fraternalism in Central Asia. But nationalist imperatives took precedence. Outspent and outgunned by the Turks and the Saudis to the north, the Islamic Republic focused increasingly on Central Asia, emphasizing its common cultural heritage via a low-cost, low-risk approach that one historian described as *siyasat-e dast-e gul*, or the diplomacy of offering little more than a polite bouquet of flowers.[54] National interests interpreted through the

[53] Ramazani, "Iran's Foreign Policy: Both North and South," *The Middle East Journal* 46, no. 3 (summer 1992): 400.

[54] Halliday, "An Elusive Normalization: Western Europe and the Iranian Revolution," *The Middle East Journal* 48, no. 2 (spring 1994): 325.

lens of Iranian nationalism trumped ethnic or religious affinity in two of the regional conflicts that arguably most involved Iranian identity issues, Nagorno-Karabakh and the Tajik civil war. In both cases, the "the strategic interests and political sovereignty concerns of the Iranian state have superseded the evangelical goals of the Islamist elements of the Iranian leadership."[55]

In the Gulf, Iran parlayed its cooperation over Iraq into an improved tenor of relations with Saudi Arabia and the other Arab states; however, conciliation did not extend to abandoning its own ambitions. In fact, the Islamic Republic viewed the containment of its Iraqi rival as an opportunity to reassert what its leadership viewed as Iran's natural hegemony in the Persian Gulf, repeatedly denouncing the U.S. military presence and engaging in what its neighbors and the United States interpreted as provocative conduct. Tehran progressively escalated a historic dispute with the United Arab Emirates over three jointly administered Gulf islands, and continued its rearmament program, which included acquiring unconventional naval capabilities as well as alleged investment in developing weapons of mass destruction. These aspects of Iranian foreign policy are profoundly resonant in the context of its historic self-conception as a "great power" in the Persian Gulf. Iran's arms buildup has primarily focused on reconstituting its capabilities in the wake of the depletion of the war, and even the acquisition of submarines—which raised many anxieties across the Gulf—essentially represented "status buys."[56] In addition, Iran's long breach with the United States has maintained elements of its revolutionary identity by cultivating an environment of unfamiliarity and paranoia; this in turn has contributed to its isolation. As the Islamic Republic perceived itself excluded from the development of the region, through the now-defunct U.S. policy of "dual containment" or through U.S. insistence on bypassing Iran in transporting Central Asian petroleum resources, Iran's historic suspicions became more obvious in its policies and rhetoric. These dueling misperceptions locked the two governments in a self-perpetuating cycle of threat and isolation, and both governments lacked either the political will or the overriding strategic necessity to extend a meaningful overture.

The Second of Khordad and Its Impact on Iranian Identity and Foreign Policy

The stalemate between the United States and Iran has been substantially altered by a dramatic change in the style and substance of domestic politics in the Islamic

---

[55] Hanna Yousif Freij, "State Interests vs. the *Umma:* Iranian Policy in Central Asia," *The Middle East Journal* 50, no. 1 (winter 1996): 82.

[56] Description from Chubin, as quoted in Darius Bazargan, "Iran: Politics, the Military and Gulf Security," *Middle East Review of International Affairs* 1, no. 3 (September 1997). The journal can be found on the Internet at: http://www.biu.ac.il/Besa/meria/journal/1997/issue3 /jv1n3a4 .html.

Republic. Since 1997, the Iranian media have been littered with references to the "message of 2nd Khordad"—that is, May 23, or the date of the 1997 presidential elections that catapulted Mohammad Khatami, the moderate former culture minister, to the presidency. The date has served as a rallying cry for the acceleration of political and economic reform and as a potent admonition to opponents of the president's programs of widening political participation and relaxing restrictions on the everyday life of Iranian citizens. Despite this opposition and spectacular setbacks such as the unrest that convulsed Tehran in July 1999, Khatami has been moderately successful in institutionalizing a new agenda for the Islamic Republic. His tenure has seen most of the senior provincial administration replaced; the election of municipal authorities for the first time in Iranian history; the emergence of a vibrant independent press (although within limitations and subject to arbitrary closure); and the transition to a strenuously reformist majority in the parliament. Substantive modifications to the legal framework of Iran's social, political, and economic policies have come far more slowly, however, and their advocacy has exacerbated the struggle for power, provoking a bitter and sometimes violent reaction from hard-line factions.

The reform program has been accompanied by a re-evaluation of Iran's foreign policy and a renewed effort placed on détente within the region and the industrialized world. However, unlike the polarization over the domestic agenda, the international dimension of Iran's latest transformation has been carefully orchestrated to ensure the broadest possible support from the country's fragmented political elites. Thus, with apparent "bipartisan" consensus, Iran has engaged in a major program of generalized rapprochement since 1997. These efforts have been most prominent, and most productive, within its immediate neighborhood; since May 1997, Tehran has established constructive relations with the Gulf Cooperation Council (GCC) states; played a relatively honest broker in advancing peace negotiations in the Azeri/Armenian conflict and the Tajik civil war; hinted at new flexibility in its opposition to the Middle East peace process; and withdrawn the small coterie of Revolutionary Guards still positioned in southern Lebanon.

The moderation has extended beyond the region, as the Iranian government has undertaken major initiatives to woo investors and government envoys alike from across Europe and Asia. In addition, Khatami engaged in an extraordinary bit of "tele-diplomacy" with a groundbreaking interview broadcast on CNN in January 1998; the interview jump-started the latent public debate concerning renewed relations with the United States. This savvy gesture, as well as Khatami's state visits to Italy, France, China, Germany, Japan, and Russia (as well as to regional powers such as Saudi Arabia and Syria), reaped inestimable public-relations benefits along with the financial rewards of reinvigorated trading relations with the West. Khatami trumpeted his international agenda under the banner of "Dialogue Among Civilizations," and the timing of this undertaking was reinforced by Iran's assumption of the presidency of the Organization of the Islamic Conference. The contrast with his mixed record at home has been striking; the Khatami era has been judged profoundly positive in terms of its transformation of Iran's international image and opportunities.

Conventional political analysis has explained the domestic political reform program and the increasingly cooperative and less ideological international agenda of the Khatami administration by linking both of these developments to the triumph of realism within the Iranian political elite.[57] However, this disregards the enduring, and in fact intensifying, importance of identity politics in the strategic calculus of the Iranian leadership. Over the past decade, the rapid deflation of the post-war economic boom and the perpetuation of factional infighting has prompted something of a mid-life crisis among the Iranian leadership, particularly among the left-wing Islamist factions forced to the sidelines in 1992. Khatami's term is both a measure of and an inspiration for Iran's national soul-searching, which can be seen in the popularity of tomes such as the best-seller by Tehran University political science Professor Sadeq Zibakalam, *How Have We Become Who We Are? Roots of Underdevelopment in Iran.*[58] To some extent, this introspection represents a consequence, albeit not an intentional one, of the strenuous top-down effort to promote an Islamicized and revolutionary Iranian identity under the new state, just as Mustafa Kemal Ataturk's bid to inculcate a "European" identity produced in Turkey what some have described as a moral and intellectual crisis.

In this respect, changes in Iran's foreign policy since 1997 reflect a broader transformation in the political articulation of Iranian post-revolutionary identity that was generated by the convergence of Khomeini's death and the war's conclusion and accelerated by the unfettering of public debate via the Khatami-era media renaissance. This transformation has fundamentally altered the domestic playing field of Iranian politics, generating new alliances and opportunities, and focusing the leadership on an agenda composed of mundane performance expectations rather than on the existential dilemmas and survivalist demands of the revolution and the war. These new political alignments and agendas in turn have reoriented the factional divide in Iran and the political debate over the conceptualization of the Islamic Republic. Parallels can be noted here with other states in the region; for example, in chapter 2 Marc Lynch demonstrates the catalytic impact of domestic political changes and the severing of claims to the West Bank on the evolution of Jordanian interests and foreign policy.

[57] See, for example, Mahmood Monshipouri, "Iran's Search for the New Pragmatism," *Middle East Policy* 6, no. 2 (October 1998): 95–112, and Robin Wright, "Iran's New Revolution," *Foreign Affairs* 79, no. 1 (January/February 2000): 133–45.

[58] Zibakalam, *Ma Cheguneh Ma Shodim? Rishehyab-ye Elal-e Aqabmandegi dar Iran* (Tehran: Rozaneh, 1378/1997). For a review in English, see Afshin Matin-asgari, "Review Essay," *Critique* 13 (fall 1998): 103–7.

Unlike Jordan, however, Iran has not yet arrived at a comfortable consensus on its reoriented identity. Although the shifts have relatively marginalized the ideological component within a more narrow spectrum of foreign-policy issues, its relevance to the factional struggle for power maintains it as an important operational element of Iran's domestic politics and its international relations. For example, efforts to fully normalize relations with Egypt have engendered a protracted struggle within the elements of the government still bitter over late Egyptian President Anwar Sadat's hospitality to the dying shah and his peace accords with Israel; also, much still hinges on an absurdly minor issue that strikes at the core of both states' identities: the naming of a street in central Tehran in honor of Sadat's assassin. Still, a less polarized conceptualization of Iranian identity and interests may yet prevail. President Khatami's much-heralded program of reaching out to the West is predicated on the assumption of an ideational divide between the two cultures, albeit one that the Islamic Republic now claims to be prepared to help bridge. Dialogue among civilizations appears to be an ingenious effort to revert to a predominantly nationalist conception of Iranian interests while implicitly retaining its Islamic referents and prickly sense of sovereignty. In that respect, the government is endeavoring to implement perhaps the most balanced reflection of Iranian identity.

One cannot understand the foreign policy of the Islamic Republic without appreciating the political factors and the conditioning force of its ideology; at the same time, "(w)e cannot understand fundamentalist foreign policy simply by inferring from the domestic ideology."[59] A principal danger in analyzing Iran's post-revolutionary foreign policy is the tendency to overstate the influence of Islamic ideology. The government's identification as inexorably "fundamentalist" has obscured the dynamic context and multiple influences on its decision-making, as well as the powerful impact of bureaucratic politics on its international agenda. Even a religious rationale has been operative in framing Iran's policy options and rhetoric, it has always been mitigated and exacerbated by a strong sense of nationalism and revolutionary antipathies. And its utility, as well as the efficacy of the competing conceptualizations of Iranian identity, has derived from their deployment in the bitter factional rivalries that have dominated the politics of the Islamic Republic since its inception.

As a result, the gradual but evident evolution of Iranian foreign policy since 1979 exposes the fallacy of juxtaposing identity and *realpolitik*, or the instrumental and the essential; equally so, it argues against a literalist interpretation of identity, or confusing correlation with causation in understanding the impact of identity on foreign policy. The Iranian case demonstrates that identity operates across a broad and ever-evolving spectrum, which can endow foreign policy

[59] Zachary Karabell, "Fundamental Misconceptions: Islamic Foreign Policy," *Foreign Policy* 105 (winter 1996–97): 76–90.

with texture and flexibility, or entrap it within the assertion of contentious claims. Revolutions and their aftermath offer a unique and critical juncture for analyzing the dynamic interaction between the various layers. Today a new identity crisis is emerging in Iran. Approximately two-thirds of the Iranian population is younger than 25, and literacy within the population has expanded dramatically, with a nearly universal rate for young Iranians.[60] Their perceptions of Iran and its place in the world will increasingly dominate the foreign policy of the Islamic Republic or any successor government. Weary of war and deprivation, infused with a sense of their own political entitlement, the children of the Islamic Revolution are likely to redefine Iranian identity in a powerful fashion. Their interpretation will determine Iran's international role in a new millennium.

[60] Statistics regarding the relative youth of the Iranian population are used quite casually in the media, often without reference. Thus, one sees some variation in the estimates. In mid-1998, *Agence France-Presse* published an interview with Abbas-Ali Zali, head of the Islamic Republic's statistics center, in which he asserted that 37 million Iranians (out of a total population at that time of 62 million) were younger than 24, and that 4.8 million students were enrolled in high school and university programs. See "800,000 To Join Iran's Labor Force Each Year: Official," *AFP* (May 3, 1998). The Economist Intelligence Unit in London, in mid-1999, estimated that by the year 2000, more than 43 percent of Iran's population would be *younger than* 14. See *EIU*, "Economic Forecast: Social Indicators" (May 7, 1999). Media estimates indicate that overall literacy had increased from approximately 50 percent in the pre-revolutionary period to nearly 80 percent by the mid-1990s. The Central Bank's statistics indicate that 93.5 percent of those younger than 30 (that is, primarily educated since the revolution) can read and write. See Ahmad Reza Roshan, "Per Capita Income Drops But Consumption Goes Up," *Sobh-e Emrooz* 26 (Nov. 20, 1999); "Iran: Indicators," Reuters (Aug. 1, 1999).

5. Footprints in the Sand

The Definition and Redefinition of Identity in Iraq's Foreign Policy

ADEED DAWISHA

Iraq's foreign policy from the birth of the state in the 1920s and throughout the twentieth century clearly illustrated the interdependence of domestic factors and foreign-policy outputs.[1] Such a formulation posits that a country's domestic conditions and peculiarities decisively affect its foreign policy, and the outcome of the policy may affect the state's internal situation.[2] Within the parameters of this interactive relationship, the role of the ruling elites is paramount. It is, after all, they who formulate and execute their state's foreign policy in accordance with their perception of the possible international consequences on the one hand, and the imperatives of the domestic environment of the country on the other hand. In their foreign-policy system model, Michael Brecher, Blema Steinberg, and Janice Stein liken foreign policy to a flow into and out of a number of structures and processes that produce decisions. Their foreign-policy system consists of "an environment or setting, a group of actors, structures through which they initiate decisions and respond to challenges, and processes which sustain or alter the flow of demands and products of the system as a whole."[3] The decision makers, therefore, lie at the center of their model. Similarly, in a

---

[1] The emphasis on the domestic sources of foreign policy has been a topic of intense scholarly scrutiny. See, for example, Howard H. Lentner, *Foreign Policy Analysis: A Comparative and Conceptual Approach* (Columbus, Ohio: Charles E. Merrill, 1974); K. J. Holsti, ed., *Why Nations Realign: Foreign Policy Restructuring in the Postwar World* (London: Allen and Unwin, 1982); David O. Wilkinson, *Comparative Foreign Relations: Framework and Methods* (Belmont, Calif.: Dickinson, 1969); James N. Rosenau, *The Study of Political Adaptation: Essays on the Analysis of World Politics* (New York: Nichols, 1981); Jerel A. Rosati et al., editors, *Foreign Policy Restructuring: How Governments Respond to Global Challenge* (Columbia: University of South Carolina Press, 1994).

[2] Expressed succinctly by Wilkinson, *Comparative Foreign Relations*, 4.

[3] M. Brecher, B. Steinberg, and J. Stein, "A Framework for Research on Foreign Policy Behaviour," *Journal of Conflict Resolution* 13, no. 1 (March 1969): 79.

study of Egyptian foreign policy, this author conceptualized foreign policy as a system in which policy inputs (influences) are converted into policy outputs (decisions) through the process of policy formulation by the decision-making elite. Thus, "influences from the operational environment . . . comprise the inputs into the psychological environment of the decision-making elite, in which objectives are formulated *according to a set of perceptions that the decision-makers hold of the environment. . . .*"[4] (emphasis added). One crucial element of this environment, on which much intellectual effort has focused in recent years, is the question of "identity."

This chapter explores the relationship between identity and foreign policy in Iraq, discussing the role and motivations of the ruling elites as the crucial intervening variables. Writers on identity and nationalism argue that the cultural and political elites are the ones responsible for "constructing" national identity. Eric Hobsbawm and Terence Ranger even titled a book that they edited *The Invention of Tradition*. The volume is based on the premise that traditions are invented for the purpose of building and cementing a sense of nationhood.[5] The word "invention" as it relates to the development of nations is also used by Ernest Gellner, who insists that the concept of a nation based on "objective" elements is nothing but a myth.[6] Benedict Anderson takes issue with the argument that nations are forcibly, even artificially, invented. His position is that a national identity, as with any other kind of collective identity, is not so much "invented" by an elite as "imagined" by the community.[7] Anthony D. Smith, however, sees a discernible historical *process* in the development of a national identity, which he bases on an innovative concept, that of the *ethnie*. To Smith, an *ethnie* is a community in which cultural myths, symbols, memories, and values are transmitted from generation to generation in the area that the community perceives as its "historic territory" or "homeland."[8] Regardless of whether they are invented, imagined, or historically developed, however, collective identities always have been the focus of peoples' loyalties. In Iraq, competing sub-national, national, and supranational identities inevitably have influenced foreign policy. Similarly, the existence of competing identities has afforded the ruling elites countless opportunities to define and redefine the country's identity in accordance with their own interest and the dictates of policy at any given time.

[4] A. I. Dawisha, *Egypt in the Arab World: The Elements of Foreign Policy* (London: Macmillan, 1976): 68.

[5] Eric Hobsbawm and Terence Ranger, eds., *The Invention of Tradition* (London: Cambridge University Press, 1983).

[6] Ernest Gellner, *Thought and Change* (London: Weidenfeld and Nicholson, 1964):169; also, Gellner, *Nations and Nationalism* (Ithaca: Cornell University Press, 1983): 48–49.

[7] Benedict Anderson, *Imagined Communities: Reflections on the Origin and Spread of Nationalism* (London: Verso, 1983).

[8] Anthony D. Smith, "The Origins of Nations," *Ethnic and Racial Studies* 12 (1989): 344–5.

Iraq's Multiple Sub-National Identities

Iraq was created in 1921 as part of the reorganization of British interests in the Middle East. The infant state was put together from three provinces of the defunct Ottoman empire, Baghdad, Basra, and Mosul. It was a forced and artificial creation, lacking the essential underpinnings of nationhood. The south of the country was overwhelmingly Shiite, the central part Sunni, and the north contained substantial non-Arab populations, primarily Kurdish and to a lesser extent Turkoman. In addition to this diversity, the state contained smaller, yet influential, concentrations of Christians and Jews who were mainly city dwellers, except for the Christian Assyrians who lived in villages north of Mosul.

Compounding these ethnic and sectarian divisions was the vast cultural and economic divide between city and tribe. Indeed, over the years "tribalism" was to be a major problem for the central authorities of the state. As late as 1965, more than forty years after the establishment of the Iraqi state, 50 percent of the population lived in the countryside, most belonging to some tribe and professing tribal values. Although that number had dwindled to 27 percent by 1989, tribal values and attitudes persisted in rural and urban areas, including among the supposed Westernized middle classes, despite claims to the contrary by the self-proclaimed modernizing and vehemently anti-tribal Ba'th Party.[9]

Successive Iraqi governments have tried to imbue this human mosaic with a sense of a shared and cohesive national identity but generally have failed. King Faisal 1 was the first Iraqi leader to realize the magnitude of the task. Twelve years into his rule, he agonized over the situation:

> There is still—and I say this with a heart full of sorrow—no Iraqi people but unimaginable masses of human beings, devoid of any patriotic idea, imbued with religious traditions and absurdities, connected by no common tie, giving ear to evil, prone to anarchy, and perpetually ready to rise against any government whatever. Out of these masses we want to fashion a people which we would train, educate and refine. . . . The circumstances, being what they are, the immenseness of the effort needed for this [can only be imagined].[10]

[9] Amatzia Baram, "Neo-Tribalism in Iraq: Saddam Hussein's Tribal Policies, 1991–96," *International Journal of Middle East Studies* 29 (1997): 2–3.

[10] Quoted in Hanna Batatu, *The Old Social Classes and the Revolutionary Movements in Iraq* (Princeton, N.J.: Princeton University Press, 1978): 25–26. For the full text of this confidential memorandum in which the king details Iraq's complex ethnic, sectarian, and tribal problems, see Naji Shawkat, *Sira wa Dhikrayat Thamineena 'Aman, 1894–1974* (Biography and Memoirs of Eighty Years, 1894–1974) (Baghdad: Maktabat al-Yaqdha al-'Arabiya, 1990): 622–31.

Over the next half century various Iraqi governments instituted policies and enacted laws designed to break tribal, ethnic, and sectarian loyalties and to construct a sense of Iraqi nationhood. Socioeconomic policies led to gradual urbanization; national education emphasized the oneness of Iraq and its secular character; and the army, pampered and vigorously expanded, was made into, and constantly characterized as, the quintessential "national" institution. Meanwhile, aggressive ideological trespassing and penetration, especially in the contemporary Ba'thist era, consistently demeaned "regional" and "particularistic" impulses as backward, even shameful, unfit for the forward-looking men and women of the "nation" of Iraq. Yet to what extent were these policies successful? As late as 1982, a leading member of Iraq's Ba'thist ruling elite lamented that "secessionism, sectarianism and tribalism . . . are tearing the unity of society to pieces."[11]

What was actually meant was that sub-national ethnic, sectarian, and tribal identities and loyalties took precedence over an Iraqi national identity. And the two most prominent and consequential of these identities that seemingly were "tearing the unity of society to pieces" were the ethnic Arab vs. Kurd identities and the sectarian Sunni vs. Shiite identities.

Making up some 20 percent of Iraq's population, the Kurds have proved to be the most difficult community to assimilate into the state of Iraq. Of a different ethnic stock and speaking an Indo-European language, the Kurds have a strong sense of a separate identity. Even though racked by clannish and tribal rivalries, the Kurds have a fully developed sense of nationhood that has been frustrated by the various Middle Eastern states and governments in which the Kurds constitute significant minorities. Residing mostly in the mountainous terrain of northern Iraq, the Kurds had been able to lead a relatively autonomous existence from the days of the Ottoman empire until about the 1920s. Since the inception of the Iraqi state in the 1920s, most Iraqi governments have considered the "Kurdish issue" one of their most difficult and enduring problems. Iraqi contemporary history is replete with Kurdish revolts, manifesting the Kurds' intense sense of separateness. Committed to defending the unity of the Iraqi state, successive Baghdad governments have been unable—and on the whole unwilling—to reach peaceful accommodation with the Kurds.

The other sub-national identity that has plagued Iraq's domestic politics and its international relations is that of the Shiites, the majority religious sect in

---

[11] Quoted in Baram, "Neo-Tribalism in Iraq," 2. Recently an Iraqi author wrote: "Any student of contemporary Iraqi society will discover . . . that the primary factor of the persistence of tension and violence [is] the brittleness of Iraqi national identity." Selim Mattar, *Al-That al-Jariha: Ishkalat al-Hawiya fil 'Iraq wal 'Alam al-'Arabi "al-Shirqani"* (Wounded Essence: Problems of Identity in Iraq and the Arab "Eastern" World) (Beirut: al Mu'assassa al-'Arabiya lil Dirasat wal Nashr, 1997): 378.

Iraq. The Shiites' perpetual—sometimes dormant, sometimes overt—rivalry with the minority, yet politically dominant, Sunnis has constituted a major fissure in Iraqi politics. From the days of the Ottoman empire, through the contemporary history of the Iraqi state, the Shiites have felt marginalized politically and economically by the Sunni establishment. However, sharing with the Sunnis an overarching Arab identity, and speaking the Arabic language, the Shiites quarrel with Baghdad does not possess the same sense of intractability that tends to characterize the Kurdish "problem." Even so, Shiite grievances and distrust of the "Sunni government" have persisted, on occasions erupting into physical violence. The central authorities in Iraq have reciprocated with a healthy dose of their own mistrust of the Shiite community in Iraq.

Arabism as a Transnational Identity

In addition to ethnic, tribal, and sectarian sub-national identities, the transnational identity of Arabism has competed with, and at times taken precedence over, an Iraqi national identity.[12] A transnational identity entails an awareness of belonging to a large group of humanity that stretches across state boundaries and which is "supposed to share a common origin, characterized by a name and by common cultural features, and above all by the bounds of the linguistic community."[13] The intellectual father of Arab nationalism is Sati'al-Husri,[14] a Syrian by birth who exerted immense influence on education in the formative years of the Iraqi state. Choosing between the French and German models of nationalism, Husri rejected the French idea, propagated by the nineteenth-century historian and philosopher Ernest Renan, that a nation is a voluntary contractual exercise, a "daily plebiscite" dependent entirely on the will of the people.[15]

[12] Islam is the other transnational force that has affected the politics of various Middle Eastern states. However, in the case of Iraq, it has not been significant so far.

[13] Maxime Rodinson, *The Arabs* (London: Croom Helm, 1981): 25.

[14] Eminent historian Albert Hourani found in al-Husri's writings "a pure theory of nationalism with all its assumptions clearly understood and accepted, all its problems faced. . . ." Hourani, *Arabic Thought in the Liberal Age, 1798–1939* (London: Oxford University Press, 1962): 312. To another noted historian, Majid Khadduri, al-Husri "formulated perhaps more clearly and consistently than any other writer a systematic and coherent theory of Arab nationalism." Khadduri, *Political Trends in the Arab World: The Role of Ideas and Ideals in Politics* (Baltimore: Johns Hopkins University Press, 1970): 199. For the fullest treatment of the life and ideas of Sati' al-Husri, see William L. Cleveland, *The Making of an Arab Nationalist: Ottomanism and Arabism in the Life and Thought of Sati' al-Husri* (Princeton, N.J.: Princeton University Press, 1971); and Bassam Tibi, *Arab Nationalism: A Critical Enquiry*, 2d ed. (New York: St. Martin's Press, 1990).

[15] Ernest Renan, "What Is a Nation?" in Homi K. Bhabha, *Nation and Narration* (London: Routledge, 1990).

Husri instead opted for the concept of cultural nationalism, promoted by the Germans of the Romantic school, Johann Gotfried Herder, Johann Gotlieb Fichte, and Ernest Moritz Arendt.[16] In this formulation, a nation cannot depend on ephemeral bases such as "the will of the people"; rather, a nation is objectively constituted through the coherence of its history and, most of all, by the unity of its language. A nation is both predetermined and eternal. Thus, to Husri an Arab national identity cannot be a matter of choice. Like one's physical features, it is something one is born with and is expected to live with. He puts it this way:

> Every Arabic-speaking people is an Arab people. Every individual belonging to one of these Arabic-speaking peoples is an Arab. And if an Arab does not recognize this, and if he is not proud to be an Arab, we must look for the reasons that have made him take that stand. His view may be an experience of ignorance: in that case we must teach him the truth. It may spring from a false consciousness: in that case we must enlighten him and show him the right way. It may be an expression of his egoism: in that case we must limit his egoism. But under no circumstances, should we say: "He is not an Arab so long as he does not wish to be one, and does not accept his Arabism." He is an Arab whether he wishes to be one or not . . . although perhaps an Arab without feeling, without consciousness, and perhaps even without conscience.[17]

These are the stark words of a committed Arab nationalist who either would not see, or would not wish to see, other identities that were bound to clash with, and at times supersede, the Arab identity. Michael Hudson, while conceding the existence of certain homogeneous features in the Arab world, nevertheless argues that in a culture dominated by primordial identifications, the Arab identity continues to compete with other "parochial but intensely held corporate identifications."[18] Hudson's words are especially true of Iraq with its multiple sub-national identities, the adherents of which would perceive an overarching Arab identity as serving the interests of the politically dominant Sunni establishment. Thus, the constant swaying in contemporary Iraqi history between *al qawmiyya al 'arabiya* (Arab nationalism) and *al wataniyya al 'Iraqiya* (Iraqi patriot-

---

[16] For a full exposition of the ideas of the German thinkers of the Romantic school and the turbulent era in which they lived, see Hans Kohn, *Prelude to Nation-States: The French and German Experience* (Princeton, N.J.: D. Van Nostrand Co., 1967): 118–266.

[17] Tibi, *Arab Nationalism*, 136.

[18] Michael C. Hudson, *Arab Politics: The Search for Legitimacy* (New Haven, Conn.: Yale University Press, 1977): 56.

ism) is a symptom of the country's multiplicity of identities, which has influenced—and has been influenced by—the direction of Iraqi foreign policy.

Identity and Foreign Policy in Pre-Saddam Iraq

The earliest illustration of this tension between an Arab identity and an Iraqi identity was the 1936 military coup, reputed to be the first intervention of the military in politics in the modern Arab world. Until then, Iraqi governments, dominated by Arab Sunni elites, had propagated the pan-Arab idea. However, the three primary figures in the government that was established after the 1936 takeover were Bakr Sidqi, a Kurd; Hikmat Suleiman, a Turkoman; and Ja'far Abul Timman, a Shiite. Not surprisingly, the government, led by Suleiman, "contained not a single advocate of the pan-Arab cause on which all previous governments had been founded."[19] Here was the first conscious effort to define an identity for Iraq that took into consideration the country's non-Sunni and non-Arab communities. The Suleiman government developed and publicly advocated an "Iraq First" policy with the support of the army under Sidqi.[20] Almost all of the government's utterances and policy statements focused on cementing national unity and fostering societal harmony to create a strong Iraqi identity. References to Iraq's Arab affiliations were rare. This was in stark contrast to the orientation of the preceding prime minister, Yassin al-Hashemi, whose policy was so Arab-oriented that he was called "the Bismarck of the Arabs."[21]

In concurrence with its efforts to define an Iraqi identity, the Suleiman government pursued a foreign policy that emphasized closer relations with Turkey, Iran, and Afghanistan. In 1937 Iraq joined with these three states in the Sa'dabad Pact, as the Suleiman government relegated relations with the Arab world almost to an afterthought.[22] This, however, generated the ire of Arab nationalists, who continued to demand Iraq's unwavering commitment to Arab nationalism.

[19] Phebe Marr, *The Modern History of Iraq* (Boulder, Colo.: Westview Press, 1990): 73.

[20] Abbas Kelidar, "A Quest for Identity," *Middle Eastern Studies* 33 (1997): 411; see also Liona Lukitz, *Iraq: The Search for National Identity* (London: Frank Cass, 1995): 87–88; also Michael Eppel, *The Palestine Conflict in the History of Iraq* (London: Frank Cass, 1994): 50–66.

[21] 'Abd al-Razzak 'Abd al-Daraji, *Ja'far Abul Timman wa Dawrahu fil Haraka al-Wataniya fil 'Iraq* (Ja'far Abul Timman and His Role in the Iraqi National Movement) (Baghdad: Wizarat al Thaqafa wal Funoon, 1978), fn. 220, 437.

[22] Najda Fathi Safwat, *Al-'Iraq fi Mudhakirat al-Diblomasiyeen al-Ajanib* (Iraq in the Memoirs of Foreign Diplomats) (Baghdad: Maktabat Dar al-Tarbiya, 1984): 111–13; also, Talib Mushtaq, *Awraq Ayami, al-Jus'i al-Awal, 1900–1958* (The Papers of My Days, Part One: 1900–1958) (Beirut: Dar al-Tali'a lil Tiba'a wal Nashr, 1968): 247; see also Marr, *Modern History of Iraq*, 73, and Eppel, *The Palestine Conflict*, 51.

One editorial reminded the government that "Arab nationalism is rooted in Iraq, and [Iraqi] history is full of great struggle for its sake."[23] The uncompromisingly Arab nationalist *al-Muthana* magazine warned darkly that "no government of this country could succeed if it did not follow the (Arab) nationalist line. . . ."[24] This was no idle threat, because the Sunni-dominated officer corps were becoming restless as a result of rumors that Kurdish officers were replacing Arabs, and that "70 percent of the students at the Military College in Baghdad were now Kurds."[25] Indeed, within a year, Sidqi had been assassinated in a plot involving Sunni Arab nationalist officers, who then hastened the resignation of Suleiman. These officers, vigorously propagating an Arab identity, forced an activist Arab policy that focused on pressuring the British to solve the Palestine problem in a manner commensurate with Arab desires. This episode ended in the brief and ill-fated 1941 war against the British in which the Iraqi army was defeated and a less radical government was installed.

That, however, did not mean the end of Iraq's Arab orientation; the Arab Sunni ruling elite continued to be involved in Arab affairs. In January 1943 Iraq submitted to the British a plan for a "Fertile Crescent Union." The Iraqi government, under its wily prime minister, Nuri al-Sa'id, proposed a two-stage process for a comprehensive Arab union. In the first stage, Syria, Lebanon, Palestine, and Transjordan would be united into one state. Once this state of "Greater Syria" had been formed, it would join Iraq in an "Arab League" to which other Arab states could later adhere if they so wished. The League would be responsible for defense, foreign affairs, currency, communications, customs, and the protection of minorities.[26] The plan was presented as a first step in a process that would lead to a union of the Arabic-speaking world, the governmental form of which would depend on the preferences and ultimate decisions of the Arab populations.

Undoubtedly, the plan had more to do with Hashemite ambition and Iraq's rivalry with Egypt over Arab leadership than with any consuming attachment to the cause of Arabism. Nevertheless, the mere submission of the plan testified to the recognition by Iraq's political elite of their Arab identity. After all, the basis of the union was the Arab character of these states; if the union were to come to fruition, Iraq could become just one part of a larger Arab entity. To an Arab nationalist, this would be a dream come true. To the non-Arab Kurds, however, it was not much short of a nightmare. Constituting a significant 20 percent of Iraq's population, the Kurds would become a tiny and unimportant island in an ocean of Arabic-speaking peoples. The Arab Shiites too were hardly thrilled by

[23] *Al-Istiqlal* (Baghdad, Nov. 6, 1936), quoted in al-Daraji, *Ja'far Abul Timman*, 437.

[24] *Al-Muthana* (Baghdad, Nov. 12, 1936), quoted in al-Daraji, *Ja'far Abul Timman*, 437–438.

[25] Safwat, *Al-'Iraq fi Mudhakirat*, 128.

[26] Patrick Seale, *The Struggle for Syria: A Study of Post-War Arab Politics, 1945–1958* (New Haven, Conn.: Yale University Press, 1986): 11–12.

the Fertile Crescent plan. While they were a substantial majority in Iraq, they would constitute a small minority in a predominantly Sunni Arab world. It was not that the Shiites did not think of themselves as Arabs; it was simply politically disadvantageous for them to subsume their Shiite identity into an Arab one. Iraqi Shiites, therefore, perceived such a union as essentially a plan to cement Sunni hegemony and further marginalize the Shiites.[27] Shiite and Kurdish response was accordingly negative, constituting one factor in the plan's ultimate failure.

The failure of the Fertile Crescent plan prompted Egypt to submit a counterplan for a "League of Arab States," which came to fruition in 1945 when representatives of the seven Arab states signed a pact creating the League. The prologue to the agreement characterized the members as "desirous of strengthening the close relations and numerous ties which link the Arab states and anxious to support and strengthen these ties upon a basis of respect for the independence and sovereignty of these states."[28] In a sense, the League represented for Iraq a perfect compromise between the Iraqi and Arab identities. It was a clear affirmation that Iraq was part of a larger Arab system in which all of the constituents were enjoined to seek closer ties, yet it asserted unequivocally the independence and sovereignty of the Arab states. As a foreign-policy output, the Arab League was a confirmation that the tension between the two competing identities in Iraq need not constitute a zero-sum game. That it did not, in this instance, was also a function of the goals and interests of the ruling elites.

The interplay between the Iraqi and Arab identities did take the form of a zero-sum game in the wake of the 1958 revolution in Iraq. The Arab world of the mid-1950s had seen a surging nationalist tide that promised to deliver the Arabs from their allegedly "present subservience to the imperialist West" into a new heroic age of assertion and power. The prophet of this radical and activist Arab nationalism was Egypt's charismatic leader, Jamal Abd al-Nasir (or Nasser). He had single-handedly frustrated Western efforts to enlist the Arab countries into an anti-Communist alliance; he had defied Western military domination in the area by buying arms from the Eastern Communist bloc; and, in the perception of most Arabs, he had achieved the unthinkable: the defeat of Britain and France, the two great imperial powers, in the 1956 Suez crisis. Under Nasir, especially in the 1950s, Arab nationalism symbolized for the Arab populace the means by which their glorious past would be transformed into an equally glorious future. In those days, there were times when a meeting of minds and a sharing of dreams existed between Nasir and much of the popula-

[27] Yitzhak Nakash, *The Shi'is of Iraq* (Princeton, N.J.: Princeton University Press, 1994): 133–34.

[28] For a succinct exposition of the roots and development of the Arab League, see Cecil A. Hourani, "The Arab League in Perspective," *The Middle East Journal* 1 (April 1947): 125–32.

tions of the Arab world. His fiery, radical brand of Arab nationalism seemed to permeate most levels of Arab society, breaking barriers between regime and people, state and citizens.[29] Those were indeed heady days, when "Arab organic unity" ceased to be an unattainable fantasy. In February 1958, Egypt and Syria joined together into the United Arab Republic (UAR), representing to most Arabs, as well as to the outside world, the first step in the road to the ultimate and inevitable unity of all Arabic-speaking peoples. Revolutionary turmoil, adulation of Nasir and his pan-Arabism, and beleaguered, baffled, and increasingly impotent status-quo leaderships suggested that soon other Arab states would surrender to the seductive powers of the UAR. This assumption gained dramatic credence on July 14, 1958, when a military coup toppled the monarchical government of Iraq,[30] which had been Nasir's bitterest enemy and the bastion of Western influence in the area, bringing in young military officers who shared the revolutionary ideology of the UAR's president.

The euphoria that Arab nationalists felt in the wake of the 1958 Iraqi revolution soon diminished as a result of the power struggle between the coup's leader, Brigadier Abd al-Karim Qasim, and his second-in-command, Colonel Abd al-Salam Arif. The latter, a vigorous propagator of Iraq's Arab identity, was considered to be the representative of the "unity now" forces; he had traveled to Syria and discussed without authorization the possibility of Iraq joining the UAR. He further intimated that Qasim, who approached unity with the UAR with far more caution, was irrelevant to the process.[31] Arif had blazed through the length and breadth of Iraq, making umpteen speeches in which he extolled the virtues of Arab unity and the leadership of Nasir. The Egyptian president was undoubtedly his hero, which moved one foe to remark that in his speeches, Arif "ignored the leader of the revolution (Qasim) and praised Jamal Abd al-Nasir. Was Abd al-Nasir the leader of the revolution?"[32] Indeed, Qasim himself was hardly enamored with his second-in-command and was busy strengthening his own power base while Arif gallivanted around the country, making speeches. By the fall of 1958, Qasim had fostered a competitive identity by encouraging Iraqi

[29] Nasir's charisma extended beyond the Arab world, even to such an unlikely place as the Iranian Shiite religious city of Qom. See Roy Parviz Mottahedeh, *The Mantle of the Prophet: Religion and Politics in Iran* (New York: Simon and Schuster, 1985).

[30] The coup in Iraq also has been attributed to the alienation of the Westernized middle stratum of Iraqi society, the *effendiyya*, whose upward mobility was retarded by a traditional elite unwilling to share power. See Eppel, "The Elite, the *Effendiyya*, and the Growth of Nationalism and Pan-Arabism in Hashemite Iraq, 1921–1958," *International Journal of Middle Eastern Studies* 30 (May 1998): 227–50.

[31] Marr, *Modern History of Iraq*, 159.

[32] Quoted in Benjamin Shwadran, *The Power Struggle in Iraq* (New York: Council of Middle Eastern Affairs Press, 1960): 35.

constituencies that shared his wariness about unity, the so-called "Iraq First" forces. The Communist party was at the helm of these forces, and its membership was dominated by non-Sunnis. The majority of non-Sunni communal groups saw the efforts at Arab unity as essentially a Sunni project, and they fought it either through their communal identity, or, if they felt the need for an ideological affiliation, through joining the Communist party.[33] Either way, they formed the backbone of the popular forces that Qasim used to promote the "Iraq First" identity.[34] That helped Qasim arrest the penetration of the Arab unity tide into Iraq throughout his five-year rule.

Qasim's unwillingness to join the Arab unity bandwagon is considered by many analysts as the beginning of the end for the pan-Arabist march. From 1958 until 1963, when Qasim was overthrown, Iraq's foreign policy was aimed at undermining Nasir's United Arab Republic; Iraq also was one of the first states to recognize and to promise help to the 1961 Syrian secessionist government. To the Iraqis, the Syrian secession constituted a return to the status quo, where the interests of the various Arab states were paramount, in no way to be subjugated to a larger, overarching ideology. Supported by the domestic forces that made up the "Iraq First" constituency, Qasim's foreign policy was vehemently anti-unionist, emphasizing Iraq's sovereignty and its own national (*watani*) interests.

This episode, and indeed the entire span of Qasim's rule (1958–63), points to the ability of political leaders to mobilize public support by appealing to one of a number of available identities. On the other hand, Qasim's years in power also show that this "menu" is neither limitless nor determined solely by the leader's preferences at any particular time. The identities available to Qasim had to resonate with the Iraqi public. As the editors note in the introductory chapter, identity "conditions what government leaders can entertain and is considered legitimate by their societies." Thus a "Communist" identity was never an option, even at the height of the party's power in Iraq during 1958–59. In a similar vein, Qasim never invoked a "Gulf" identity for Iraq when he made a bid to incorporate Kuwait into Iraq in 1961 (for that matter, nor did Saddam Hussein in 1990). The long-standing patronizing attitude—even contempt—felt by Iraqis toward the inhabitants of the Gulf precluded the possibility of utilizing a "Gulf" identity to mobilize domestic and regional support for the leaders' policy.

[33] Nakash, *Shi'is of Iraq*, 135–36; Lukitz, *Iraq: The Search*, 151–53.
[34] Part of the effort to distance Iraq from the Arab nationalist tide was to emphasize the country's status as the cradle of great pre-Arab civilizations. Thus Qasim added the Akkadian eight-point star of Ishtar to the national flag, as well as incorporating the insignia of the sun god Shamash to Iraq's national emblem. See Amatzia Baram, "Mesopotamian Identity in Ba'thi Iraq," *Middle Eastern Studies* 19 (October 1983): 427.

The tension between the politically dominant Sunni minority and the other Iraqi communities continued after the demise of Qasim. In Saddam Hussein's rise to prominence as the leader of the vigorously Arabist Ba'th Party, whose slogan is "one Arab nation with an eternal mission," Arabism was systematically propagated through the vigorously mobilizing institution. Even so, communal and particularistic loyalties persisted, necessitating frequent shifts in foreign policy, as well as a number of redefinitions of Iraq's identity by the country's ruling elite.

Immediately after taking power in a military coup in July 1968, the new Ba'thist rulers faced the perennial problem of a separatist Kurdish national identity. A Kurdish rebellion throughout the 1960s had militarily and financially drained the country. The new rulers, all committed to the Ba'th Party's uncompromising Arab nationalist ideology and to achieving pan-Arab unity through revolutionary struggle, succeeded only in fueling Kurdish fear and mistrust. As the Kurdish rebellion intensified, the Ba'thists tried to suppress it militarily but failed. Consequently, a 1970 settlement with the Kurds incorporated most of the Kurdish demands. A further setback to the Ba'thists' pan-Arab designs occurred in September that year, when King Hussein of Jordan unleashed his army against the Palestinian guerrillas, and Iraq watched the bloody spectacle unable to deliver on its fiery pan-Arab rhetoric. These two embarrassing episodes seemed to generate an internal debate led by Saddam Hussein to reevaluate Iraq's single-minded pan-Arab orientation, which found its public expression in a resolution of the party's Eighth Regional Congress:

> There were deficiencies and mistakes in the understanding and definition of the dialectical connection between the local (watani) tasks with which the party is being confronted . . . and the . . . pan-Arab tasks. The bitter experience through which the party had to go during the events of September 1970 was the natural outcome of all [these] mistakes. . . . Before the [September] events, the party was pushed into the pan-Arab arena, and in particular the Palestinian question, in a way that largely exceeded its capability . . . and before . . . many tasks were accomplished on the local Iraqi level . . . such as stabilizing the regime . . . and [fully] solving the Kurdish problem.[35]

It was not that the Ba'thist regime no longer cared about Iraq's Arab identity; rather, the regime felt that focusing on the country—achieving political harmony, reviving the economy, building the infrastructure, and especially solving the country's ethnic and sectarian problems—would be a more effective stepping-stone to-

---

[35] Quoted in Baram, "Qawmiyya and Wataniyya in Ba'thi Iraq: The Search for a New Balance," *Middle Eastern Studies* 19 (April 1983): 193.

ward the regime's Arab nationalist concerns and ambitions. These goals required not just an intellectual and political reorientation toward Iraq, but also sensitivity to Iraq's internal problems. In instructing an educational committee, Saddam Hussein said: "When we talk of the [Arab] nation we should not forget to talk about the Iraqi people. . . . When we talk of the Arab homeland we should not neglect to educate the Iraqi to take pride in this piece of land . . . in which he lives. . . . [Iraqis] consist of Arabs and non-Arabs. . . . When we talk of the great [Arab] homeland, we must not push the non-Arabs to look for a country outside Iraq."[36] Hussein was signaling the regime's intent to nurture an Iraqi identity, without necessarily abandoning the country's Arab identity.

Throughout the 1970s, the regime embarked on a political and cultural program designed to create a continuous link between modern Iraq and the ancient civilizations that had resided in the same land.[37] Plays depicting the achievements of Sumeria, Akkadia, Babylonia, and Assyria were performed throughout Iraq and internationally. Massive archeological work was done to resurrect and/or to reconstruct such ancient cities as Hatra, Assur, Nineveh, and Babylon. New museums of Iraqi history were built and old ones were lavishly refurbished. The political leadership made sure they became "a focal point of pilgrimage for the adult populations as well as for school children."[38] And artists and intellectuals were encouraged to incorporate Iraq's pre-Arab heritage in their work.

Iraqi foreign policy followed the path of this domestic orientation. After 1970, the Iraqi leaders began to gradually abandon their aggressively revolutionary and expansionist policies in the Arab world, and instead adopted a largely non-interventionist stance. By emphasizing domestic development, the Ba'thist leaders hoped to make Iraq the role model for the rest of the Arab states. If Iraq were to lead the Arab world, it would be because other Arabs would see it as the area's greatest and most dramatic success story. And in such a milieu, diplomacy and politics gradually replaced coercion and revolutionary trespassing.

By the mid-1970s the change in Iraq's foreign policy was discernible. Iraq was quickly shedding its image as a "base for Arab nationalist revolution," adopting instead a pragmatic, state-centered posture based on diplomacy and moderate policies.[39] Relations with Sadat's Egypt, Pahlavi Iran, Saudi Arabia, and the Gulf

[36] Ibid., 196.
[37] The following information is taken from Baram, "Mesopotamian Identity," 426–55.
[38] Ibid., 428.
[39] See for example, Dawisha, "Iraqi Foreign Policy: Motives, Constraints and Performance," in *Sources of Domestic and Foreign Policy in Iraq*, ed. Z. Michael Szaz (Washington, D.C.: American Foreign Policy Institute, 1986): 30–42; Ahmad Yousef Ahmad, "The Dialectics of Domestic and Role Performance: The Foreign Policy of Iraq," in Bahgat Korany and Ali E. Hillal Dessouki, *The Foreign Policies of Arab States* (Boulder, Colo.: Westview Press, 1984): 147–83; Dawisha, "Iraq: The West's Opportunity," *Foreign Policy* 41 (winter 1980–81): 134–48; Marr, *Modern History of Iraq*, 244–46.

states were normalized, and Iraq's radical stance on oil pricing was tempered, bringing it in line with Saudi thinking. Iraq even established diplomatic relations with, and extended financial loans to, Sultan Qabus of Oman, whom the Iraqis had vilified as a "British stooge" and a "lackey of imperialism."[40] This moderate orientation was crowned in 1980, when Saddam Hussein proclaimed his "Arab National Charter." The Charter stated that the "recourse to armed force by one Arab state against another Arab state [would] be prohibited, and any dispute arising between Arab states [would] be resolved by peaceful means. . . ." The use of force against neighboring non-Arab countries was also prohibited "except in the case of self defense or the defense of sovereignty." Further, all Arab states were enjoined to cooperate in opposing any aggression against "the territorial sovereignty of any Arab state. . . ."[41] Applauded by the other Arab states, the Charter, while reiterating Iraq's membership in the Arab family, was an unequivocal affirmation of the principle of Arab solidarity among independent and sovereign states. And in this sense, it was not coincidental that the proclamation of the Charter occurred at a time when Hussein and the other Iraqi leaders were working hard to make Iraqis proud of their uniqueness.

The Iraq-Iran war, begun in September 1981, shifted Iraq's foreign-policy priorities away from the Arab world to Iran. In fact, the war claimed all of Iraq's attention and energies in its foreign as well as its domestic policies. One of the conflict's domestic by-products was a reemphasis by Hussein and the ruling elite concerning Iraq's Arab identity.[42] The roots of the conflict lay in the advent in 1979 of the virulently Shiite Islamic Republic of Iran and the realization by one and all that the only consequential Muslim country with an indigenous Shiite majority was neighboring Iraq. The momentous happenings across the border clearly enhanced Iraqi Shiites' awareness of their sectarian identity. Meanwhile, the Iranian ayatollahs were bent on inciting the Iraqi Shiites against their secularist Ba'thist leaders. Thus, throughout 1980 reports of disturbances in the Shiite-dominated area of southern Iraq were rampant. Terrorist acts increased, and a hitherto small Shiite underground organization named *al-Da'wa* gained membership rapidly. In March 1980 a bomb was thrown at Tariq Aziz, the only Christian member of the Iraqi leadership, by members of *al-Da'wa* who, accord-

[40] See *al-Thawra* (Baghdad, Feb. 18, 1971, and Nov. 2, 1972). In the early 1970s Sultan Qabus depended on British military personnel in his struggle to defeat the Dhofari rebellion, which was vigorously supported by a then-ally of Iraq, the Marxist and equally radical Democratic Republic of South Yemen.

[41] Muhamed Tawaliba, *al-Qadhiya al-Qawmiya bein al-Manhaj al-Kifahi wal Tadhlil al-Maqsood* (The National Issue between the Program of Revolutionary Struggle and Deliberate Falsification) (Baghdad: Wizarat al-Thaqafa wal I'lam, 1980): 101–02.

[42] For a more detailed exposition of Hussein's usage of "identity" as a function of his regime's political survival, see Dawisha, "Identity and Political Survival in Saddam's Iraq," *Middle East Journal* 53 (autumn 1999): 553–67.

ing to Baghdad, had been receiving arms, training, and equipment from Tehran. This incident and another bomb attack a few days later prompted Hussein to execute Imam Baqr al-Sadr, the most influential Iraqi Shiite cleric, and to expel some 35,000 Iraqi Shiites, supposedly of Iranian descent, to Iran. So while the causes of the Iraq-Iran war were many, a primary cause was the mounting exasperation that Hussein felt in the face of persistent Iranian incitement of the Iraqi Shiites and his growing fear of a heightened Shiite identity at odds with a "Sunni" government pursuing "secularist" policies. In the September 1980 speech in which he abrogated the 1975 Iraq-Iran treaty, he declared:

> The ruling clique in Iran persists in using the face of religion to foment sedition and division among the ranks of the Arab nation despite the difficult circumstances through which the Arab nation is passing. The invocation of religion is only a mask to cover Persian racism and a buried resentment of the Arabs. The clique in Iran is trying to institute fanaticism, resentment and division among the peoples of the area.[43]

The statement reflected Hussein's strategy. In responding to the sectarian appeal of the Iranian ayatollahs, he decided to invoke Iraq's "Arab identity." The use of Arabist symbolism drew a clear ethnic distinction between the "*Arab* Iraqis" and the "racist and resentful *Persian* Iranians."

The ayatollahs naturally countered with religious/sectarian appeals. When the Iranians finally expelled the Iraqis from Iranian soil in the summer of 1982, mounting their own invasion of Iraq, Ayatollah Khomeini went on the radio to appeal to the "beloved Muslim people of Iraq." He did not mention Shiism, no doubt in order to attain the widest possible religious support against the "Godless rulers of Iraq." Yet the Shiite dimension was evident. The Iranian military assault was aimed at southern Iraq, where the bulk of the Shiite population lived, and in his address, he singled out the inhabitants of Basra, the largest Shiite city in Iraq, and the two holy Shiite cities of Najaf and Karbala:

> Beloved Iraqis: Rise up, and with the inspiration of the great religion of Islam attack the enemies of Islam, because with the valuable help of you beloved ones, your Iranian brothers will excise these cancerous tumors from the body of your Islamic country and will make the noble Iraqi nation govern their destiny. You the zealous inhabitant of Basra, welcome your faithful brothers and cut short the oppressive hands of the blasphemous Ba'thist from your land. You the respectable inhabitant of the holy shrines of Najaf and Karbala, you zealous youths who have attacked these

[43] *Al-Thawra* (Baghdad), Sept. 18, 1980.

filthy ones at every opportunity, use the opportunity offered to you by God and rise up in a manly manner and fulfill your own destiny.[44]

Hussein could have countered the Iranian effort at cementing a Shiite identity in Iraq by continuing to emphasize the "Iraqi identity." In fact, unlike Arabism, Iraq identity had the added advantage of not excluding the Kurdish population. But Hussein seemed to have calculated that the ayatollahs' "Persian" ethnicity was perhaps their main point of weakness; after all, it was on the notion of ethnicity that Kurds differed from the Iraqi Arabs. In terms of surviving the Iranian onslaught, therefore, Hussein's main preoccupation was to unite the various religious and sectarian communities under the banner of Arabism, and if that would alienate the Kurds, it would be a loss worth taking. His most pressing concern was to impress on the Shiites, who made up some 80 percent of the army's rank and file, that they were first and foremost Arabs, just as their "Sunni brothers," and that their government shared in their Arabism. In this way, Hussein hoped, the Sunni identity of his government—along with its narrow Takriti identity—would be forgotten as Shiites and Sunnis patriotically stood shoulder to shoulder in defending their cherished "Arabism" against the "racist Persians." Consequently, Hussein's counterattack contained emotionally charged and historically laden Arabist symbolism. For instance, the war against Iran was likened to the battle of Qaddisiya when a Muslim army from the Arabian Peninsula defeated Sassanid Persia in A.D. 637, capturing Ctesiphon, the Sassanid capital on the banks of the Tigris River, and expelling the Persians from Iraq. Indeed, the war, popularly and in vigorous government propaganda, became known as the Qaddisiya of Saddam.

Another example of the use of historical Arabist imagery in emphasizing the ethnic divide between the *Arab* Shiites of Iraq and the *Persian* Shiites of Iran was the government effort to remind the Iraqi Shiites of the Arab ethnicity of the founders of their sect. Thus, the government placed a banner at the entrance of the Imam Ali mosque in the city of Najaf—the holiest mosque and city in Shiite Islam—that declared: "We take pride at the presence here of our great father Ali, because he is a leader of Islam, because he is the son-in-law of the prophet, and because *he is an Arab*" (emphasis added).[45]

Arabism was not the only identity that the Hussein regime invoked. Throughout the Iraq-Iran war Hussein referred to the unity of Iraq as a nation, adding that it was not Saddam Hussein who was fighting the Iranians; rather, it was "the Sunnis, Shiites and other religions and sects in Iraq . . . , the whole

[44] The British Broadcasting Corporation, *Summary of World Broadcasts*, ME/7079/A/10–11, July 16, 1982.

[45] Quoted in Dawisha, "Iraq: The West's Opportunity," 142.

unified Iraqi people, who [were] fighting to safeguard their values and their new spirit."[46] Similarly, Hussein, faced with Iran's religious/sectarian onslaught, found it prudent to reiterate his own commitment, as well as Iraq's adherence, to Islam and its principles. Thus, one of the country's main newspapers, *al-Thawra*, attacked the Iranian leaders for accusing Iraq of being anti-Islamic. The paper retorted:

> We tell you that Iraq is a true Islamic state, and the people of Iraq, as well as its leaders, believe in God and in the teachings of Islam as a religion and as a heritage. Indeed, President Hussein's regular visits to the holy shrines and his continuous efforts to provide for these shrines is a clear proof of his deep and his unequivocal belief in the glorious message of Islam.[47]

Other references to Islam and the unity of Iraq were made throughout the war, but neither was emphasized as much as Iraq's Arab identity. And, more often than not, the Arab dimension was present or implied in the references to Iraqi unity or to the Islamic character of the country. For instance, in the previous passage, the newspaper referred not just to the "teachings of Islam," but also to its "heritage," which, as both Iraqis and Iranians know, is fundamentally Arab. During the Iraq-Iran war Hussein and the other members of Iraq's ruling elite vigorously emphasized the country's Arab identity, because they considered it to be the most potent weapon in maintaining unity, thus maintaining their political power.

Conclusion

This chapter has examined the interplay between identity and foreign policy during five episodes in Iraqi political history—the Suleiman-Sidqi political leadership of 1936, the Fertile Crescent and Arab League plans of 1943–45, Qasim's response to Abd al-Nasir's Arab nationalism in 1958, Hussein's response to the Kurdish problem and to Black September in the 1970s, and the Iraq-Iran war in the 1980s. These five episodes strongly confirm the editors' contention in the introductory chapter that societies generally have a menu of choice regarding their national identities, and that leaders, while unable to impose an identity that does not resonate with their public, nevertheless can and do *choose* from among various identities that are acceptable to their societies.

The analysis should help answer critical questions: How do national identities emerge and develop? Are they constructed or primordial? Does a discernible relationship exist between identity and a state's foreign policy? In other

[46] *Al-Thawra*, March 3, 1981.
[47] *Al-Thawra*, Jan. 16, 1982.

words, can the analyst detect patterns of foreign-policy behavior that could be attributed to a particular identity, and conversely, do shifts in foreign policy reverberate back onto the domestic arena, affecting identity?

"Nations as a natural, God-given way of classifying men," writes Gellner, "are a myth. Nationalism . . . sometimes takes pre-existing cultures and turns them into nations, sometimes invents them. . . . That is a reality."[48] This is the *constructivist* position, which postulates that nations are created, even invented. This is achieved purposefully by a determined elite when "dead languages [are] revived, traditions invented, and quite fictitious, pristine purities restored."[49] On the opposite spectrum of the argument lies the *primordialist* conception, which posits that a nation is culturally determined through an immemorial past. To the primordialist, national sentiment and solidarity are intrinsic to human nature, and as such they are not only natural but inevitable.[50] A middle position is suggested by a number of authors in which primordiality is accepted but with the connotation that it "is continually imagined, and continually reconstructed."[51] Anthony Smith puts it lucidly:

> Do not nationalists themselves claim that they are engaged in awakening the nation by reminding their co-nationals (through festivals and rituals, education and political struggle) of their common history and destiny? . . . The task, therefore, of those who set out to forge modern nations is more one of reconstructing the traditions, customs and institutions of the ethnic community or communities which form the basis of the nation than of inventing new traditions. . . . Traditions, myths, history and symbols must all grow out of the existing, living memories and beliefs of the people who are to compose the nation. Their popular resonance will be greater the more continuous with the living past they are shown to be.[52]

[48] Gellner, "Nationalism and High Cultures," in John Hutchinson and Anthony D. Smith, *Nationalism* (London: Oxford University Press, 1994): 63–64.

[49] Gellner, *Nations and Nationalism*, 56.

[50] Leonard Binder, "Introduction: The International Dimensions of Ethnic Conflict in the Middle East," in *Ethnic Conflict and International Politics in the Middle East*, ed. Binder (Gainesville, Fla.: University Press of Florida, 1998): 6. Although Binder uses the term "ethnic," the analysis is just as relevant for "national." See also Ernest B. Haas, *Nationalism, Liberalism and Progress* 1 (Ithaca: Cornell University Press, 1997): 41.

[51] S. N. Eisenstadt, "The Construction of Collective Identities: Some Analytical and Comparative Indications," *European Journal of Social Theory* 1 (1998): 235.

[52] Anthony D. Smith, "The Nation: Invented, Imagined, Reconstructed," in *Reimagining the Nation*, ed. Marjorie Ringrose and Adam J. Lerner (Buckingham, England: Open University Press, 1993): 13–16.

This middle position seems most relevant to the case of Iraq. A sense of primordialism does indeed exist in both the Arab and Iraqi identities. Excluding the Kurds, the Iraqis, whether Sunnis, Shiites, or Christians, city dwellers or bedouin, *are* indeed Arabs, in the sense that they are bounded not only by the linguistic community but also by a history that includes the 500-year Abbasid dynasty and its capital of Baghdad. Moreover, long before the Arabization of Iraq, Mesopotamia (the area now called Iraq) was the custodian of some of the earliest and most glittering civilizations. All of this is historical reality; it was *not* invented by the fertile imaginations of contemporary Iraqi elites. Instead, Iraqi elites could draw from either legacy in their effort to define the identity that would be most beneficial to their interests and most suitable to existing sociopolitical imperatives. Thus, Qasim, utilizing ethnic and sectarian fears of a Sunni-dominated Arab nationalism, could advocate his "Iraq First" policy, secure in the knowledge that an "Iraqi identity" was an intellectually valid concept, based on a long historical legacy. Hussein and the Ba'th could promote Iraq's "Arab identity," knowing that they easily could defend the legitimacy of the concept on historical and linguistic grounds. In the case of Iraq, therefore, identities hardly could be said to have been invented from nothing, but, based on the living past, they certainly were constantly reconstructed and redefined.

The question now is: Once redefined, would a particular identity influence the direction of foreign-policy behavior? This is, after all, the central objective of the book. As the editors note, the various contributions of the book address "how a particular identity makes certain kinds of state behavior possible or probable, and why." This chapter clearly shows that a relationship between identity and foreign-policy direction exists. Take, for instance, the policy of the 1936 Suleiman government. As we have seen, the leaders of that government promoted an "Iraq First" orientation, which was a striking contrast to the Arabist policies of its predecessor. And it was no coincidence that the Suleiman regime enunciated a foreign-policy oriented less toward the Arab world and more toward Turkey, Iran, and even distant Afghanistan. In this case, a causal relationship could be established: Identity (independent variable) produced a specific foreign-policy behavior (dependent variable).

The causal flow (direction) in other instances of Iraqi foreign-policy behavior, however, has not been not so clear-cut. Qasim's advocacy of an "Iraqi identity" certainly generated a particular foreign-policy behavior, which was vigorously anti-unionist. But the development of "Iraqi identity" itself was, if not totally, then at least partially, caused by an international phenomenon, namely, Nasir's expansionist Arab nationalism. In this case, "identity" could be said to have been both a dependent and independent variable. In the case of the Iraq-Iran war, "identity" clearly constituted the dependent variable, since Saddam Hussein's redefinition of the country's identity as "Arab" came as a clear response to the non-Arab, Persian characteristics of the "other," the Iranian enemy.

In the case of Iraq, a direct relationship between "identity" and foreign-policy behavior clearly does exist. This is a function not just of the contemporary Baʿthist era, but of the monarchical period as well. Indeed, as we have seen, the many reconstructions and redefinitions of the country's identity resulted from the impact of domestic imperatives and/or international events and phenomena. And given the dynamic nature of the foreign-policy system, these redefined identities in turn led to changes in the country's foreign-policy priorities and behavior.

6. The Evolution of Political Identity in Syria

YAHYA SADOWSKI

Choices of Political Identity

An ancient ritual is repeated daily in cafes, cabs, and caravansaries across Syria. When two strangers meet in the course of business, they begin a long conversation that resembles a game of twenty questions. They inquire about each other's origins, families, and background, blessing each other's children and expressing sympathy for each other's troubles with many pious phrases, while sharing cigarettes or tea. Such conversations allow people to establish some common component of identity that permits them to treat each other with a greater degree of intimacy, perhaps to offer one another the "special price" reserved for friends and relatives. Precisely which common denominator is established does not seem to matter much; it need not be something as obvious as a common religion or regional identity. Perhaps both have brothers who have emigrated or have children who studied at the same university—the connection can be quite tenuous. The conversation permits people to rotate facets of their identities like the faces on a Rubik's cube until they have found facets that match, transforming them from strangers into acquaintances who can trust each other and do business.

This fluidity of identity plays an important role in politics. Years ago, in one of the most penetrating discussions of Syrian politics ever written, Alasdair Drysdale noted:

> A Syrian officer may act like an officer in a restaurant if he feels that this will get him quicker service; he may be very conscious of his kin group when choosing a marriage partner; he may act as a member of a particular Alawi tribe during an intra-Alawi dispute within the armed forces; he may act as an Alawi, villager, peripheral non-Sunni or Ba'thi—or all five—during a coup d'etat, as a socialist during regime economic policy formation and as a Syrian during war with Israel. The relative importance of any of these identities may vary from person to person; thus many Alawi officers will reject their ethnic identity or feel it to be of no importance while

others may consider themselves Alawis first and Syrians second. That a particular officer is Alawi may be interesting if one is partial to ethnic arithmetic, but it does not necessarily reveal anything about that individual's behavior and political allegiances.[1]

Drysdale argued that the identity of Syrians is often "situation specific," open to redefinition according to circumstances or, as it would be fashionable to say today, "socially constructed."[2]

The truth of Drysdale's observation is evident to anyone who has lived and worked in Syria. But it raises certain questions. Does the fact that Syrians can invoke many facets of their identity mean that they have no fundamental notion of identity that underlies all the rest? Does the fact that an officer is an Alawi and a socialist and a Syrian mean that all three of those identities are of equal weight? What happens when an individual is forced to choose? If an officer has to decide to support one of two cabals that are planning a military coup, one consisting of Alawi officers and the other of socialist officers, which facet of his identity determines his choice? Individual Syrians make choices about their political identities. Thus, Syrian President Hafiz al-Asad, according to every reliable account, turned his back on his Alawi origins when he was quite young and has insisted ever since that he is an Arab. Other individuals, however, do not always accept such choices. Many urban Sunni Syrians insist that Asad is "really" an Alawi—and their conviction carries real social weight. Who prevails?

Individuals make choices about their political identity, but not under circumstances of their own choosing. A complex variety of social structures constrain and pattern individual choices, diverting individuals into groups, making society more diverse or more homogenous. Over the last two centuries, the pattern of identity that these social structures have produced has varied dramatically from one period to the next. During the decades after the Ottoman *tanzimat* (the state-building reforms of 1838–60), Syria's urban elites began to acquire a proto-nationalist consciousness of themselves as Ottoman citizens; but the rest of the population retained parochial identities that blended tribe, sect, and class.[3] When the Ottoman empire collapsed and the French occupied the country after World War I, urban elites transferred their loyalty to Arabism; the lower classes—urban and rural—began to experiment with new, farther-ranging

---

[1] Alasdair D. Drysdale, "Ethnicity and the Syrian Officer Corps: Some Theoretical Perspectives," paper presented at the annual meeting of the Middle East Studies Association in Louisville (Nov. 28, 1975): 6.

[2] For a cogent critique of the current fashion, see Ian Hacking, *The Social Construction of What?* (Cambridge: Harvard University Press, 1999).

[3] Hanna Batatu, "Some Observations on the Social Roots of Syria's Ruling Military Group and the Causes for Its Dominance," *Middle East Journal* 35 (summer 1981): 331–44.

political identities: pan-Arabist, pan-Syrianist, Islamist, sectarian, and city patriotic, to name a few.[4] After independence in 1946, a slow and irregular process of homogenization began, with the state promulgating an Arabist identity through the schools, the media, and national policy.

The state is only one—albeit the most potent—of many forces that shape the political identity of Syrians today. Yet state institutions, sometimes bolstered by economic trends, seem to be gradually bringing about a homogenization of the Syrian population; parochial identities are slowly declining. What is ironic, however, is that the state is not incubating the pan-Arabism that the ruling political elites endorse. Contrary to the plans of those who govern, the governed in Syria are developing a *Syrian* character that not only supersedes parochial identities but also tends to offset the country's official Arabist ideology.

Evidence of Recent Changes in Syrian Identity Patterns

Social trends that appeared during the 1980s and gained momentum during the 1990s seem likely to reshape the foundations of identity in Syria. These trends have not had time to decisively change the pattern of Syrian politics, but they will if they continue. They all seem to point toward the growing homogeneity of Syria's political cultures and values and the growth of a local or Syrianist sense of national consciousness.

THE DECLINE OF IDEOLOGY

The first trend has been the decline of formal political ideology. The enthusiasm for Arabism in Syria probably peaked in the 1970s and then began a steady decline. Even as recently as 1984–85 large numbers of adolescents still believed passionately in Ba'thist doctrine, and the Asad regime could easily mobilize squads of young women to beat up their peers who resisted secularization and insisted upon veiling themselves. But various events in the late 1980s combined to dampen the political ardor of even the most naïve elements of the Arabist camp. Throughout the 1980s the Asad regime's Arabist credentials had been frayed by the spectacle of proxy wars that it waged with the PLO, various Lebanese factions, Jordan, and Iraq. In 1988–89 Syria abandoned its policy of seeking "strategic parity" with Israel and entered into an alliance with Egypt that involved de facto acceptance of the Camp David accords. And in 1991 Syrian troops not only joined with the American-led forces assaulting Iraq but Syrian negotiators also began a direct engagement with Israeli diplomats in a

[4] James L. Gelvin, *Divided Loyalties: Nationalism and Mass Politics in Syria at the Close of Empire* (Berkeley: University of California Press, 1998).

search for peace, a decision that provoked public protest.[5] More than one pan-Arab idealist was driven to despair.

In many other Arab countries the decay of Arabism in the 1980s was mirrored by a rising interest in Islamism. Syria was an interesting exception. Islamist urban guerrilla groups had already risen against the Asad regime in a civil war that lasted from 1978 until 1982. The Asad regime's savage repression of this insurrection, culminating in the death of 20,000 people during the leveling of Hama, convinced many Islamists that militarism was a mistake. The dominant faction among the surviving Muslim Brothers adopted a strategy of seeking change through peaceful means. A wave of Islamic conservatism spread among middle-class urban Sunnis, but it focused on personal affairs and remained distinctly apolitical. The most dedicated young Muslims seemed drawn toward quietistic movements, such as certain Sufi groups or the reform movement of Muhammad Shahrur.[6]

Economic forces compounded the decline of ideology. From 1985 until 1990 Syria wrestled with a protracted economic crisis triggered by a sudden decline of foreign aid and oil prices, but rooted in a long history of excessive arms spending, government regulations that stifled economic initiative, and political corruption that drained resources and distorted markets.[7] This crunch did not breed any rebirth of radicalism, however. Instead, it made people focus on their short-term, concrete interests at the expense of their dreams of collective action. Older cadres, both Arabist and Islamist, complained that Syria's youth had grown cynical and materialistic.[8] Ali Haydar, one of Asad's oldest friends and the commander of his Special Forces, moaned in private about the death of political commitment among the rising generation.

THE CAPITALIST CONSENSUS

The economic crisis of the late 1980s had a second noteworthy effect: It forced many Ba'thists and government officials to radically revise their economic philosophy. As a result, bureaucrats and businessmen found themselves speaking

[5] "Troops Surround Cities After Pro-Iraqi Protests," Paris Agence France-Presse report translated in *FBIS* (Aug. 30, 1990): 47. But also see "Reports of Pro-Iraqi Protests Unfounded, Observers Say," *MEED* (Sept. 14, 1990): 29.

[6] For an anecdotal view of the return to Islam, see Robert Satloff, "Anxious Days for Syria," *Jerusalem Report* (July 16, 1992): 29–30. The main text for Dr. Shahrur's liberal interpretation of Islam is *al-Kitab wal-Qur'an: Qira'a Mu'asira* (Damascus: al-Ahali lil-Taba'a wal-Nashr, 1994).

[7] For a description of the economic crisis by one of Syria's leading economic policy experts, see Nabil Sukkar, "The Crisis of 1986 and Syria's Plan for Reform," in *Contemporary Syria: Liberalization between Cold War and Cold Peace*, ed. Eberhard Kienle (London: British Academic Press, 1994): 26–43.

[8] For indications of cultural trends in Syria, see John Lancaster, "Syria: The Hollywood of the Middle East?" *Washington Post* (Feb. 2, 1998): A14; and Robert S. Greenberger, "Rock-and-Roll Seems Here to Stay in Assad's Syria," *Wall Street Journal* (Jan. 21, 1994): A1.

the same language. As ties between these social groups flourished, a second ho-mogenizing trend took hold: A broad public consensus emerged in favor of a capitalist economy, provided that the state would continue to play a central role.

The Ba'thists who took power in Syria in 1963 represented the left wing of the party and were committed to a "socialist" economic program that included a state monopoly over finance, nationalization of major industrial plants, agrarian reform, and a highly protectionist trade regime. These programs, directed against prosperous urban Sunnis by a party that recruited heavily among reli-gious minorities in the countryside, succeeded in eliminating the political power of Syria's capitalists, impoverishing some, driving many into exile. For the next two decades, businessmen and bureaucrats viewed each other as poisonous rivals.

Asad, who knows little about economics and is primarily interested in foreign policy, thought that this social conflict weakened Syria in the face of its external enemies, so he and his clique have worked to liberalize the Syrian economy. The first restorations of nationalized properties took place immediately after Asad's November 1970 coup. Major rounds of economic liberalization followed in 1973, 1979, 1987, and 1991.[9] By the late 1970s Elizabeth Picard had discerned one of the major products of this trend: the emergence of alliances between Syria's po-litical and economic elites, or the birth of what she called a "military-mercantile complex."[10] This alliance has expanded vastly ever since.

For some time scholars dismissed the "military-mercantile complex" as a largely parasitic affair that contributed little to economic development. Its core comprised a handful of individuals who had parlayed their tight connections with the political powers in Damascus into opportunities for private profit. This group included a few regime loyalists like the Alawi opportunist Muhammad Haydar and a handful of non-Ba'thists/non-Alawis like Uthman al-A'idi (a hote-lier who parlayed his political connection into profits from Syrian Arab Airways contracts) and Sa'ib Nahhas (a Shi'i who combined his political connections in Damascus and Tehran into a tourism monopoly involving Iranians visiting Syria).[11] However, as opportunities for private business have expanded, new groups that do not rely on political connections have emerged—and old groups have begun to invest in ventures where their political connections are much less important. Syria's "crony capitalism" has evolved into something much more entrepreneurial.

[9] For a good periodization, see Volker Perthes, "Stages of Economic and Political Liberal-ization in Syria," in *Contemporary Syria*, 44–71.

[10] Elizabeth Picard, "Ouverture Economique et Enforcement Militaire en Syrie," *Oriente Moderno* (July–December 1979).

[11] For profiles of Syrian business leaders, see David Butter, "Who's Who in Syrian Busi-ness," *MEED* (Nov. 18, 1994): 13–14.

This change was the result of new economic policies that expanded the opportunities for private initiative. When the economic crisis began in 1985, the Syrian government responded with massive cuts in public spending. The currency was devalued, many government commodity subsidies were repealed, and, in 1988, Syrian arms expenditures were reduced by almost one-third. Save for a brief shopping spree made possible by Saudi grants after the liberation of Kuwait, weapons spending has remained around $2 billion per year ever since.[12] But these reductions were not enough to fully stem the crisis, so the regime began to listen more closely to its minister of economy, Muhammad Imadi, a non-Ba'thist with an economics degree from Columbia University. Imadi had been urging the government to adopt policies to encourage foreign investment and to lure back capital from Syrian émigrés.[13] In May 1991 the government issued a law that provided tax holidays for private investors and allowed businesses to retain up to 75 percent of their foreign exchange earnings.[14] In September 1994 another law substituted commercial profit criteria for central planning in the public sector and made other policy changes in an attempt to facilitate private investment in joint projects with public-sector firms.[15]

These policy changes, along with a rise in the value of Syrian oil exports, ushered in a period of economic prosperity unmatched since the "cotton boom" of the 1950s. This, in turn, galvanized public and elite support for further economic reforms. In 1998, Syrian experts agreed that the next four steps in economic liberalization should be:

1. Unification of the system of multiple exchange rates;
2. Repeal of a law that created risk for private citizens dealing in foreign currencies;
3. Creation of a stock market;
4. Creation of a private banking sector.[16]

Important differences over economic policy remained, of course, but these concerned primarily the pace of the reform program or how groups disadvantaged

[12] See SIPRI Military Expenditure Database (1997) and Andrew Rathmell, "Syria's Insecurity," *Jane's Intelligence Review* 6 (September 1994): 414–19.

[13] For an outline of Imadi's economic philosophy, see "Interview with Dr. Muhammad Imadi: 'Hadha Khittatna li-Jadhib Amwal al-Mughtaribin," *al-Majalla* (May 17–22, 1989): 35–41. Other influential Syrian economists promoted a similar program; see Cherif Cordahi, "A Blueprint for Economic Progress," *South* (June/July 1991): 48.

[14] For the text of the law, see "Syria: Main Articles of Investment Law," *MEED* (May 24, 1991): 29.

[15] For the text of the law, see "'Text' of Decree on Public Sector," translated from *al-Ba'th* in *FBIS* (Oct. 21, 1994): 47–53.

[16] Ibrahim al-Hamdi, "al-'Aqabat al-Arba'a imam al-Istithmar fi Suriya," *al-Wasat* (April 22, 1996): 38–40.

by the process might best be protected. Even in the state-controlled press, editorials calling for these reforms became commonplace.[17]

Until the reform process began in the late 1980s, Syria's business elites had been divided not only from the political elite but also internally into discrete and mutually suspicious groups. Volker Perthes documented the rivalry among (a) the old bourgeoisie that had survived the socialist programs of the 1960s, (b) the new industrialists, who took advantage of government tolerance for the development of light industries in the 1970s, (c) the state bourgeoisie that made its fortunes directing public-sector firms, and (d) the new commercial class that exploited government licenses and contracts.[18] Under the reforms, the boundaries between these groups began to blur. Members of the new commercial class, such as Nahhas, who had focused his investments in trade and tourism, began to branch out and invest in industry.[19] Alawis who once might have been expected to play on their connections to the regime became independent entrepreneurs—such as Rema Makhluf, a relative of Asad's wife, who sat on the board of the Ebla Corporation and helped it to negotiate a deal with General Motors for setting up an assembly plant near Aleppo.[20]

Perhaps even more impressive was the wholesale movement among the *children* of the political elite to join the business community. The sons and daughters of the Ba'thist *nomenklatura* largely rejected their parents' example and avoided careers in the party, civil service, or military. The president's nephew Mudar al-Asad married Maya Haydar and joined the business of her father, the entrepreneur Muhammad Haydar.[21] Mudar's brother Sawmar has taken over his father's publishing interests and has launched a satellite television network based in London.[22] The children of Syria's other vice president, Abd al-Halim Khaddam, have also gone into business—but have been tarnished by their involvement in a toxic-waste scandal.[23] Probably the most prominent and successful of these *née Ba'thist* businessmen is Firas Talas, director of the MAS business

[17] See "Paper Urges Bank Reforms to Spur Savings," a *Tishrin* editorial translated in *FBIS* (Sept. 13, 1994): 61–63; and "Daily Urges Focus on Improving Export Quality," ibid. (Sept. 22, 1994): 56–57.

[18] For a sophisticated analysis of Syria's business community, see Perthes, "The Bourgeoisie and the Ba'th," *Middle East Report* (May–June 1991): 31–37.

[19] "Nahhas Moves into Industry," *MEED* (Sept. 6, 1991): 29–30.

[20] Butter, "Who's Who."

[21] Alain Chouet, "Alawa Tribal Space Tested by Power: Disintegration by Politics," *Maghreb-Machrek* (January–March 1995): 93–119, as translated in the Daily Report of the U.S. Foreign Broadcast Information Service (FBIS) (Oct. 3, 1995).

[22] Roula Khalaf, "'Doctor' Who Wants Democratic Arab TV," *Financial Times* (May 1, 1998): 4; and Frances Greenwood, "Syrian Politics by Satellite," *Middle East International* (March 13, 1998): 4.

[23] Raymond Hinnebusch, "Asad's Syria and the New World Order: The Struggle for Regime Survival," *Middle East Policy* 2 (1993): 1–15.

group that specializes in agricultural products. Firas has also emerged as one of the most vocal proponents of economic reform.[24]

THE CONVERGENCE OF TOWN AND COUNTRY

Until recently the sharpest divide in Syrian politics—one that shaped political behavior more dramatically than either sect or ideology—was the confrontation between rural and urban society. Until the Ba'th took power, one observer noted, the rift could be described as follows:

> The antagonism between urban and rural people reaches such an extent that one can almost speak of two different populations coexisting within the same political frame but without intermingling. The peasant pays all the costs of the antagonism, because the economic and social structure is based on the incontestable primacy of the cities.[25]

The pattern of clashes during the civil war against the Islamists, particularly during the assault on Hama in 1982, indicated that old urban-rural grievances were still very much alive. Sunni villagers had more in common with their Druze and Alawi cousins in the countryside than they did with their urbane and flashy co-religionists in the major cities.

But migration from the rural areas to the cities has been strong in Syria as it has across the Third World. Most rural families now have relatives in the cities. Consider the case of the Alawis. As recently as the 1960s they formed an overwhelmingly rural population, constituting only 10 percent of the population in the city of Latakia, the capital of the province in which most Alawis were concentrated. Today Alawis constitute a clear majority in Latakia (perhaps 55 percent of 306,000 people in 1994)[26] and form an even larger share of the population in coastal towns like Tartus (population 150,000 in 1989) and Banyas. Moreover, Alain Chouet thinks that they form almost half of the population of Hims, Syria's third largest city (population 644,000, according to the 1994 census).[27] A huge Alawi community—numbering perhaps 200,000—also lives in Damascus. By the 1990s at least a third and perhaps as much as half of Syrian Alawis lived in cities.[28]

---

[24] Ibrahim Hamdi, "Firas Mustafa Talas lil-Wasat: al-Salam al-Jiz'i Yabqi al-Hajiz al-Nafsi ma'a al-Sharikat al-Isra'iliyya," *al-Wasat* (Nov. 4, 1995): 38–39.

[25] Jacques Weuleresse, *Le Pays des Alaouites,* cited in Nikolaos Van Dam, *The Struggle for Power in Syria: Sectarianism, Regionalism, and Tribalism in Politics, 1961–1978* (New York: St. Martin's, 1979): 27.

[26] For urban population figures reflecting the 1994 census, see *al-Ba'th* (Feb. 6, 1995): 4; and *Information Please Almanac: Atlas and Yearbook 1997* (Boston: Houghton Mifflin, 1997): 271.

[27] Chouet, "Alawa Tribal Space Tested by Power."

[28] Although no official statistics reflect the communal breakdown of the Syrian population, scholarly estimates suggest the Alawis constitute 12 percent to 18 percent of the total Syrian population. (I personally favor the higher estimates.) If Alawis do constitute about 15 percent of

The pattern of urbanization has had other effects that promote national integration as well. Officially, Damascus and Aleppo appear to be cities of comparable size: in 1994 the former had a population of 1,549,000 and the latter 1,599,000. However, the suburbs of Damascus have grown both more rapidly and more extensively than their Aleppine counterparts. If the suburbs are included, the population of Damascus jumps to more than 3 million people—some think perhaps even 4 million.[29] Thus, Damascus (al-Sham) will remain not only the political capital of Syria, but the economic center of the country as well. The emergence of al-Sham as the country's Paris has actually dampened some of the old urban rivalries that used to divide the Shawwam, the Halabna, the Hamasna, and the Hamawiyyin.[30]

The industrialists of Aleppo may resent this. After all, the Aleppines have a well deserved reputation for entrepreneurship, for preferring industry to simple commerce, and for developing small firms into huge plants through sheer gumption. Yet expansion of Aleppo's industries will require an expansion of its ties to Damascus. For one thing, the sheer size of Damascus means the city supplies many of the country's emerging markets. The largest source of economic growth in 1993 may have been the explosion of private transportation firms as individuals responded to the overcrowding of Damascus's public transportation system by importing hundreds of microbuses.[31] Damascus is also the financial capital of the country, and will probably remain so even after the state gives up its monopoly in the banking sector. The growth of Aleppine industry has been constrained by the scarcity of capital in the city. An attempt by Aleppine entrepreneurs to create an "informal finance" sector by offering high interest rates for cash deposits collapsed in 1995.[32]

INTERMARRIAGE WITHIN THE RULING CLASS

The final pattern of homogenization that deserves mention is a trend toward intermarriage—across sectarian lines—within the political elite.

The most prominent example of this trend has been Asad's old companion and foreign-affairs expert, Abd al-Halim Khaddam. In fact, gossips claim that Khaddam's long career owes more to his savvy marriages than to any talent as a

---

Syria's 13.8 million citizens, that means there are about 2.1 million of them. The Alawi population of Damascus, Hims, and the four major coastal cities (Latakia, Jabla, Tartus, Banyas) totals something like 200,000 + 322,000 + 373,000 = 895,000, or 43.2 percent.

[29] U.S. Department of State, Bureau of Public Affairs, Background Notes: Syria, October 1995, 1.

[30] For years the most popular jokes in Syria were those that Damascenes told about Halabis—and vice versa.

[31] James Whittington, "Syria's Economy Shackled by Old Institutions," FT (May 11, 1993): 4.

[32] Ibrahim Hamdi, "Suriya: al-Halabiyun Yukhasiruna al-Fawa'id . . . wa-Ra's al-Mal," al-Wasat (June 11, 1995): 41.

policymaker. Khaddam's first wife was an Alawi from a prominent family of the Matawira tribe. (He later married a second woman, from his own Sunni confession.)[33] Khaddam's marriage strategy has extended to the matches he has made for his children as well. His oldest son married an Alawi, the daughter of Major General Muhammad Nasif, the de facto director of the powerful General Intelligence Directorate. His daughter reportedly married into the family of an influential Christian intellectual.[34]

The Alawi members of the elite have been especially successful in pursuing interdenominational marriages. The children of Ali Haydar, a boyhood friend of Asad who commanded the key Special Forces Division until 1994, married outside the Alawi community. His son married a Sunni; his daughter married a Shi'i. The record for intermarriage by an Alawi family may go to the children of Shafiq al-Fayyad, until recently commander of the Third Armored Division; al-Fayyad also is a close friend and a key ally of the president. One of al-Fayyad's sons married into a Christian family and the other into a Shi'i one, while his daughter married a son of his political rival, Rif'at al-Asad, the president's brother.[35]

Intermarriage is even accepted within the president's own family. Asad supported his daughter, Bushra al-Asad, when she accepted a marriage proposal by a young Christian, although the latter's parents eventually blocked the match. The president's brother, Rif'at, has had at least four wives—two Sunnis, one Lebanese, and one Syrian. Nothing in traditional Alawi doctrine prevents such matches, but the advances in the community's power means they have become much more common. This may have important consequences. Alawi religious doctrine is never taught to women, nor to any man who is not descended from Alawis on both sides of his family. Thus, the growing trend toward intermarriage may mean the slow death of Alawism as a faith. This does not appear to be causing much alarm. The generations of Alawis who flocked to the Ba'th party were not only not especially religious; they also positively reveled in the way that secularism gave them a way to escape the stigma that orthodox Muslims tried to cast on their origins.

Other internal forces also promote a common Syrian identity. There are obvious economic factors: people employing the same currency, following the same regulations, being encouraged to trade with each other and discouraged from trading beyond their borders. Political factors also deserve mention: people serving in the same army or militia[36]; being made to salute the same flag and sing the same anthem; joining one of the "cults" that have developed

[33] Batatu, "Some Observations."

[34] Chouet, "Alawa Tribal Space Tested by Power."

[35] Ibid.

[36] One school of thought insists that the demand of military conscription, the need to form a common culture of discipline among people of diverse regional origin, is *the* dominant force

around various Asads (Hafiz, Rif'at, and Basil); even attending schools that teach a common curriculum. (Although the curriculum in Syria is Arabist rather than Syrianist, Syrian teachers effectively extol the virtues of the Syrian regime while decrying the crimes of its rivals.)

Even a common high culture is emerging. The cultural activities of Damascus and Aleppo (not to mention the folk festivals at Bosra) no longer live in the shadow of Iraqi and Egyptian models, as they did through the 1960s. Majda Rumi is recognizable as the *Syrian* diva. Sa'adallah Wannus is the national playwright. Adonis is probably the national poet, Nizar Qabbani having become a collective property of the Arabs. Several voices compete for the role of national author—Hanna Mina, Zakariya Tamir, Ghada al-Samman—although perhaps no one has yet written "the great Syrian novel."

As a collective sense of "being Syrian" develops, the understanding of what it means to be an Arab evolves. The 90 percent of the Syrian population who can claim Arab ancestry (basically everyone except the Kurds, the Armenians, and the shrinking Jewish community) have not stopped thinking of themselves as Arabs—indeed, they continue to take great pride in that identity. But they are Arabs today in much the sense that the French are Europeans: The cultural identification is solid, but how much political collaboration that entails depends on changing circumstances. Syrian citizens can give their primary loyalty to their own state without ceasing to think of themselves as Arabs—indeed, they continue to think of themselves as exemplary Arabs.

This sense of common Syrian identity has not yet developed into an articulate political ideology. It is still manifest mostly in rather subtle indicators, such as the fact that the acronym for Firas Talas's firm, MAS, stands for *min ajli Suriya:* "for Syria." Yet the sentiment is tangible. As Perthes has explained:

> While the [Asad] regime and its leadership certainly lack legitimacy, the legitimacy of the state is not in doubt. . . . People from all parts of Syria have come to regard Damascus as their legitimate capital and to accept the Syrian state as the proper frame for national politics—Greater-Syria or pan-Arab visions, and regional ties and animosities notwithstanding. The existence and extensive utilization of primordial loyalties has not prevented the development of a strong sense of Syrian identity; and almost all societal groups—including the bourgeoisie and the military who will both have a say in determining Syria's future—are interested in maintaining the state, its stability, and if possible its regional role.[37]

---

in the birth of nationalism. See Barry R. Posen, "Nationalism, the Mass Army, and Military Power," *International Security* 18 (fall 1993): 80–124.

[37] Perthes, *The Political Economy of Syria under Asad* (London: I. B. Tauris, 1995): 269.

If current trends continue, Syrians will develop a growing consciousness of themselves not as Arabs, Muslims, or socialists but as Syrians—citizens of a state called Syria, a country distinct from Lebanon and Iraq, who as a result share common interests and a common culture. This does not mean Syrians will be immune to appeals by wider causes; even in the United States ardent patriots can still persuade themselves that they are part of a larger entity called "the West."[38] It does not mean that they will ever develop an aggressively passionate Syrian nationalism of the type that emerged in Serbia. Instead, Syrian nationalism is more likely to resemble Belgian nationalism, which is almost invisible in everyday life but which can be quickly aroused by foreign invasion.

To date, Syrian nationalism remains a sentiment. No intellectual has yet stepped forward to articulate and advocate such an ideology (and intellectuals are almost universally the inventors of nationalism). This is hardly surprising; Arabism is still the official ideology of the Ba'thist regime, which quickly silences anyone who dissents too publicly or too effectively. But beyond this, other intellectuals would be unlikely to tolerate a noisy Syrianist in their midst. Arab intellectuals, whether they follow Arabism or Islamism, are quite wedded to their regional connections; they enjoy being read and recognized in neighboring capitals, and they have done much of their best work in exile.[39]

However, the structures—the realities of power and behavior—on which a Syrian identity might someday be erected are already visible. If it is generally true that the prevailing ideas of philosophy and "common sense" reflect the realities of social life,[40] this Syrian identity may yet blossom into a full-scale nationalist ideology.

---

[38] Samuel Huntington, *The Clash of Civilizations and the Remaking of World Order* (New York: Touchstone Books, 1998).

[39] Despite all of the great analyses of the decadence of Arab intellectuals, this phenomenon seems to have escaped attention. On the one hand, intellectuals are lambasted for how readily they compromise their principles and collaborate with particular Arab governments; see Fouad Ajami, *The Dream Palace of the Arabs* (New York: Pantheon Books, 1998). Yet in the midst of such collaboration, Arab intellectuals rarely advocate local or particularist ideologies like Syrianism; instead, they remain loyal to region-wide ideologies. This is true despite strong incentives to localism—particularly in Iraq (where the regime has pressed its Mesopotamian heritage) and among Palestinians (who have been consistently betrayed by other Arabs). We lack good explanations of why this is so. Even the Islamists in the Arab world tend to be internationalists rather than localists (unlike their counterparts in Turkey and Iran, who are often "religious nationalists"); see Mark Juergensmeyer, "The New Cold War? Religious Nationalism Confronts the Secular State," *Comparative Studies in Religion and Society* 5 (Berkeley: University of California Press, 1994).

[40] Or, as a German intellectual who rejected nationalism argued 140 years ago: "The mode of production of material life conditions the social, political and intellectual life-process in general. It is not the consciousness of men that determines their being, but on the contrary their social being that determines their consciousness." Karl Marx, preface to *The Critique of Political Economy* (1859).

Foreign Affairs and the Importance of "Otherness"

The political and economic forces that bind Syrians together centrifugally are mirrored in centripetal forces abroad that exclude Syrians from other identities. Syrians are not Iraqis, or Jordanians, or Palestinians. The Israelis and the Lebanese, in particular, have had a profound impact on the way Syrians understand themselves.

The Syrians fear the Israelis in a way few Americans are likely to understand. Israel has defeated Syria in four wars (1948, 1967, 1973, and 1982), occupied a fertile swath of its territory, bombed and strafed the elite residential quarters of Damascus, destroyed much of its industrial infrastructure (1973), and infiltrated the highest circles of the Ba'th party. Some Damascenes will not hold sensitive conversations outdoors because they fear that the Israeli electronic surveillance posts on Mount Hermon may be eavesdropping on them. These fears are not the result of political manipulation and propaganda; whether realistic or not, they are completely homegrown. Israel has supplied the Syrians with a common enemy for fifty years. Israel forms the critical "other" against which Syrians define themselves, the out-group whose existence promotes their own solidarity. They measure their progress in terms of their ability to narrow the economic gap with Israel. They measure their security in terms of their ability to deter Israel. Israel is the challenge to which the Syrians view themselves as a Toynbee-style response.

The other group that has played an important role in shaping Syria's identity is the Lebanese. Viewed from the perspective of Beirut, the Lebanese hardly appear as a "group" at all; they are a dozen sects and a hundred clans who can barely tolerate sharing the same political framework and who, in the words of Ghassan Tueni, would set the entire country aflame if they needed a light for a cigarette.[41] Yet, in their attitudes toward the Syrians, the Lebanese display surprising unanimity. The great majority of Lebanese resent the Syrian military and intelligence presence in their country. And even those Lebanese who are politically allied with the Syrians still tend to look down on their neighbors to the east. The great majority of Syrians working in Lebanon, whether in the military or among the 250,000 who visit each year as agricultural laborers and construction workers, are of peasant origin. Even Syrians from Damascus and Aleppo appear unsophisticated and rustic by the standards of the Beirut jet set. Likewise, Syrian officials who regularly dominate their Lebanese counterparts complain that the latter subtly patronize and silently despise them.

This has impressed the Syrians because the differences between themselves and the Lebanese are clearly minor. From a Syrian perspective, the differences

[41] Jonathan C. Randal, *Going All the Way: Christian Warlords, Israeli Adventurers, and the War in Lebanon* (New York: Viking Press, 1983).

between a Beiruti and a Damascene are no more profound than those between a Damascene and an Aleppine. Lebanese and Syrians eat virtually identical cuisines, they speak the same general dialect, they cite the same proverbs and jokes. Syrian businessmen look at their Lebanese counterparts and envy their freedom. But they look at the Lebanese political system and recoil from its anarchy and disorder. The Lebanese rejection of Syrians is mirrored in a Syrian distaste for the Lebanese. The Syrians think the Lebanese are corrupted, infected by the West, superficial, and urbane in the worst sense of the term. They view themselves as purer, capable of greater courage and stronger resistance, as more "authentic" than the self-hating Arabs of Beirut who they think are ambivalent about their own origins. The Lebanese, like the Israelis, also supply the Syrians with an image of otherness—but one that gives them a more fine-tuned perception of their own identity. They view Lebanon as a region that was once an integral part of Syria but that has now become so divisive and decadent that its reintegration may be neither possible nor desirable.

Cultural contact, economic exchange, and military clashes with Israel and Lebanon have given Syrians a stronger sense of their own identity, and foreign policy has reinforced the trend. If isolation or marginalization within Arab politics has imposed on Syrians a sense of otherness, the Asad regime's own foreign policy—which departs from the wider Arab consensus on the peace process, relations with Iran and Russia, and the future of Lebanon—has forced on them a sense of their own togetherness.

Asad's foreign policy has been so obstinately independent that some scholars have been driven to rather extreme hypotheses to explain it. Daniel Pipes claims that in international affairs Syria plays a "dangerous double game."[42] He argues that Asad and key Syrian policy makers think of themselves primarily as Alawis. They are not actually interested in pan-Arabism; they use it only to conceal their real interest: pan-Syrianism. They seek the unity of Greater Syria, or the lands that today comprise the states of Syria, Jordan, Lebanon, Israel-Palestine, and parts of southern Turkey. Why would Asad and the other Alawis prefer pan-Syrianism to pan-Arabism? Pipes suggests that as minorities they seek to dilute the Sunni majority of Syria by unifying with Lebanon and perhaps Iraq. (Of course, this doesn't explain why the Alawis would want to unify with the Sunni majorities in Jordan and Palestine.) To defend a rigid and simplistic conception of political identity in Syria, Pipes posits a massive conspiracy, a hidden foreign-policy agenda, and a hypothesis that (since it is based on unobservable Alawi duplicity) is unfalsifiable.

Less far-fetched explanations also address Syria's foreign policy. In the 1950s Syrian politics were so internally divisive that (as later happened in Lebanon)

[42] The *locus classicus* for this argument is Pipes, *Greater Syria* (New York: Oxford University Press, 1990).

virtually all of the country's neighbors were able to finance local proxies. Turkey, Iraq, and Egypt took turns sponsoring military coups in Damascus.[43] Anyone who wished to stabilize the situation in Syria, whether Ba'thist or Islamist, was going to have to undercut these networks of foreign penetration—perhaps by counterattacking and fostering surrogates for Syrian power in the surrounding states. This is just what Asad did, deploying ideology, cash, and terror, as necessary. Through Kurdish movements like the PKK he developed leverage against Turkey. Through sponsorship of Ba'thist, communist, and Islamic opposition, he sought influence in Baghdad. Through support for rejectionist elements of the PLO, he gained the ability to affect both the Palestinians and the Israelis. And through alliances with sundry militias in Lebanon (including Amal, the Syrian Social Nationalists, Sa'iqa, and Maronite independents such as Elie Hobeika and Sulayman Franjieh), he became a force in Beirut even after Syrian troops officially withdrew from the city. As even his opponents say, he turned Syria from a game into a player.

Syria's foreign policy under Asad does not show a strong ideological dimension; instead, it flows primarily from structural considerations. Asad's approach to Israel reflects more a fear of the Jewish state's military capabilities and the threat that Israel poses to Syrian influence rather than any ideological abhorrence of Zionism.[44] Despite his own preference for secularism, Asad has been equally comfortable wooing Iran and Saudi Arabia despite the fundamentalist bases of these regimes. Henry Kissinger would probably have followed the same policies if he had been president of Syria. In other words, Asad has tended to act as neither a pan-Arabist nor a pan-Syrianist but as a Syrian. He is not playing a double game but a single one. And when Arabist ideology and Syrian *realpolitik* have pointed in different directions, interests have usually prevailed over passions.

This has, as we have noted, cost him some support. It was a major force in the decline of Arabist ardor among rank-and-file Syrian Ba'thists during the 1980s. More recently, "realistic" changes in economic and foreign policy have caused rifts between Asad and some of the oldest members of his inner circle, such as Major General Ali Haydar (dismissed as commander of the Special Forces in 1994) and Abd al-Halim Khaddam (who remains vice president for foreign affairs even though Asad clearly now prefers to work with the foreign

---

[43] The best description of this period remains Patrick Seale's wonderful study, *The Struggle for Syria: A Study of Post-War Arab Politics, 1945–1958* (London: Oxford University Press, 1965).

[44] I am not suggesting that Asad does *not* loathe Zionism—or imperialism or the Americans, for that matter. Rather, whatever his personal feelings are, he judges all political movements and events by a calculus of pure power. If he has not read Machiavelli he must certainly have read its medieval Syrian counterpart, *The Subtle Ruse: The Book of Arabic Wisdom and Guile* translated by Rene Khawam (London: East-West Publications, 1980).

minister, Faruq al-Shar'a). Throughout this painful process, Asad has managed to keep most Syrians behind him.[45] Today a majority of Syrians agree (however they felt at the time) that Asad's decision in 1990 to join the coalition against Saddam Hussein proved very profitable for the country. Likewise, most now seem to endorse Asad's decision to negotiate a "peace of the brave" with Israel.[46]

IMPLICATIONS FOR THEORIES OF NATIONALISM

In the 1950s and 1960s, modernization theorists claimed that the unification of national culture was an inexorable consequence of the defeat of traditional society. National unity was portrayed as a natural part of modernity, as was an industrial economy and a democratic polity. The slow emergence of a sense of Syrian identity does not mean that the predictions of modernization theory were correct, however. First, there has been nothing inevitable (or even highly probable) about this trend; Arabist and Islamist interpretations of collective political identity might well have prevailed. Indeed, even today the growth of Syrian identity depends on the strengthening of state institutions and economic integration—either of which might be reversed.[47] Despite being home to the oldest continuously inhabited cities in the world, Syria is still a young country and anything might happen.

Second, although the emergence of Syrian nationalism is part of a worldwide trend, it is not something everyone views as progress. Nationalism is one of the most two-faced of all social phenomena. It can trigger both altruistic love of country and genocidal xenophobia. The persistent strength of nationalism has often been an embarrassment to modernization theorists, particularly when nationalism helps suppress democratic liberties or when it is invoked to curb trade and the movement of ideas across borders. Some scholars have suggested that the greatest danger to world peace in this century will come from hypernationalism, from radical nationalist movements that promote persecution of local minorities and aggression against neighboring states. Fortunately, the developing nationalism in Syria seems to be both subdued and realistic in temper. In fact, Syrian nationalism seems to be almost as much of an embarrassment to the Syrians themselves as it is to modernization theorists. Where Syrians once viewed themselves as the vanguard of Arab or Islamic unities that stretched from the Atlantic to the Indian Oceans, they now find themselves working to build a more prosperous home for their children in a smaller world, one that stretches from Majdal Shams to Hassakeh.

[45] This is the opinion of the leading CIA analyst who studies Syria.

[46] See, for example, Jonathan Ferziger, "The Price Is Right: Bring on the Israeli Tourists, Urge Market Traders in Damascus," *Jerusalem Report* (Dec. 1, 1994): 24.

[47] For an account of how high oil prices used to promote pan-Arabism, see Saad Eddin Ibrahim, *The New Arab Social Order: A Study of the Social Impact of Oil Wealth* (Boulder, Colo.: Westview Press, 1982).

People attempting to understand the evolution of nationalism and identity in Syria would do well to attend to the work of the late Ernest Gellner. Alone among the major Western students of nationalism, Gellner knew something about the Arabs and worked them into his theorizing. Gellner was no modernization theorist, but he too thought that nationalism would follow whenever a society began to industrialize. He suggested structural reasons for this: Successful industrialization requires that societies emphasize rationalistic social thought, egalitarian mores that permit the easy reallocation of labor, and a new system of universal education that ensures that everyone speaks the same language and shares a single work ethic. It was this last element, he contended, that laid the foundation for nationalism:

> Time was when education was a cottage industry, when men could be made by a village or clan. That time has now gone, and gone forever. (In education, small can now only mean beautiful if it is covertly parasitic on the big.) Exo-socialization, the production and reproduction of men outside the local intimate unit, is now the norm, and must be so. The imperative of exo-socialization is the main clue to why the state and culture *must* now be linked, whereas in the past their connection was thin, fortuitous, varied, loose, and often minimal. Now it is unavoidable. That is what nationalism is about, and why we live in an age of nationalism.[48]

In Syria, where industrialization is still in its early stages, it is hard to see how economics demands a homogenous culture bred in state educational institutions. It is easier to see how the development of the state itself demands, or at least encourages, such homogeneity. The modern state has an easier time imposing its authority as culture homogenizes and communications between center and periphery improve, as schools teach not only a common language but also elementary disciplines such as queuing and the "show of hands." The state promotes the homogenization of culture through instruments other than schools, however.[49] For example, the state fosters homogeneity through the courts, where the diversity of traditional codes and arbitrators has been replaced by a centralized body of law enforced by a nationally controlled police force. The state also advances homogeneity particularly through the military. In Syria, as in many other societies, the single most important event in the march toward development of a homogenous national culture may have been the imposition of universal military conscription.

[48] Ernest Gellner, *Nations and Nationalism* (Ithaca: Cornell University Press, 1983): 38.

[49] For some highly original ideas about the subtle ways in which the state may promote national homogeneity, see the works of Norbert Elias; particularly *The Germans: Power Struggles and the Development of Habitus in the Nineteenth and Twentieth Centuries* (Cambridge: Polity Press, 1996).

Nationalism has shown a surprising tenacity in our century. Hutus and Tutsis, who had thought of themselves as different castes within a single society only fifty years ago, now view themselves as distinct nations, each demanding control of a state. Pathans, Punjabis, and Sindhis have fought each other for centuries, but intellectuals from the three groups are still working to unite them in a single nation called Pakistan. In the advanced industrial societies evidence indicates that nationalist passions are cooling, that both internationalist and regional loyalties are on the rise.[50] But in countries where the state is still in the process of formation, the urgency of nationalism also seems to be growing. It seems likely that Syria will participate in this trend.

[50] Ronald Inglehart, *Modernization and Post-Modernization: Cultural, Economic, and Political Change in 43 Countries* (Princeton, N.J.: Princeton University Press, 1997).

7. Identity and Foreign Policy

The Case of Egypt

IBRAHIM A. KARAWAN

Unlike many of the countries examined in this book, Egypt does not have the acute communal cleavages that can easily get translated into sharp ethnic conflicts regarding political identity or identities. Within its region, Egypt is a clear case of ethnic and cultural homogeneity. Egyptian leaders and political activists of different ideological persuasions have been keenly aware of that historical and societal specificity and tended to see it as one of the factors that could justify Egypt's ability to play a central role in the Arab world. After all, historically shaped features of state-society relations may actually prevent, reduce, or facilitate state action in the area of foreign policy relative to other regional actors.[1]

Though the prominent Arab nationalist writer Mohamed Hassanein Heikal might not have been the first to characterize Egypt as the only nation-state in the Arab world—characterizing the rest as tribes with flags—he clearly popularized that notion. In 1995, when the Ibn Khaldun Center for Development Studies in Cairo embarked on organizing a conference on ethnic and religious minorities and identity formation in the Arab world, Heikal insisted that Egypt be excluded: It had virtually no minorities to study. In my own interviews with Islamists in Egypt, I have been struck by their strong sense of Egyptian centrality within the boundaries of Islamic action. For them, any force working against Islam must strive to weaken Egypt before it targets any other country, due to Egypt's centrality in the Muslim world. The leadership of Islamic movements in the region, they believe, could not possibly be assumed by countries such as the Sudan, Iran, or even Saudi Arabia. From such perspective, regional leadership belongs naturally to Egypt. Thus, even for leaders of transnational movements,

---

[1] See Pierre Birnbaum, "The State Pattern as a Determinant of Foreign Policy," *Jerusalem Journal of International Relations:* 6 (1982): 36–48, and Steven Jackson, "The Limits of State Action" (Ph.D. dissertation, Yale University, 1982).

which, from an ideological perspective, do not focus on territorial states, the distinctiveness and centrality of Egypt's state and societal identities has loomed large in elite self-images.

Regarding foreign-policy issues, Egyptian elites have engaged in debates at certain critical junctures (the aftermath of political succession, regional wars, and disengagement from external conflict), about which identity should assume primacy in shaping Egypt's foreign-policy behavior. The identities they have identified include national identity, Arab identity, Islamic identity, Middle Eastern identity, African identity, and Mediterranean identity. Thus, even in a society with significant ethnic and linguistic homogeneity, different identities have been constructed and employed to shape the country's orientation and its identification of allies and enemies. If this type of identity construction can take place in Egypt, which has been associated with sociocultural integration and po-litical continuity, then there are strong reasons to believe in the relevance of identity factors in foreign-policy formation with regard to much less integrated societies in the region.[2]

However, in recent decades it has not always been possible to have meaningful debates in Egypt about identity issues because of strong state control over society and its determination to depoliticize the polity. At times, the state has claimed to have settled the complex issues of Egypt's cultural and political identities and has even insisted on making its determination of the primary identity virtually beyond discussion. Under such conditions any societal challenges to the state-determined collective primary identity have become essentially illegitimate.

Nevertheless, debates have developed in Egypt during the last three decades about identity and its role in shaping Egyptian foreign-policy choices. What has made those debates possible has been the political decompression or relative weakening of state restrictions on the political discourse. The most important debates have taken place as Egypt has embarked on restructuring its foreign policy by disengaging from the Arab-Israeli conflict or by defecting from the Arab coalition. These debates have involved advocates of state-centered politi-cal identity on one hand and proponents of Arab-centered political identity on the other; at stake have been the main foreign-policy options that each of these political identities would encourage or discourage.

Identity and "State Arabism"

Egypt was transformed during Nasser's era by an activist state that aspired to re-structure not only the economy and society, but also the cultural and political

---

[2] See chapter 5 in this volume, in which Adeed Dawisha discusses the communal identities that have threatened the unity of Iraq. Egypt has nothing similar to such communal fragmentation.

identities of the country according to the outlook of the new ruling elite. Much has been written about *ishterakiyat al-dawlah* or the state socialism during the 1960s; a parallel development during the Nasserist era that did not receive similar attention can be called *urubat al-dawlah* or "state Arabism." In fact, the beginning of this state Arabism, or the restructuring of Egypt's national identity, could be traced to the mid-1950s. Nasser did not "invent" Arab nationalism in Egypt, but he saw it as a relevant dimension of Egypt's identity in light of his experience in the Palestine War. In fact, in the immediate aftermath of his military takeover, Nasser identified a number of politically relevant identities for Egypt: Arab, Islamic, and African. By 1955 and certainly after the Suez War the following year, the state machinery emphasized Arabism; other identities were deemed relevant but clearly not crucial.[3]

The "state Arabism" that Nasser promoted should not be equated with the sheer invention of political Arabism in Egypt. Arabist attitudes had a presence in Egypt before Nasser and his military group seized power in July 1952. What the Free Officers had attempted to do, however, was to make Arabism a central part of the state ideology and to make disagreeing with their reinterpretation of Egyptian history nearly impossible. This made the adoption and advocacy of non-Nasserist ideas of political Arabism in Egyptian society punishable by law. For example, in 1965, Egyptian security agencies arrested some cadres of the Socialist Youth Organization on suspicion that they had come under the ideological influence of the Popular Front for the Liberation of Palestine; the latter organization was then an Arab nationalist group that held beliefs similar, though not identical, to those of Nasser's sole political organization, the Arab Socialist Union. That is why it was not possible for a major book like "*Awdat al-Wa'y*" ("*The Return of Consciousness*") by the leading Egyptian intellectual and writer Tawfiq Al-Hakim, which generated wide debates about identity issues in Egypt, to appear until two years after Nasser's death in September 1970. Al-Hakim, who believed in the uniqueness of the Egyptian culture and identity, argued again in 1978 that Egypt should not involve itself in Arab issues and that the best foreign policy for Egypt was a Swiss-like neutrality.[4]

Although the majority party under the monarchy, the *Wafd* Party, was not anti-Arabist, the Nasserist regime contended that it lacked "broad horizons" in the 1919 revolution with regard to Egypt's political identity. Nasser's regime criticized the Wafd for failing to depict Egypt's independence as part of the Arab world's struggles and aspirations for freedom and unity. Regarding foreign policy, the Wafd was accused of lacking vision and of focusing primarily on the Su-

[3] Dawisha, *Egypt in the Arab World* (London: Macmillan Press, 1976): 131.

[4] See Tawfiq Al-Hakim, *The Return of Consciousness*, translated by Bayly Winder (New York: New York University Press, 1985). See also the article by Al-Hakim on Egyptian neutrality in *Al-Ahram* (March 3, 1978). The secular intellectual Hussein Fawzy supported Al-Hakim's views with regard to this matter in *al-Akhbar* (March 23, 1978).

dan. The "correct" direction, however, according to the realities of history and geography (as adopted by the Nasserist regime) was to focus on the east and north east, a sign of a strong Egypt marked by historical vision and political dynamism.

Thus, when comparing the revolutions of 1919 and 1952, the political documents and the official media of the Nasserist regime stipulated that the earlier revolution had failed to grasp the centrality of Egypt's Arab identity and role, but the second revolution was cognizant of their political significance and centrality. The Wafd Party, whose leaders were mostly in prison or under house arrest after being described as counterrevolutionaries and enemies of the people, was not able to express its disagreement with the official characterization of its ideology or its political stands.

In that regard, the case of Egypt under Nasser particularly during the 1950s was not exceptional among developing countries where statist reinterpretations and reevaluations of history reshape political identity, build regime legitimacy, and discredit domestic opponents. These efforts can make it possible for wide segments of society to accept or to tolerate sustained high costs of state policies based on a core identity.[5]

However, more than once Nasser admitted that Arab identity had been weak in Egypt. As he pointed out in the early 1960s, part of the state's function and responsibility was to nourish the Arab identity in society. This task was to be carried out by organizations such as the Arab Socialist Union, the Socialist Youth Organization, the state-controlled mass media, and the educational system. To make such ideational transformation from above, all of the aforementioned state-run organizations had to engage in sustained and overlapping attempts to reshape the beliefs of the "rising generation" and also to re-socialize their beliefs along Arab nationalist, and particularly Nasserist, political lines. Left to themselves, members of this generation were not likely to adopt the politically and historically correct identity.

Making an effort to reshape political identity in society does not, however, guarantee its success. In the 1963 talks intended to prepare for an Arab unity scheme involving Egypt, Syria, and Iraq, Nasser ended up recognizing the severe limitations—if not failure—of his attempt to reconstruct political identity in Egypt via "state Arabism." He also accepted the notion that for a host of historical reasons, Arab political identification had been decidedly stronger in Syria than in Egypt and that state efforts to construct such a transnational political identification would have to confront major societal and historical obstacles in Egypt.

[5] See Lisa Anderson, "Legitimacy, Identity, and the Writing of History in Libya," in *Statecraft in the Middle East*, ed. Eric Davis and Nicolas Gavrielides (Miami: Florida International University Press, 1991).

In the Nasserist historiography, Arab identity formation in Egypt was often compared with the case of Syria, particularly from the perspective of crucial formative experiences of the two countries. According to this perspective, Arab nationalism in Syria served a defensive function to safeguard a cultural identity threatened by Turkification and later by French cultural penetration. It also served an integrative function to transcend ethnic factionalism in Syrian society. In Egypt, the Ottoman rule was much less repressive, the British occupation did not emphasize identity transformation, and society was not fragmented along ethnic lines. Thus, the primacy of Egyptian national identity over Arab national identity had a wide base in Egypt.[6] The Nasserist state machinery and political organizations had to work hard to develop and to deepen the Arabist idea in Egyptian society, to make the dominant cultural norms congruent with the state's definition of the primary political identity and to reduce, if not get rid of, any societal opposition to the Egyptian state's choices.[7]

From that time until the end of the Nasserist era in 1970, however, the level of societal support for Arabist identity in Egypt declined. Two wars contributed to that outcome. The first was a costly war in Yemen in which Egypt got entangled for years and suffered heavy losses. The Egyptian involvement stemmed from the principles Nasser had advocated about Arab identity and Arab unity. In such a context, the option of doing nothing was inconceivable, regardless of the material cost.

The second war, the June 1967 "Six-Day War," was more disastrous not only for Egypt's resources but also for the legitimacy of the Nasserist regime. In fact, the defeat in 1967 was widely perceived in Egypt as much larger in impact than the 1948 defeat that contributed to the demise of the monarchy and helped bring Nasser's Free Officers to power. The decision by Egypt's leaders to escalate the confrontation with Israel in May 1967, just like their decision to intervene in Yemen, was justified by using pan-Arabist norms and by citing the supposed absence of alternatives. In choosing to stand by Syria against Israel, Egypt responded to some Arab states that had challenged Egypt's Arab nationalist credentials. It was around this time that the Islamist identity grew stronger in Egyptian society. The Islamists attributed the 1967 defeat to what they saw as the deviation of the Nasserist regime from the straight path of

[6] Abdel 'Atti Muhammad, *"Tatawur al-Fikrah al-'Arabiyah fi Misr"* (The Evolution of the Arab Idea in Egypt) in *'Urubat Misr* (The Arabness of Egypt), ed. Saad Eddin Ibrahim (Cairo: Al-Ahram Press, 1978): 47–49; and Eberhard Kienle, "Syrian and Egyptian Policies toward the Arab World," paper presented to the Middle East Studies Association meeting, Research Triangle Park, North Carolina, Nov. 11–14, 1993.

[7] For a general conception of the Nasserist state, see Ellen K. Trimberger, *Revolutions from Above* (New Brunswick, N.J.: Transaction Books, 1978).

Allah and the regime's political emphasis on secular causes as pan-Arabism and Arab socialism.[8]

Analysts, however, differ with regard to the argument of the absence of foreign-policy alternatives in light of the pan-Arabist identity of Nasser's Egypt. In my own judgment this argument is not convincing; the regime used it for political purposes. After all, despite the regime's radical Arab nationalist rhetoric between 1956 and 1967 wars—the period that witnessed the consolidation of Nasser's regime—Egypt's borders with Israel were perhaps the quietest in the area. When Israel was about to complete its diversion of Jordan River water and Syria escalated its support of Palestinian military action against Israel, Nasser refused to be dragged into confrontation with Israel through the actions of Syria, which was trying to outbid Egypt in terms of its commitment to the Palestinian cause.[9]

The primacy of Arab identity in Egypt's foreign-policy behavior after 1967 was challenged by Egyptian acceptance of the Rogers initiative. When the Syrian, Iraqi, and Palestinian leaders denounced the Egyptian state decision to accept that American initiative as a serious and costly defection from the Arab camp, the Egyptian leadership under Nasser declared that it would not accept any *wisayah* (sponsorship) over its decision making and over the Egyptian people, even in the name of pan-Arabism. It was also clear that Nasser, despite his regime's Arab nationalist statements, did not consult with Arab leaders before accepting the U.S. proposals, even though he had met them only few days before. According to Mohamed Heikal's account at the time, if Egypt had asked for an Arab vote on its political move "it could not have moved. Egypt had to assume its responsibility and to act."[10] Thus, the roots of the territorial state's outlook on political identity have grown even under the shadow of a regime committed to the primacy of pan-Arabist political identity.[11]

The "Egypt First" Identity

Conventional wisdom argues that Sadat's era witnessed the restructuring of Egypt's identity and that this restructuring played an important role in reshaping the country's foreign policy. After all, foreign policy is primarily shaped by

[8] See Ali Hillal Dessouki, "Arab Intellectuals and al-Nakba: The Search for Fundamentalism," *Middle Eastern Studies* 9 (1973): 187–95.

[9] Ibrahim Karawan, "Sadat and the Egyptian-Israeli Peace Revisited," *International Journal of Middle East Studies* 26 (1994): 260.

[10] See Heikal's articles in *Al-Ahram* (Aug. 7, 1970, and Sept. 4, 1970).

[11] A similar trend regarding the decline of the pan-Arabist ideology and identity in Syria is persuasively analyzed by Yahya Sadowski in chapter 6.

how leaders simplify and organize a complex environment. The lenses performing such functions determine the information they deem important, their images of other actors, diagnosis of political situations, and the norms guiding policy choices. For instance, the shift in Egypt's foreign policy toward Israel is attributed to the way President Sadat and the core elite in his regime defined Egypt's primary political identity. Advocates of this explanation focus on the primacy of Egyptian nationalism in Sadat's beliefs and in influencing his political objectives and actions. "If Sadat saw himself principally as an Arab, then his definition of any given situation, his objectives, and his strategy have to be tied to Arab aspirations, acceptance, and support. But if he saw himself as an Egyptian first of all, then his definition of the situation would be more flexible."[12]

Accordingly, when Sadat concluded that Egypt's interests could be served by seeking a cease-fire at the end of the October 1973 war, accepting disengagement agreements (1974–75), and negotiating and settling with Israel (1977–78), he did not care to maintain the Arab coalition that made the October war possible. These moves were condemned in the Arab world as manifestations of Egypt's "defection," which left other Arab fronts vulnerable. After all, in the Arab world, Egypt had the strongest army, one-third of the total Arab population, a central geostrategic location, and the longest experience in modernization. With Egypt out of the war equation, Arab political and military options were seriously curtailed.[13]

Sadat did not reconsider his policy to disengage from the conflict with Israel because he believed that linking all fronts would have given Syria and the radical Palestinian groups veto power over Egypt's policy regarding its national territory. This option was unacceptable to Sadat, who rejected any "Arab tutelage" over Egypt's policy; as he himself put it, "It is not conceivable that the fate of my country should be dependent on the consent of other Arabs."[14]

However, the political identity adopted by the leader is not enough by itself to account for the shift in foreign-policy behavior. The Sadat-centered argument overlooks his adoption of diametrically opposed positions, which could

[12] See Salwa Sharawi Jum'ah, *al-Diplumasiyiah al-Misriyah fi 'Aqd al-Sab'inat* (Egyptian Diplomacy in the Seventies) (Beirut: Center of Arab Unity Studies, 1988); and Shaheen Ayubi, *Sadat and Nasser* (Wakefield, N.H.: Longwood Academic, 1922): 100–11.

[13] For comparison with the "Iraq first" policy that was developed and advocated under Prime Minister Hikmat Suleiman in the late 1930s, see chapter 5 by Adeed Dawisha.

[14] See Daniel Dishon, "Sadat's Arab Adversaries," *Jerusalem Quarterly* (summer 1978): 13–15. On the debate concerning the status of political Arabism, see Fouad Ajami, "The End of Arab Nationalism," *The New Republic* (Aug. 12, 1991): 23–27; As'ad Abu Khalil, "A New Arab Ideology? The Rejuvenation of Arab Nationalism," *Middle East Journal* 46, no. 1 (winter 1992): 22–36; Karawan, "Arab Dilemmas in the 1990s: Breaking Taboos and Searching for Signposts," *Middle East Journal* 48, no. 3 (summer 1994): 433–54; and Ibrahim, "Arabism: Eclipse or Renewal," paper presented to the Conference of the Center for Contemporary Arab Studies, Georgetown University, Washington, D.C., March 30, 2000.

not be attributed to the same belief system. For years Sadat refused to negotiate with Israel as long as it occupied Arab land, and he characterized negotiating under these conditions as total capitulation. A review of Sadat's political statements confirms that he had viewed Israel in demonic terms and consistently attributed to it expansionist designs, reflecting Robert Jervis's "inherent bad faith model." Sadat's anti-Israeli and even anti-Jewish attitudes, at least until November 1977, were not a well kept secret! Studies that analyzed his speeches to track his search for political identity have found it difficult to explain Egypt's foreign-policy shift since the mid-1970s in light of the weight of his sheer personal characteristics and political beliefs.[15]

The role of external and internal settings that made certain courses of state action more acceptable at one time than another is equally important. Although the basic norms of the leader are relevant—particularly in regimes with a high concentration of power—they do not by themselves predetermine all policy outcomes. Whether the road to the Geneva conference was hopelessly blocked because of differences over Palestinian representation and the format of negotiations remains inconclusive. However, even if such differences had been overcome, any negotiations based on collective bargaining and mutual vetoes over the issues of security, sovereignty, refugees, water resources, and Jerusalem were bound to stall, because of the gap between Israeli and Arab interests. While Israel emphasized its security and its historical claims to the West Bank, Arab demands concerned two issues: achieving Palestinian statehood and Israeli withdrawal to the June 1967 boundaries.

While the stalemate over a settlement seemed to preclude an early exit from the conflict with Israel via a multilateral track, escalating domestic tensions and the socioeconomic crisis provided the context in which Egypt's disengagement from the conflict with Israel and defection from the Arab coalition reflected more than just Sadat's primary identity. Severe socioeconomic hardships led to a change in the "national mood," and Egyptians became much more inclined to favor decreasing Egypt's external commitments. The regime used this mounting war fatigue to forge congruence between state and societal preferences for disengagement from the conflict.

In Bahgat Korany's words: "Tired of war and the threat of war, and skeptical about the capability of most Arab regimes to face up to the next crisis, a large number of Egyptians were ready to give their leader a chance to explore the peace road." Egypt's best military performance in the 1973 war had demonstrated that after six years of mobilizing its resources for war, it could not liberate more than a portion of the occupied land.[16] While many Egyptians opposed

[15] Karawan, "Sadat and the Egyptian-Israeli Peace Revisited," 249–66.

[16] Bahgat Korany, "The Cold Peace, the Sixth Arab-Israeli War and Egypt's Public," *International Journal* (autumn 1983): 661.

normalizing relations with Israel, most accepted bringing the historical conflict to a halt. Though Mohamed Heikal disagreed with this foreign-policy shift, he recognized the wide endorsement of the "peace initiative" and argued that although this initiative began as a one-man decision, "the decisive popular support it gained made it ultimately a collective decision."[17]

Certain features of state-society relations may prevent, postpone, or reduce the scope of foreign-policy change, even if desired by the state managers along the lines of political identity. Thus, some have argued that Sadat was able to take certain foreign-policy risks because Egypt—unlike Syria, for instance—had a long historical tradition of centralized political power and an ethnically homogeneous society.[18] In light of this, one can understand how some of the strongest Egyptian critics of the foreign-policy shift toward Israel under Sadat ended up warning its Arab opponents that their attempts to influence Egypt's domestic politics by addressing its people over the heads of their own government were doomed to failure.[19]

A comparison with Lebanon further illustrates this link between the policy change and the nature of communal identity in society. On May 17, 1983 Lebanon became the second Arab country after Egypt to conclude a peace agreement with Israel. However, this attempt to alter Lebanese foreign policy failed drastically. The state was vulnerable to strong crosscutting communal pressures triggered by a lack of understanding among Lebanese groups about how to define the nation's identity and how to determine its friends and enemies. One group's closest ally was the other's worst political enemy and vice versa. In this setting, a radical shift in foreign-policy behavior was unlikely either to materialize or to be sustained. In fact, Lebanon's abortive foreign-policy change exacerbated rather than alleviated its communal strife.[20]

[17] Mohamed Heikal, al-Mustaqbal (Feb. 11, 1978): 10–11. See also Nahed Ramzi et al., *Public Opinion Attitudes toward President Sadat's Visit to Jerusalem* (Cairo: Center for Social Studies, 1977) and Stephen Cohen and Edward Azar, "From War to Peace," *Journal of Conflict Resolution* 25, no. 1 (March 1981): 87–114.

[18] Fouad Ajami, *The Arab Predicament* (Cambridge: Cambridge University Press, 1981): 101; Michael Hudson, *Arab Politics: The Search for Legitimacy* (New Haven, Conn.: Yale University Press, 1977): 243–46; and Tahseen Basheer, "The Egyptian State in Transition," in *Egypt at the Crossroads: Domestic Stability and Regional Role*, ed. Phebe Marr (Washington, D.C.: National Defense University Press, 1999): 3–16, and *Reflections on the Middle East Peace Process* (Washington, D.C.: The American Enterprise Institute, 1981): 5–8.

[19] See Heikal, *"Khitab Maftuh ila al-'Aqid Mu'ammar al-Qadhafi"* (An Open Letter to Colonel Mu'ammar Qaddafi), *Al-Ahram* (July 1, 1975).

[20] Ghassan Salame, "Is a Lebanese Foreign Policy Possible?" in *Toward a Viable Lebanon*, ed. Halim Barakat (London: Croom Helm, 1988): 347–60. See also Mark Tessler, "Center and Periphery within Regional International Systems," *Jerusalem Journal of International Relations* 11, no. 3 (September 1989): 74–89.

The comparison between Egypt and Lebanon offers further insights regarding the maintenance of foreign-policy shifts against external pressures to undo them. Sinai II, the Jerusalem trip, and the Camp David accords were opposed in the Arab world with as much, if not more, vehemence than was the Lebanese-Israeli agreement. However, Egypt's ethnic homogeneity and an Egyptian self-image of primacy in the Arab world accounted, at least in part, for the failure of attempts by some Arab states to make Egypt undo its foreign-policy shift.

Lebanon, on the other hand, was vulnerable to manipulation by regional powers, contributing to its communal fragmentation. Stronger regional actors backed different Lebanese factions and used patron-client relationships to influence Lebanon's domestic and foreign policies. As a result, the country became a familiar cockpit for regional conflicts during Nasser's 1950s conflict with the West and during the Palestinian-Israeli confrontations of the 1960s and 1970s. The Lebanese civil war resulted in "the virtually complete collapse of all barriers between the domestic politics of Lebanon and the international politics of its immediate region."[21] Inasmuch as the Israeli-Lebanese agreement reflected the weight of Israel's invasion one year before, it was opposed by Syria, which, allied with Muslim and leftist groups, first made the agreement moot and then successfully exerted pressures for its abrogation in March 1984.

States can play an active and purposive role when faced with such highly contested situations, and the mass media can prove crucial in providing the necessary political legitimation or, at least, societal acquiescence. The mass media can be used as a transmission belt between the state and society. It can be utilized for foreign-policy purposes by appealing to shared values and emotive symbols, manipulating the information available to the public, inflating the success of new policies, and by deflecting opposition to the foreign-policy shift.[22] By using its control over most of the mass media, the Egyptian state embarked on a systematic effort to influence the way Egyptians were to define their political identity. Egypt's major economic malaise was justified against the backdrop of its prolonged involvement in the Arab-Israeli conflict. Egyptians were told time and again that their country, the area's richest, had almost become the poorest because of that protracted involvement. At the societal level in Egypt, feelings of war fatigue, inward-looking attitudes, and resentment of the high price of wars had been increasing since 1967. The mass media articulated these attitudes and

[21] Leonard Binder, "Lebanon and the Regional State System," *Middle East Insight* 6, no. 1 (summer 1988), and Raymond Hinnebusch, "Syrian Policy in Lebanon and the Palestinians," *Arab Studies Quarterly* 8, no. 1 (winter 1986): 1–20.

[22] See Stephen Krasner, "Approaches to the State," *Comparative Politics* 16, no. 2 (January 1984): 235; Michael Handel, *The Diplomacy of Surprise* (Cambridge, Mass.: Harvard University Center for International Affairs, 1981): 252; and Gordon Clark and Michael Dear, *State Apparatus, Structure, and Language of Legitimacy* (Boston: Allen and Unwin, 1984): 97–103.

in so doing nourished them by making an exit from the Arab-Israeli conflict synonymous with overcoming the domestic crisis. Thus, the state-run mass media used societal grievances, which had exploded between 1975 and 1977 against the state's economic policies, to build support for Egypt's foreign-policy restructuring.

During that time, one of the media's favorite themes was that the quantum leap in oil prices would not have occurred without Egypt's war efforts. In this way, economic aid from the oil-rich Arab countries was portrayed as a moral obligation and as compensation for Egypt's huge sacrifices. After large-scale outbreaks of socioeconomic unrest, *Al-Ahram* published articles under such evocative headlines as "Petrodollars and Petroblood" and "A Sea of Money and a Sea of Blood." *Al-Ahram* also criticized rich Arabs and emphasized that it was only because of "the sea of blood that Egypt had given for the Arab cause, that their sea of wealth had come into being."[23] The media also stressed that since 1975 a decline had occurred in aid from oil-rich Arab states in the Gulf[24] that had joined the IMF in insisting that aid to Egypt be contingent on reduced food subsidies.[25]

Against this background many Egyptians came to see pan-Arab entanglements as producing more costs and fewer benefits.[26] Arab condemnations of Egypt's foreign-policy change led to further backlash regarding Egyptian attitudes toward "political Arabism": "What right had the rich Arabs, who had been so niggardly in sharing the exorbitant wealth they won from Egypt's fight, to dictate her foreign policy?" "If the Egyptians are an Arab People, why do other Arab people treat them as if they were Egyptian only? If other Arabs don't acknowledge the Arab character of the battle why don't the Egyptian people acknowledge only its Egyptian character and accept a separate deal?"[27] "Why should Egypt allow a veto on its search for a settlement by those who totally reject the concept of a settlement and/or those who insist on some conditions that frustrate any likelihood of reaching a settlement?"[28] "What should be done if it becomes clear that among the 'brothers' there are those who want neither war nor peace?"[29]

[23] Hassan al-Tuhami, "A Sea of Money and a Sea of Blood," *Al-Ahram* (Jan. 22, 1977), and Lutfi al-Kholi, "Petrodollars and Petroblood," *Al-Ahram* (Jan. 30, 1975). *Al-Ahram* estimated Egypt's war losses from 1948 until 1975 to be $40 billion (Aug. 22, 1975).

[24] Adel Hussein, *al-Iqtisad al-Misri Min al-Istiqlal Ila al-Tabʾiyah* (The Egyptian Economy from Independence to Dependency) 2 (Cairo: Dar al-Mustaqbal al-'Arabi, 1982): 261–63.

[25] *Ruz al-Yusif* (Jan. 31, 1977).

[26] See Mahammad Sid-Ahmad, "Breaking Taboos," *The Middle East* (April 1978): 45; and Ajami, "The Struggle for Egypt's Soul," *Foreign Policy* 35 (summer 1979): 3–30.

[27] *Ruz al-Yusif* (Jan. 31, 1977): 16.

[28] *Al-Ahram* (April 21, 1978).

[29] *Al-Akhbar* (May 12, 1978).

In such a setting it was possible to formulate, implement, and sustain a foreign-policy shift and to mobilize societal support for Egyptian disengagement from the Arab-Israeli conflict. By all accounts, the Egyptian state has in fact never considered encouraging its own society to accept Israel as a legitimate political community or to normalize economic and cultural relations with it.

Under Mubarak's regime—or the "Third Republic," as some call it—debates in Egyptian society about identity and foreign policy have flourished. In a symbolic gesture, Mubarak started his era by releasing hundreds of political prisoners, most of them with Nasserist, leftist, Islamist, and liberal convictions. Each of these groups had its views about Egypt's primary identity and the impact of that identity on foreign policy. Despite Mubarak's notion of "democracy in doses" the press has enjoyed significant degree of freedom,[30] which at first was utilized mostly to criticize the prevailing views and practices under Nasser and Sadat.

Arabist political language also has been loudly heard during Mubarak's era, not only in the discourse of the political opposition, but also in the official pronouncements of the state. In the name of political Arabism, Egypt has supported the Palestinians and has linked more normalization with Israel to settlement of the remaining issues of the Arab-Israeli conflict, including Israel's monopoly of nuclear weapons in the Middle East.[31] Egypt reestablished relations that were broken off with other Arab states after its peace agreement with Israel, and it supported lifting economic sanctions imposed on Libya, Iraq, and the Sudan. The Mubarak regime also played an active role in helping Syria avoid a likely military confrontation with Turkey in 1998. The decision to recall the Egyptian ambassador from Tel Aviv to protest Israel's response to the second Palestinian *intifada* is also a case in point.

Most opposition groups in Egypt appreciated these foreign-policy moves, even though these groups continued to criticize Mubarak's domestic policies. These foreign-policy changes also allowed Egypt to gradually reassert its leadership role in the Arab world without undermining the state interest in maintaining relations with Israel and the United States. Egyptian policy makers have argued that "because of Egypt's long experience in dealing with the Israelis, its close ties with the United States, its diplomatic history, Cairo can be a benefit to the Arab negotiating parties."[32] Instead of expecting the search for a peaceful

[30] Ann Lesch, "Domestic Politics and Foreign Policy in Egypt," in *Democracy, War and Peace in the Middle East*, ed. David Garnham and M. Tessler (Bloomington: Indiana University Press, 1995): 226–30.

[31] For a coherent articulation of "Mubarak's diplomacy," see Mustapha al-Fiqi, "al-Shari' Al-Misri wa al-Siyassah al-Kharijiah" (The Egyptian Street and Foreign Policy), *Al-Ahram International* (May 19, 1997): 12.

[32] Gregory L. Aftandilian, *Egypt's Bid for Arab Leadership* (New York: Council on Foreign Relations, 1993): 34.

settlement to erode Egypt's regional role, the regime anticipated its strengthening.[33] When other Arab actors, including the Palestinians, Jordan, and Syria, embarked on the path of negotiated settlements with Israel, the regime argued that their policy alteration proved the wisdom of Egyptian disengagement from the conflict. Mubarak's pragmatic foreign policy has often helped to bring his regime and the opposition closer on matters of foreign policy, and with its focus on Arab solidarity—not radical Arabism—the regime has taken steps to narrow the gap between "the logic of the state" and "the logic of the nation."

Conclusion

Even in the ethnically homogenous Egyptian society, identities are characterized by unmistakable multiplicity. At least five political identities with a potential for shaping Egypt's foreign policy have been recognized. But these identities are far from being equal in terms of their ability to influence societal attitudes and foreign policy in Egypt. Inequality in the hierarchy of political identities in Egypt has tended to persist over long periods. There is no definitive way of knowing when and under what conditions that hierarchy may change drastically, but the role of the ruling elites is crucial in constructing and in reconstructing political identities. Future research should distinguish between relevant identities in ruling-elite circles, among attentive publics, and in the wider society at large.

Although political identities change over time, attempts to construct identities from above, as well as to change societal attitudes toward core foreign-policy issues, are fraught with difficulties. In Egypt's case, for instance, Nasser failed to make Arab nationalism the primary identity of most Egyptians despite his charisma and the political resources available to the Egyptian state. Moreover, sharing, or imagining that one shares, cultural traits with other societies is one thing, but translating such perceived identification into political perceptions that actually shape foreign policy is an entirely different matter.

The case of Egypt suggests that knowing the declared political identity of the regime at any historical juncture does not reduce the foreign policy choices available to the principal decision makers to one. This is similar to the problems faced by systemic analysis. International structures and state capabilities cannot account fully for the specific external behavior of states, and systemic constraints by themselves cannot account for considerable divergence of foreign-policy outcomes across states located in similarly structured systems. Mere position and relative power do not tell us much about particular patterns of

[33] See Mustapha al-Fiqi's article in *Al-Ahram International* (March 21, 2000): 13 and the sharp critique by Osama al-Ghazali Harb in *Al-Ahram al-Dawli* (March 27, 2000): 10.

foreign-policy behavior. They can point to what is *not* possible but provide less guidance about what *is* desirable and feasible when state survival is not at stake.[34] The same applies to the ways in which identity factors can lead to quite different, if not diametrically opposed, positions and actions. Identity and norms can be used to justify specific choices in foreign policy but in opposite directions.

The case of Egypt illustrates the difficulty of determining the relevance of political debates in society for understanding the identity of the community and the policy behavior of the state. This is particularly difficult to assess in Arab regimes marked by what has been called "restricted political pluralism," such as in the case of Egypt. These regimes have acted in repressive ways when they perceived regime security to be threatened. In essence, such regimes have engaged in a sort of "managed liberalization from above" without losing their ability to control the polity or to unleash vigorous repression, to demonstrate that the regimes could use their "sharp teeth" if opposition forces failed to act in a disciplined and "constructive" way.[35] In such a setting, open intellectual and public debates about identities and the degree to which the regime's foreign policies reflect or ignore them may become difficult, if not impossible. If it is true that identities are basically products of ongoing societal debates, the existence of a certain political space is needed to allow these debates to unfold.

However, whenever such regimes face serious challenges, they tend to tighten their control over the mass media and to narrow the scope of public debates, to weaken the opposition forces in the parliament and the professional associations, to rely more on military and security organizations, and to put certain issues and decisions above the realm of permissible discussion. Despite all of these limitations, the case of Egypt illustrates that political-identity factors are indeed relevant for shaping and reshaping the country's foreign policy; even so, these factors are not always crucial in every case or in every issue area.

[34] See Richard Herrmann and Michael Fischerkeller, "Beyond the Enemy Image and the Spiral Model: Cognitive-Strategic Research after the Cold War," *International Organization* 49, no. 3 (summer 1995): 418–19.
[35] Karawan, "ReIslamization Movements According to Kepel: On Striking Back and Striking Out," *Contention* (fall 1992): 174–75.

8. Conclusion

*Thinking Theoretically about Identity
and Foreign Policy*

STEPHEN SAIDEMAN

The contributions to this volume address the connections between identities
and foreign policy in the Middle East in a variety of ways, disagreeing about
the sources of communal identities and their causal impact on foreign policies. Thus, this chapter cannot and will not attempt to provide a single
theory of identity and foreign policy. Instead, I assess whether the contributors met the goals set out by Telhami and Barnett in the introduction, consider the continuities and contradictions among the various accounts, extend
the implications of the chapters, and consider the next steps in this research
agenda.

The primary goals set out by the editors were to determine how identity
influences foreign policy and to understand why particular identities emerge.
Thus, the first part of this chapter deals with identity's impact on foreign policy;
the second section addresses identity formation. I then consider some key omissions and logical extensions. I conclude by addressing broader issues about the
relevance of this project: its applicability beyond the Middle East, its implications for future theoretical work, and logical suggestions for policy.

Identity's Impact on Foreign Policy

How does identity influence foreign policy? There are at least four possible answers: that identity does not matter; that it constrains foreign policy; that identity essentially constructs the world so that perceptions of one's state and the
others are defined by one's identity; or that it influences the ethnopolitical
strategies (and, thus, the foreign policies) of rational politicians. These four approaches largely coincide with current approaches in the field of international
relations: realism, institutionalism, constructivism, and liberalism as defined as a

theory of preferences.[1] I will spend more time on the latter three than on realism since Barnett and Telhami cover realism well in the introduction.

THE INSIGNIFICANCE OF COMMUNAL IDENTITIES

Rather than driving policy, identity may just be a gloss over the real forces shaping international relations: material interests in the form of security or economic desires. Realists and neorealists argue that communal identities of
Middle Eastern populations do not shape the policies of states, as states maximize either power or security. Making decisions based on whom one is like—
for example, being of the same race or religion—may sometimes coincide with
security-motivated policies. However, when a conflict exists between security
concerns and identity, the state will likely follow its security interests. One can
further argue that identities may be epiphenomenal. That is, external threats
cause leaders to create, enhance, or mobilize identities to facilitate the extraction of resources from the society to confront the external threat.[2]

Economic interests are often said to drive foreign policy, regardless of the
identities at stake.[3] States, or the firms that influence foreign policy making, are
said to be more concerned with profits and protecting investments than with the
color of skin involved, beliefs that are practiced, the language that is spoken, or
the family ties that are shared. States, then, may ally with countries because of
desirable markets, subsidies, or investments, rather than because of shared communal attributes. Marxist approaches (as well as others focusing on economic
concerns) play down the role of state and national identity. Indeed, a harder test
of the relevance of identities than that presented here would be to consider their
impact on foreign economic policy.

If identity does not shape foreign policy, but economic and/or security interests determine the foreign policy of Middle Eastern states, several puzzles arise.
First, if identity does not matter, why would leaders care about pan-Arabism,
the spread of Islam fundamentalism, and other identities? Were Nasser and others foolish to think that such appeals would carry weight? The chapters of this
volume suggest that leaders have good reasons to be concerned with identities,
both for domestic concerns and international politics.

Second, these broader identities might be epiphenomenal. For example,
Maloney's discussion of Iranian leaders mobilizing support during the war with

---

[1] See Andrew Moravcsik, "Taking Preferences Seriously: A Liberal Theory of International
Politics," *International Organization* 51, no. 4 (autumn 1997): 513–54; and Jeffrey W. Legro and
Moravcsik, "Is Anybody Still a Realist?" in *International Security* 24, no. 2 (fall 1999): 5–51.

[2] Barry Posen, "Nationalism, the Mass Army, and Military Power," *International Security* 18,
no. 2 (fall 1993): 80–124.

[3] David N. Gibbs, *The Political Economy of Third World Intervention: Mines, Money, and U.S.
Policy in the Congo Crisis* (Chicago: University of Chicago Press, 1991).

Iraq suggests that identity may merely be an intervening variable between external threat and domestic mobilization.[4] Likewise, pan-Arab ideology may have merely justified the policies of countries that already shared a common interest in defeating Israel. Once these countries no longer felt threatened by the same state, Arab nationalism may have declined in its utility. This approach has various problems, however, as several chapters and Barnett's work elsewhere indicate. One, leaders and peoples in the region seemed to care a lot about something that, according to realists, was unimportant. Two, constructivists argue that justification is an important political dynamic worthy of exploration and significant in influencing outcomes,[5] so if Arab nationalism "only" justified what states wanted to do, then that still is quite important. The failure to justify means that the policies might be perceived as illegitimate.

Third, if material interests drive policy, it is not clear why politicians delay or refuse to alter their behavior according to new international circumstances. If material and security interests drive policy, then why have Arab states chosen not to embrace Israel? Given its economic and military capabilities, Israel could have been a valuable trading partner and military ally. Recent Turkish engagement of Israel provides evidence of Israel's value as a friend. While Israel might be a military threat to some of its neighbors, these states face other threats, so why not ally with one threat to balance another?[6] Given the threat that Syria posed to Jordan, shouldn't Jordan have allied with Israel in the 1970s and 1980s? Although tacit cooperation occurred, it was limited. What constrained these states from cooperating more openly, if not identity politics? Further, Maloney shows that the identity choices made by Iranian elites constrained them later, so supporting groups in Lebanon was not an easy decision to reverse. In these cases, identity politics is path dependent; past decisions limit the possibilities of current policy, and states are not simply responding to changing material conditions.

While most of the authors suggest that identity does matter in various ways, two suggest that international concerns may outweigh the impact of state and national identities. Sadowski compares Asad of Syria to Henry Kissinger, suggesting that a power-maximizing decision-maker runs Syrian foreign policy. Because Syrian foreign policy has focused on the most threatening actor in the region, Israel, and has taken advantage of the most internally divided state, Lebanon, it is hard to argue with Sadowski. He admits that there are domestic costs to Syrian foreign policies that run counter to particular identities, but adds

[4] Even if this were the case, intervening variables often play crucial causal roles.

[5] Friedrich V. Kratochwil, *Rules, Norms, and Decisions: On the Conditions of Practical and Legal Reasoning in International Relations and Domestic Affairs* (Cambridge: Cambridge University Press, 1991).

[6] Marc Lynch raises this issue well in chapter 2.

that the existence of such costs does not deter Asad. Karawan raises the possibility that identities are so elastic that they may not meaningfully constrain Egyptian foreign policy. Still, he allows that the strength of Egyptian nationalism helped to weaken the costs of the Arab response to Egypt's separate peace with Israel. The remaining authors convincingly argue that identity dynamics, particularly the relationship between state and national identities, critically shape what countries do.

VULNERABILITY AND POLICY

If conflicts between state and national identity influence foreign policy at all, vulnerability might inhibit states from engaging in assertive foreign policies. The conventional wisdom on the international relations of ethnic politics asserts that vulnerability to ethnic conflict deters states from supporting separatist movements in other countries.[7] "The greatest deterrent to territorial revisionism has been the fear of opening a Pandora's box. If any one boundary is seriously questioned, why not all the boundaries in Western Africa."[8] Separatism is a serious threat because most African states face serious racial, religious, tribal, and/or linguistic divisions. Leaders fear that once a group successfully questions one tenuous, artificial African boundary, then all boundaries would be subject to challenges.[9] Thus, in this context, countries that have severe identity conflicts should not engage in assertive foreign policies.

---

[7] For a more complete discussion of the vulnerability hypothesis and evidence against this line of thinking, see Stephen M. Saideman, "Explaining the International Relations of Secessionist Conflicts: Vulnerability vs. Ethnic Ties," *International Organization* 51, no. 4 (fall 1997): 721–53, and *The Ties That Divide: Ethnic Politics, Foreign Policy, and International Conflict* (New York: Columbia University Press, 2001).

[8] I. William Zartman, *International Relations in the New Africa* (Englewood Cliffs, N.J.: Prentice-Hall, 1966): 109. Also see Lee C. Buchheit, *Secession: The Legitimacy of Self-Determination* (New Haven, Conn.: Yale University Press, 1978); William J. Foltz, "The Organization of African Unity and the Resolution of Africa's Conflicts," in *Conflict Resolution in Africa*, ed. Francis M. Deng and Zartman (Washington, D.C.: Brookings Press, 1991); Jeffrey Herbst, "The Creation and Maintenance of National Boundaries in Africa," *International Organization* 43, no. 4 (autumn 1989): 673–92; Robert H. Jackson and Carl G. Rosberg, "Why Africa's Weak States Persist: The Empirical and the Juridical in Statehood," *World Politics* 35, no. 1 (October 1982): 1–24; Jackson, *Quasi-States: Sovereignty, International Relations, and the Third World* (Cambridge: Cambridge University Press, 1990); Benjamin Neuberger, *National Self-Determination in Postcolonial Africa* (Boulder, Colo.: Lynne Rienner Press, 1986); and Saadia Touval, *The Boundary Politics of Independent Africa* (Cambridge, Mass.: Harvard University Press, 1972).

[9] Some have even argued that there need be no rational basis for such fears; see Neuberger, *National Self-Determination*, 97. For an excellent discussion of precedent setting and violating, see Elizabeth Kier and Jonathan Mercer, "Setting Precedents in Anarchy: Military Intervention and Weapons of Mass Destruction," *International Security* 20, no. 4 (spring 1996): 77–106.

Scholars have argued that international organizations and international norms have helped to restrain states from supporting ethnic rebels in other countries.[10] "Since all countries are at risk from disgruntled minority groups, there is a general sense that all states gain crucial protection from the current system."[11] The "current system" refers to the international organizations and norms that are produced by the mutual vulnerability and that reinforce inhibitions about supporting separatists.

Debates on these issues have greatly overstated the matter of African cooperation while ignoring the Middle East. Has vulnerability to ethnic conflict deterred states from supporting separatists in their neighbors in the Middle East? Logically, it should have, as the lines drawn in the Middle East are just as artificial as those in Africa. The example of the Kurds, however, is enough to challenge the vulnerability argument since several states with significant Kurdish separatist movements have supported Kurdish separatists in neighboring states, especially Iraq and Iran. While Iran may have given Iraq's Kurds support to fight but not enough to win, the example still challenges the logic of the vulnerability argument since it focuses on reprisals and precedent setting. Even weak Iranian support risks a backlash from Iraq and other states opposed to separatism. The Kurdish example suggests that identity conflicts within states do not necessarily prevent states from getting involved in the identity conflicts of other states.

ETHNIC POLITICS, STRATEGIC POLITICIANS, AND FOREIGN POLICY

Instead of focusing on the meaning of identities (which is a focal point for constructivists), an ethnic politics approach stresses the incentives and constraints that politicians face as they compete for power and office, and how the strategies they develop for domestic political purposes influence states' foreign policies.[12] If politicians are motivated by the desire to gain and to maintain positions of power,[13] then they will consider identities within their states as critical opportunities and constraints. Ethnic politics can serve as a critical dynamic, compelling some politicians to support particular ethnic groups abroad while constraining others.

[10] Herbst, "Creation and Maintenance"; Jackson and Rosberg, "Weak States"; and Jackson, *Quasi-States.*

[11] Herbst, "Creation and Maintenance."

[12] While there are other ways to consider how strategic politicians use or are influenced by ethnicity, what I present is a logic that underlies several contributions to this volume as well as work I present in *Ties That Divide.*

[13] David R. Mayhew, *Congress: The Electoral Connection* (New Haven, Conn.: Yale University Press, 1974); and Barry Ames, *Political Survival: Politicians and Public Policy in Latin America* (Berkeley: University of California Press, 1987).

Each politician requires the support of others to gain and to maintain political office, the supporters forming the politician's constituency. How the constituency supports a decision maker varies, depending on the regime type and on existing political institutions. In a democracy, the constituency's support primarily comes through voting, though campaign contributions also matter. In an authoritarian regime, the leaders' constituencies generally consist of those who control the means of repression, such as the officer corps of the military as well as the security apparatus. Regardless of the particular support mechanisms, incumbent politicians care most about preventing these supporters from leaving their coalition, i.e., exiting.[14] Who is exiting determines how politicians respond.

In addition, identities influence the preferences of potential and existing constituents, and, therefore, who might wish to exit and why.[15] Identities influence whom constituents want to support and to oppose in international relations. If ethnic identity influences individuals' preferences toward domestic policies, these same identities should influence preferences toward foreign policies for several reasons. First, ethnic identity inherently creates feelings of loyalty, interest, and fears of extinction.[16] International boundaries do not cause members of ethnic groups to stop caring about their ethnic kin's condition. Constituents care most about those with whom they share ethnic ties, or about those with whom a history of ethnic enmity exists. Israeli Jews, for instance, have shown much concern for the plight of Jews in Ethiopia, Russia, and elsewhere. Second, ethnic ties influence foreign policy making because showing support for ethnic kin abroad can be a litmus test for a politician's sincerity on ethnic issues at home. Politicians lack credibility if they take symbolic stands on issues but do not follow up when a related foreign event develops. Third, politicians can use the circumstances of ethnic kin to emphasize certain ethnic identities at the expense of other identities and issues. When constituents focus on economic problems or other troublesome issues, a politician can use a foreign event to increase the salience of ethnic identity, creating unity at least for the short term.

Politicians care about the ethnic composition of their supporters, as this may determine who might exit and over what issues. Thus, politicians avoid certain issues and embrace others to prevent their supporters from exiting and to attract the constituents of their competitors. Obviously, these dynamics matter only for issues that are "loaded" with ethnic content—education, language issues, immi-

---

[14] Albert O. Hirschman, *Exit, Voice, and Loyalty: Responses to Decline in Firms, Organizations, and States* (Cambridge, Mass.: Harvard University Press, 1970).

[15] For a rational choice theoretic explanation of why followers care about ethnic identities, see Russell Hardin, *One for All: The Logic of Group Conflict* (Princeton, N.J.: Princeton University Press, 1995).

[16] Donald Horowitz, *Ethnic Groups in Conflict* (Berkeley: University of California Press, 1985), especially chapter 4.

gration, and the like. Taxing and spending is likely to activate ethnic politics if current policies seem to favor some groups over others. Regulation of sewage treatment is much less likely to invoke identity politics. For foreign policy, identity conflicts within other states are most likely to resonate and affect ethnic politics at home while complex negotiations over non-tariff barriers are much less likely to mobilize groups along ethnic lines. For instance, if a politician needs Muslims for political support, then the role of religion in the state will be a prominent area of interest for both the politician and his or her supporters. The ethnic identities of those who might leave a constituency not only restrain politicians but also can provide opportunities. Politicians can use the circumstances of ethnic kin to emphasize certain ethnic identities at the expense of other identities and other issues. For instance, suppose that one's constituents are both Arab and Muslim and that other politicians may be able to use religion to attract one's supporters; in such a case, it makes sense to emphasize the Arab identity. A similar hypothetical example would be: Israeli politicians under fire domestically would support Jewish groups in trouble elsewhere because Israeli Jews, despite their differing ideologies and conflicts over the meaning and impact of religion on government, would share concern over the plight of Jews elsewhere.

When constituents become focused on economic problems or on a particularly problematic ethnic identity, a politician can use a foreign event to increase the salience of a specific ethnic identity domestically, creating unity at least for the short term. Consequently, if ethnic ties determine the foreign-policy preferences of constituents, then such ties also influence the politician's foreign-policy choices—both as constraint and opportunity. If the politician can influence foreign policy, the existence of ethnic ties and antagonisms between the politician's supporters and external actors will shape the state's foreign policy.[17]

This approach focuses more attention on political institutions and domestic political competition. These factors influence whether supporters' threats to exit really matter. Politicians confronting the most competition will more strongly support the ethnic kin of his or her constituents, and politicians facing little competition—and, consequently, no credible exit threats—can weakly support such groups or ignore them. The distinction here is not between democracies and authoritarian regimes but between highly competitive democracies and authoritarian regimes and weakly competitive democracies and authoritarian regimes.

Obviously, religion matters in Israel's domestic politics, and, as a result, in its foreign policy. The relevance varies, depending on whether the reigning coalition needs the support of the smaller religious parties. When such parties are

[17] See David R. Davis and Will H. Moore, "Ethnicity Matters: Transnational Ethnic Alliances and Foreign Behavior," *International Studies Quarterly* 41, no. 1 (March 1997): 171–84.

relatively unimportant, one would expect Judaism to matter less in Israel's foreign policy; when such parties are vital for maintaining a governing coalition, then the religious identity should greatly influence foreign policy. One can read Barnett's argument about Israeli politics as largely a rationalist account of strategic politicians responding to changing incentives and opportunities. Elections have produced different results because of demographic changes (the large inflow of Russian immigrants) and institutional changes (separate election of the prime minister), rather than because any changing of preferences by politicians or supporters. Changing costs may cause constituents to increase or decrease their support of the peace process not because such variations cause reconsiderations of identities but simply because of new expected utility calculations.

One could view Jordan's foreign policy through the same lens. King Hussein could be viewed as manipulating debates about key issues, including opening and closing the public sphere, to preserve his position. While such an account might not be able to address all of the preferences of powerful groups in Jordanian society, it could anticipate Hussein's efforts to co-opt or to marginalize these groups as he tried to stay in power.

Maloney's analysis of Iran indicates that leaders relied on various strands of identity to build support for policies during the war and to serve as resources for factional politics. However, her discussion reveals one of the practical problems with this argument: Who are the important constituents? In times of transition, revolution, and situations in which parallel institutions exist, determining which constituents matter the most is often difficult. Of course, Maloney's chapter suggests that these situations produce conflicting policies as politicians with differing audiences pursue policies that inherently contradict.

Saddam Hussein's efforts reveal the strengths and the weaknesses of the ethnic politics approach. As Dawisha's chapter indicates, Hussein has tried to use every potential identity to mobilize support and to weaken his opposition, including: developing a secular identity to overcome more divisive ones; using narrow identities, such as tribe, to bind his supporters together; and appealing to pan-Arabism to justify his attack on Iran.[18] However, despite his power, Hussein has not been able to rely on identity and ethnic ties to maintain his rule, which seems to largely depend on coercion.

---

[18] As further proof of ethnic politics at work, smaller groups, Kurds, and Shiites in Iraq have always opposed pan-Arabism, as any real union with other Arab countries would increase the threat non-Arabs and non-Sunnis would face. This is similar to the concerns and strategies of ethnic groups elsewhere, such as Yugoslavia, as they compete for influence and fear for their security. See Saideman, "Is Pandora's Box Half-Empty or Half-Full? The Limited Virulence of Secession and the Domestic Sources of Disintegration," in *The International Spread of Ethnic Conflict: Fear, Diffusion, Escalation*, ed. David A. Lake and Donald Rothchild (Princeton, N.J.: Princeton University Press, 1998): 127–50.

The key puzzle for the ethnic politics approach is not why politicians resort to using ethnic cards, but why the strategy sometimes works and sometimes fails. Scholars have come to no agreement on this, and this volume does not provide a definitive answer either. In the following sections I address further some of the conditions under which politicians use ethnicity and identity—with varying results—to suit their purposes.

CONSTRUCTING IDENTITY AND SOCIETY

Constructivists view international politics as a social interaction in which the actors (usually states) shape the structure of international society and are shaped by it.[19] One of constructivists' main interests is identity.[20] According to this approach, state identities are shaped through an interactive process between the choices of the state, the choices of other states, and the impact of international society. A common critique of constructivists is that they do not take domestic politics as seriously as one might expect. The two self-consciously constructivist accounts in this book, chapters by Barnett and Lynch, demonstrate the power of constructivist theorizing when domestic politics is made a central part of the story. One of the key constructivist insights is that multiple consequential pathways exist between identity and foreign policy. In the following section, I consider how the contributors demonstrate identity's influence on foreign policy through the five possibilities suggested in the introduction to the volume: identity serves as a prop; identity shapes what is possible and legitimate; identity influences preferences; identity raises the costs of policies pursued for other reasons; and identity shapes outcomes.

Identity as Prop

Barnett and Telhami start with the most minimal notion of identity's influence on foreign policy—as a justification for what leaders already planned to do. The various articles raise and largely answer a few important questions: If leaders are motivated by more material interests, why do they resort to identities and norms to justify their behavior? Why not merely appeal to their populace's material interests?

Politicians seek to justify their policies with reference to particular identities, even if more material interests drive these policies. A policy may favor one audience materially, and thus cause the politician to support that policy, but hurt other significant constituencies. By invoking identities, however, the politician

[19] Alexander E. Wendt, "The Agent-Structure Problem in International Relations Theory," *International Organization* 41, no. 3 (summer 1987): 335–70.

[20] See Jonathan Mercer, "Anarchy and Identity," *International Organization* 49 (spring 1995): 229–52.

can minimize opposition or even mobilize support from those who do not benefit from the policy change. Lynch notes how King Hussein and his regime appealed to Jordanian definitions of interests and identity to justify peace with Israel, even if peace with Israel was motivated by more material concerns. Further, cognitive psychology suggests that people engage in bolstering—in finding several reasons to do something, rather than just one reason.[21] Thus, even if material interests provide impetus to pursue a particular foreign policy, a politician may be comfortable in making that decision only if other reasons, such as coincidence with primary collective identities, support that decision. The same cognitive process applies to citizens, who may favor a particular policy because of its benefits but be more energized and perhaps even mobilized by a policy's ideational appeal.

Further, politicians may not want to portray their constituents as selfish cynics who desire only material gain. By relying on the apparent imperatives of a particular identity, such as pan-Arabism, politicians can appeal to citizens without demeaning themselves or their supporters, even if a material interest motivates the policy.

An additional wrinkle is that policies are often complex and may not have a clear material benefit to supporters, even if the benefits to the politicians might be clear. In such situations, politicians may justify the policy based on how it fits with the society's norms since appeals to material interests will not work.

Influencing the Possible and the Legitimate

For constructivists, identities shape perceptions of oneself and of others, which, in turn, influence foreign policy. Identity defines a state's reality—who it is, who the threats are, and which policies are possible. In the constructivist view, Egypt's pan-Arab identity greatly influenced Egypt's domestic and foreign policies by giving meaning to reality, by even defining which policies were permissible and which policies were unthinkable.[22] The changing identification of Egypt from pan-Arabism to Egyptian nationalism[23] made possible the Camp David accords. A leader and a society, defining the world in terms of pan-Arabism, could not imagine agreeing to a separate peace with Israel. Of course, this example suggests that a consensus might not exist regarding which identity should or does prevail—for example, Sadat was killed for his actions. Sadat's death suggests that the formation of identities and competition between them is intensely political.

[21] Robert Jervis, *Perception and Misperception in International Politics* (Princeton, N.J.: Princeton University Press, 1976).

[22] See Michael N. Barnett, "Sovereignty and Nationalism in the Arab World," *International Organization* 49, no. 3 (summer 1995): 479–510.

[23] See chapter 7.

Barnett argues that collective identity helps to define the interests of the state, by legitimating some courses of action while making others unimaginable. Barnett's analysis works at all levels: Cognitive psychology, pluralist and institutional dynamics, and inter-state relations all shape the narratives and frames that shape how individuals think about and how groups fight about foreign policy. Barnett shows that debates about the peace process are largely driven not merely by material interests but also by conflicting definitions of what the nature of Israel's community is supposed to be—liberal or Jewish. What does it mean to be Zionist? Changing and competing definitions of Zionism crucially constrain Israeli politicians.

How important is it for scholars to understand how identities are constituted? In the introductory chapter, Barnett and Telhami quote Barnett and Finnemore's analogy of DNA research, arguing that understanding how identities are constituted should make possible a variety of causal claims. The question is whether this volume demonstrates that the analogy holds weight—does "constitutive" research do what it is supposed to do?

Maloney's chapter indicates that how identities are constituted does help to explain what causes Iran's foreign policy. She focuses on three identities: Persian/historical nationalist, political Islamist, and anti-imperialist. While each of these, in their most generic forms, can be found elsewhere, they combine in particular ways in the Iranian context to define and to limit Iranian foreign policy, much as proteins can combine in certain ways to determine a person's physical destiny. The three identities produce complementary and conflicting imperatives, so that some policies (such as an open alliance with Israel) are unimaginable, costly policies (such as involvement in Lebanon) are continued, and policy struggles remain quite heated.

Identity and Preferences

One of the most important claims constructivists make is that other approaches do not explain preferences but simply assume countries to have specific desires.[24] Constructivists argue that identities help to determine interests.[25] This volume indicates that this is, indeed, one of the advantages of taking identity seriously.

Lynch asserts that identities construct the preferences of states. He focuses on the conflicts between Arabist definitions of Jordan and more narrow ideas of what Jordan should be. He argues that King Hussein was constrained by Arabist

[24] Of course, others disagree. For instance, Moravcsik, "Taking Preferences Seriously," addresses how liberals can and should focus on the preferences of states.

[25] Indeed, a special issue of *Security Studies* (1998/1999) titled *Origins of Interests* is largely a constructivist effort to explain how identity shapes interests.

views, so first he went along with them and then tried to weaken Arabism by repressing the Jordanian public sphere. In the late 1980s, he opened up public debate, which then permitted and encouraged a Jordanian sense of nation that facilitated cooperation with the emerging Palestinian entity. Still, the existence of the Arabist challenge forced Hussein to engage in covert negotiations with Israel, limiting the extent of cooperation.

Maloney shows that Iranians—politicians and constituents—prefer certain policies because of how they identify themselves and others. When Persian nationalism is ascendant, Iran tends to act more aggressively to dominate its region, as its decision-makers want to fulfill a role. Political Islam determines which actors Iran wants to help—for instance, Bosnia—and which actors Iran chooses to oppose. The anti-imperialist component of its identity markedly shapes Iran's interests vis-à-vis the United States, as Maloney demonstrates.

While Dawisha's account of Saddam Hussein suggests that identities are simply tools for politicians to manipulate as they pursue particular policies, the discussion of Iraqi politics and behavior in the 1930s suggests that identities do shape a state's preferences. In the case of Iraq, domestic political change was associated with foreign-policy change since those coming to power focused on a different collective identity than their predecessors, explaining the swings to and from Pan-Arabism in Iraqi foreign policy. Identity in this case was not epiphenomenal since a particular view of Iraqi and Arab identities motivated the newcomers.

Of course, the relationship between identity and preference may not be a simple one, as a particular identity may allow limited policy preferences, and other factors may be needed to explain why one path is ranked higher than another.

Identity and Costs

Barnett and Telhami suggest that identities matter even if something else causes a policy, if only because the costs may be higher or lower because of the identity dynamics in play. This raises the question of how identities increase or decrease the costs that leaders face. These costs can be domestic or international and material or ideational. That is, acting contrary to the imperatives of a particular identity may actually reduce the amount of money or power available to domestic actors or to the country as a whole; likewise, such "identity violations" may affect a leader's legitimacy or a country's sense of itself, perhaps leading to an identity conflict.

Most obviously, Middle Eastern states that "consorted" with Israel risked economic penalties and the loss of allies because of Israel's identification as the "other" in many circumstances. Egypt's relations with Iran are still constrained because of the identity politics involved with Sadat's embrace of Israel and his subsequent assassination. Also, identities in foreign policy can cause some actors within a country to pay material costs as well, as the example of Sadat demonstrates.

Furthermore, when identities become implicated in particular foreign policies, the legitimacy of the regime may be endangered. While a realist might point out that Iranian elites used various identities to mobilize support for the war against Iraq, Maloney shows that this policy had costs—that invoking particular identities and then settling the war weakened the regime's legitimacy. At the least, failed foreign policies may weaken the legitimacy of the identity, if not the regime, as failed wars against Israel diminished the appeal of pan-Arabism in Egypt.

This raises a question that has generally not been addressed adequately by previous work in this area: Why or how do identities make some policies more costly than others? One way to think about the costs of violating norms and identities in international relations is to consider how offensive the behavior is to other states.[26] This cost will vary from country to country, depending on its expectations, standards, domestic politics, and more. These are things about which we can and should think theoretically. One implication of this approach is that countries may violate certain norms and betray certain identities rather than others if the new behavior tends to offend those whom one has already alienated or those whose alienation matters little. A country that is already upset and is alienated cannot impose new costs, or can impose only lesser penalties, for subsequent undesired behavior than a country that has not been alienated. So-called pariah states may be more willing to act in ways that are apparently costly since they have already alienated much of the international community and therefore have borne whatever penalties they are likely to face.

Still, because this volume does not address costs as well as it might, more work should be done on the issue of the penalties—material or not, international or domestic—that states might be assessed for acting contrary to their state or national identities. This is a more rationalist approach, but it is also likely to be a fruitful path for complementing more traditional approaches to foreign policy.

Identity and Outcomes

How would identities help to explain outcomes, independent of preferences, costs, and the like? For instance, one could argue that although realism does not address the origin of preferences well, relative power is helpful in explaining who wins wars and the like. Can identity do the same? The first approach would consider how a particular identity defines the "game" that is being played—the rules, the relevant or legitimate actors, and the like. The international relations

[26] The ethnic politics approach captures much, although not all, of the domestic political consequences of acting contrary to the national identity.

of a situation will differ depending on whether the various actors share the same identity or compatible ones, so the rules of the game are unproblematic. If the actors have incompatible identities, the conflict may focus on getting the game straight (which actors are appropriate, which instruments are fair, and so forth), rather than on playing the game—bargaining, warring, allying. The second approach would involve a somewhat more superficial premise: States that identify with each other are less likely to engage in conflict. There is an emerging constructivist response to the democratic peace, arguing that the common identity of democracy—and not an institutional factor—causes states to remain peaceful. Of course, the problem with this approach is that conflict in the Middle East has been most intense not just between states of opposing identities (for example, Zionist Israel versus pan-Arab Egypt) but also between states of similar identities (Ba'thist Syria and Iraq, Islamic Iran and Afghanistan more recently). When do shared identities cause cooperation or rivalry? Barnett's work addresses the latter,[27] but we need to address both halves of the question with the same theoretical apparatus to understand what conditions lead to conflict, cooperation, or something in between. This should be the next question for the identity research agenda.

Constructivism and Materialist Approaches

The particularly special contribution that constructivism makes for these debates is its focus on the content of identity. By focusing on what it means to be Israeli and how it changes over time, Barnett shows how the various meanings of "Israeli-ness" shape the interests of the actors and, consequently, the foreign policy of the state. Likewise, Lynch charts the inconsistencies over time in Jordanian foreign policy as a product of competing notions of what it means to be Jordanian. Maloney reveals that the inconsistencies in Iranian foreign policy are a product of contradictions between the constituent elements of identity. Karawan draws an interesting distinction between state Arabism in Egypt and political Arabism, reminding us to be careful about the concepts we apply. Dawisha could have revealed more about Iraqi foreign policy had his chapter focused more on the content, changing or fixed, of the Iraqi collective identity.

This attention to the content of various forms of nationalism separates constructivist accounts from rationalist ones that focus on strategic politicians; for the latter, the content hardly matters.

SUMMARY OF IDENTITY'S IMPACT ON FOREIGN POLICY
The chapters clearly show that identities do influence foreign policy and that identity conflicts rarely inhibit states from engaging in ethnically defined for-

[27] Barnett, *Dialogues in Arab Politics: Negotiations in Regional Order* (New York: Columbia University Press, 1998).

eign policies. However, the theoretical question this book raises but does not answer definitively is whether or under what conditions constructivist accounts are superior to rationalist ones, or vice versa. This volume was never envisioned as a test of these approaches, although one goal was to show the value in considering identity rather than relying strictly on rationalist approaches.

The contributors show how various identities at different levels of analysis come into play, constraining some leaders and compelling others. The argument that communal divisions prevent leaders from engaging in ethnically oriented foreign policies finds little evidence here. Nearly all of the states in the region face significant ethnic divergence at home but still follow foreign policies that the vulnerability argument could not predict. Thus, we can say with confidence that communal identities matter in the foreign policies of Middle Eastern states, but how they matter is still an open question. Do they construct the region and are constructed by it? Or more narrowly and simply as tools and constraints for politicians.

Distinguishing between constructivist approaches and the ethnic politics perspective is more difficult because they are not as antithetical to each other as they are to the other approaches. The logical implications of each provide similar predictions and explanations. One could argue that the ethnic politics approach provides the micro-foundation for the constructivist approach, providing a theory of agency for a larger argument that needs a theory of agents, structures, the content of identities, and their interaction. The constructivist approach may provide a fuller understanding of the context within which strategic politicians interact. Specifically, constructivism might better capture how the actions of the politicians shape not only policy but also the structure of the situation, which simultaneously shapes the interests and behavior of these actors. One important implication of this book is that rational-choice theoretic approaches and constructivist ones may have much to gain from serious consideration of each other.

Defining Collective Identity

Although identity is a basic part of human nature, it is a hard concept for analysts to define. Michael Barnett provides a sparse definition in his chapter: "An identity is the understanding of oneself in relationship to others." Identity is inherently relational—one defines oneself or groups define themselves in part by who belongs and, as important, by who does not belong. The relational nature of identity clearly suggests its relevance for foreign policy and international relations. Particular identities may mean that individuals, groups, and countries elsewhere will fit into the categories of "us" and "them," friends and enemies, shaping the range of permissible, even thinkable, policy options.

Discussions of identity can often be confusing as several kinds and multiple levels of identities can be in play and are frequently involved.[28] In the introduction Barnett and Telhami focus on two kinds of identities—state and national. As a result, this volume stresses the relationship between state and national identities as a key dynamic influencing and being influenced by foreign policy. Of course, focusing on these two kinds of identity might cause one to overlook the reality that multiple identities nearly always coexist and that actors are pushed in varying directions depending on the relative ranking and salience of the various identities. For instance, the most homogeneous country studied in this volume, Egypt, still has at least six identities—Egyptian, Arab, Islamic, African, Middle Eastern, and Mediterranean—in play. Likewise, Maloney shows that conventional understandings of Iranian identity are too simplistic, as three overlapping, complementary, and competing identities interact to shape what Iran is and is not. Dawisha details the complexity of Iraq's collective identity, as Islam, Arabism, and Iraqi nationalism provide leaders with a "menu" of possible identities to emphasize. Depending on the issues, the history, and the interaction with others (individuals, groups, and states), one or more identities may be more important than others. As the following discussion of competing identities illustrates, these battles are not between the existence of one identity and the extinction of others, but the relative salience and meaning of each. Even if either genocide or assimilation occurs, subordinate identities remain to structure future debates, competition, and the like.[29]

Barnett and Telhami argue that transnational identities are important in the Middle East. These identities appeal to individuals in more than one state.[30] Pan-Arabism is not just about a larger community to which one may belong, and that influences interests and perceptions. Of course, the meaning and relevance of pan-Arabism has changed over time. It is not simply about language, but the linguistic component is important for limiting its universality and for facilitating communication and competition within the Arab-speaking world, as Barnett and Telhami discuss in the introduction. This larger community can have equal or greater relevance in domestic politics than other identities. The same is largely true for pan-Islam, except it has no natural frontiers. While pan-Arabism is limited to the Arab world, pan-Islam contains a universalizing com-

---

[28] I am grateful to Ted Gurr for reminding us of the levels of analysis problems inherent in discussions of identity.

[29] My thanks to Marc Lynch for reminding me of this.

[30] Some forms of pan-nationalism are quite narrow, such as pan-Somalism, which focuses on Somalis in Kenya, Ethiopia, Djibouti, and Somalia. I have argued elsewhere that the appeal of pan-Somalism for Somalia was generally overrated; see "Inconsistent Irredentism? Political Competition, Ethnic Ties, and the Foreign Policies of Somalia and Serbia," *Security Studies* 7, no. 3 (spring 1998): 51–93.

ponent, relevant beyond the Middle East. When the primary identity of a state is pan-Arabist or pan-Islamist, the domestic and international legitimacy of the state become intertwined, often leading to severe conflicts between domestic and international imperatives.[31] Pan-nationalisms are more likely to create both conflict and cooperation, as states are both attracted to and challenged by any transnationalism (and somewhat less so by other identities).[32] Moreover, competition among states to lead and to define a transnationalist movement may lead to conflict within and between states.[33] Dawisha demonstrates how problematic transnationalism has been for Iraq as significant domestic conflict was related to pan-Arabism, and Karawan shows how Egyptian politics became intertwined with pan-Arab politics.

Of course, this raises an important question: Why would conflict exist among different states espousing the same transnational identity? Unless the leaders of different states are pursuing the same vision of pan-nationalism, then the efforts of one leader to define the pan-identity may undermine the efforts of others. If this were to occur, then the meaning of the identity may change, resulting in a crisis of legitimacy for states where competing visions of the pan-identity predominate. A hypothetical situation might clarify this. If leaders of Egypt, Syria, and Jordan all relied on pan-Arabism but had different notions of what pan-Arabism meant, including different foreign-policy prescriptions, the success of Egypt to define the movement might threaten the definition of pan-Arabism in Syria and Jordan and weaken the legitimacy of those regimes as a result.[34] Thus, the leaders of each state might have a strong desire to define the transnational identity, since their regime's stability depends upon it. Allowing leaders of other states to define the transnational identity leaves a ruler in a very dangerous position, vulnerable to the designs of politicians with different agendas.

On the other hand, as the cases suggest, there are limits to transnational identities. One way in which transnational identity is limited is that its impact within states is likely to be on ideas, norms, and the like, but material concerns

[31] Shibley Telhami, "Power and Legitimacy in Arab Alliances," paper presentation at the annual meeting of the American Political Science Association, New York, N.Y. (Sept. 1–4, 1994); Barnett, *Dialogues in Arab Politics*.

[32] Paul Kowert and Legro, "Norms, Identity and Their Limits: A Theoretical Reprise," in *The Culture of National Security: Norms and Identity in World Politics*, ed. Peter J. Katzenstein (New York: Columbia University Press, 1996), 451–97. Indeed, one of the puzzles raised but not yet answered by constructivist approaches is: Under what conditions will a particular identity or norm create cooperation or conflict?

[33] Telhami, "Power and Legitimacy."

[34] See Barnett, "Identity and Alliances in the Middle East," in *The Culture of National Security: Norms and Identity in World Politics*, ed. Peter J. Katzenstein (New York: Columbia University Press, 1996): 400–450.

still matter to politicians' constituents. If politicians focus too much on transnational ideas at the expense of improving people's material circumstances, the politicians may lose their positions. This is not to say that transnational identities do not matter, but that their ability to shape outcomes is remarkable, given how infertile the ground often is for such efforts.

This discussion of identity raises two questions for any research on this topic. How fluid is identity? What causes particular identities to be more—or less— salient? In the two next sections, I address these questions and place the contributors to this volume within these debates.

Affecting Identity

If we consider identity to be at least somewhat fluid, we then raise a question: What causes some identities to be more influential and more relevant than others? This section addresses these related issues, for the greater the fluidity of identity, the more important understanding identities' sources becomes.

DETERMINING THE FLUIDITY OF IDENTITY

One of the oldest debates in the ethnicity literature concerns the nature of identities: Are they fixed throughout history, or can political entrepreneurs create identities at will? Taking a stand on this debate is necessary, as everything else follows from this initial conception of identity. The primordial approach essentially argues that communal identities are "givens of social existence."[35] This approach resists the best efforts of politicians to redefine or to do away with historically relevant identities. Geertz argues that the roots of these givens can be found in the "non-rational foundations of personality" and are, ultimately, unexplainable.[36] For our purposes, this approach has one serious flaw: It cannot explain why the salience of identities and their content might vary. If ethnicity is a constant, how can this approach explain variations in the behavior of individuals, groups, and states? While analysts might not expect a simplistic, linear relationship between identity and behavior, we still cannot explain significant variation with something that is not supposed to change. None of the authors in this volume is a primordialist; each takes seriously the existence of multiple identities and their varying salience in the political process.

The opposite conception of ethnicity asserts that identity is highly fluid and is easily manipulated by politicians. Paul Brass asserts that "the study of eth-

---

[35] Clifford Geertz, "The Integrative Revolution: Primordial Sentiments and Civil Politics in the New States," in *Old Societies and New States: The Quest for Modernity in Asia and Africa*, ed. Geertz (London: Free Press, 1963): 109.

[36] Geertz, "The Integrative Revolution," 128.

nicity and nationality is in large part the study of politically-induced cultural change. More precisely, it is the study of the process by which elites and counter-elites within ethnic groups *select* aspects of the group's culture, *attach new value* and *meaning* to them, and use them as symbols to mobilize the group, to defend its interests, and to compete with other groups."[37] This approach can help to explain changes in policy as the result of competition between politicians as they define and redefine ethnicity. The problem is that such an approach cannot explain as well why some identities, and therefore policies, endure over time despite changes in leadership and in institutions. It also cannot fully account for the choices politicians make—since everything is possible—or for why politicians might fail.

Few of the volume's contributors have such a fluid view of identity. Karawan comes the closest, suggesting that identities are so elastic that they "can actually account for most or all sorts of possible foreign policy outcomes." So, identity may serve as a poor predictor of foreign policy. However, he goes on to argue that politicians may not be able to influence identity, citing Nasser as an example. He had a powerful position not only within Egypt but also as leader of the pan-Arab movement. If anyone could have made Arab nationalism Egypt's primary identity, it would have been Nasser. Resistance to Arab nationalism might actually provide support for the primordial approach, as Egyptian nationalism proved stronger.

Much work has focused on the middle ground between the primordial and instrumental approaches. Analysts such as Ted Gurr, Donald Horowitz, David Laitin, Joseph Rothschild, and Crawford Young argue that in most societies multiple ethnic identities exist because of history.[38] Each identity has meaning and significance, but which ones are most salient varies. "The set of groups which constitute plurality are not necessarily permanent, frozen collectives, but in a state of constant flux in response to the long-run forces of social change, shorter-run alternations of political context, and continuous processes of interaction with other groups."[39] Thus, politicians cannot summon up ethnic identities from anywhere, but they can try to emphasize certain ethnic identities at the expense of others. This is the approach taken consciously or unconsciously in most of the chapters, including this one.

[37] Paul R. Brass, *Ethnicity and Nationalism: Theory and Comparison* (New Delhi: Sage, 1991): 75. Italics added for emphasis.

[38] See Ted Robert Gurr, *Minorities at Risk: A Global View of Ethnopolitical Conflicts* (Washington, D.C.: U.S. Institute of Peace Press, 1993); Horowitz, *Ethnic Groups in Conflict*; David D. Laitin, *Hegemony and Culture: Politics and Religious Change among the Yoruba* (Chicago: University of Chicago Press, 1986); Joseph Rothschild, *Ethnopolitics: A Conceptual Framework* (New York: Columbia University Press, 1981); Crawford Young, *The Politics of Cultural Pluralism* (Madison: University of Wisconsin Press, 1976).

[39] Young, *Politics of Cultural Pluralism*, 12–13.

However, the authors differ regarding how fluid identities are. Lynch's and Barnett's constructivist approaches suggest that identities can be structured by politicians but also structure politicians' freedom to maneuver and even to imagine. Indeed, Barnett and Lynch argue that identities are fairly stable but can be altered during a crisis—an identity conflict.[40] While less formally constructivist, Dawisha and Maloney seem to agree with Barnett and Lynch in that multiple identities exist, constraining the choices politicians face, but still allowing significant room to maneuver. On the other hand, Sadowski considers identity to be much more fluid, particularly given the number of competing definitions of self and community in the Middle East.

The fluidity of identity is important because it determines the ability of politicians, as well as other factors, to influence identity, and how much identity serves as a constraint. If identity is very fluid, then politicians might be quite powerful, as they might be able to highlight certain identities or certain implications of a particular identity. On the other hand, if identities are fixed, then politicians and everyone else must react to the given. Ultimately, one's view on the fluidity of identity shapes one's stance on identity's impact on policy and on what influences identity. If identities are not completely fixed, we need to consider what influences the relative salience and meaning of each.

INFLUENCING IDENTITY

The contributors disagree on what causes some identities to become more salient or even hegemonic and what alters their meanings.[41] The three most prominent factors shaping identities in the case studies are leaders, internal ethnic conflict, and interstate interactions. In this section, I review how the authors treat these three influences of identity, consider two significant omissions, and then conclude by arguing that domestic political concerns are most important.

Karawan stresses the importance of rulers in Egypt, as do Dawisha and Barnett in their studies of Iraq and Israel, respectively. Karawan discusses Nasser's efforts to emphasize Arabism at the expense of other identities. While Nasser was not completely successful, it is still important that he tried and that his efforts influenced his policies domestically and abroad. Dawisha considers "the role and motivations of the ruling elites as the crucial intervening variable." Barnett argues that politicians, constrained by institutions and events, try to

---

[40] For an argument about when and why identity conflicts occur, see Legro, "Whence American Internationalism," *International Organization* 54, no. 2 (spring 2000): 253–89. Barnett and Lynch's conception of identity conflict is similar to Peter Gourevitch's notion that coalitions, and consequently policies, are fairly stable except during severe crises; see *Politics in Hard Times: Comparative Responses to International Economic Crises* (Ithaca: Cornell University Press, 1986).

[41] Laitin, *Hegemony and Culture*.

define events and processes as having particular meanings. If successful, politicians can use these frames and narratives to mobilize support and to legitimate policy. Therefore, politics is ultimately a contest of politicians responding to events by competing to frame various issues. However, the contributors agree that domestic audiences constrain leaders from manipulating identities however they wish. There is room to maneuver, but it is not limitless.

Even as a politician seeks to use or to manipulate an identity, however, he or she has to deal with competing politicians and, often, with competing identities. This volume raises questions about the power of politicians to shape the identity debates in their countries. Neither Nasser nor Hussein was able to promote a single identity to replace or to de-emphasize competing definitions of the political community. Thus, we are left with the classic and unanswered question of identity politics: *Under what conditions* will politicians succeed in emphasizing one identity at the expense of others?

One could hypothesize that important factors include the ability to repress, the nature of the identity, the history of the country, and control of the media. The case studies also suggest that some intuitions seem more accurate than others. Violent repression does not seem to work, as the Kurds of Iraq continue to challenge attempts to define Iraq's collective identity. Transnational identities may be harder to implant, as pan-Arabism's failure during Nasser's rule suggests, than altering the meaning of indigenous identities. Going with, as opposed to against, the grain of history is more likely to succeed, as Egyptian nationalism seems to be a better tool for elites. Lynch's argument suggests that leaders' decisions about whether to open the public discourse and to influence it has a powerful effect on which identities become salient. Although leaders may not be able to repress identities, they can shape the debates, and as Barnett also suggests, they can try to frame issues and to set agendas in ways that highlight the preferred identities. Given the roles played by hate radio in Rwanda and by Milosevic's control of Serbian media, this is not a surprising finding. Still, it is noteworthy that the media are crucial in Africa, Yugoslavia, and the Middle East despite varying political, economic, and cultural traditions and institutions.

The importance of various media in these conflicts raises a point of comparison between rationalist[42] and constructivist approaches. The two approaches have very different views on what the media can do. For rationalist approaches, television, radio, and newspapers can shape the agenda, highlighting certain choices, events, and dynamics while downplaying others. Further, the media can

[42] The term rationalist is often confusing, as it may refer to any approach that assumes that actors are behaving rationally (as states are, according to neo-Realism or neo-Liberal institutionalism) or to rational-choice theoretic approaches. For this chapter, rationalist refers to arguments that focus on strategic politicians seeking to safeguard their positions.

provide new information that causes individuals and groups to revise their cost-benefit calculations. On the other hand, constructivist approaches suggest that the media can persuade individuals of the worth, not just the costs and benefits, of specific courses of action. The media can render legitimate or illegitimate particular actors and strategies. These deeper, more powerful influences may more appropriately explain the media's role in identity conflicts than the more limited, rationalistic take. This point of contrast—the role of the media—might be an interesting focus for empirical study to determine the relative contributions of each approach.

Regardless of what politicians are trying to do, the identities in play in their polities are critically shaped by the existence of conflict within their states. For example, Jordan's large Palestinian population is central to definitions of Jordanian identity, as Lynch shows in his chapter. Barnett illustrates how identity conflicts are played out through political competition and party politics. While there is some room for politicians to maneuver in Barnett's view of Israel, the divisions between liberal and religious parties, between Ashkenazim and Sephardim, and the rest strongly influence what politicians can do. Likewise, Maloney shows how the contest for influence within Iran among and between parallel sets of institutions influences the relative impact of three components of Iranian identity. Dawisha demonstrates that Iraqi collective identity is contingent on competing identities within the country—Shiite versus Sunni, Arab versus Kurd, tribe versus city. Karawan shows that identities can be contested even in a relatively homogeneous state, as illustrated by the transnational identities that vie with Egyptian nationalism. Ultimately, these domestic conflicts have perhaps the strongest influence on a society's collective identity.

International factors are the third set of forces shaping the identities of states and their sub-state actors.[43] War, Israel, and transnational movements significantly shape the identities at stake within and across states.[44] Lost wars undermined Nasser's efforts to emphasize pan-Arabism at home. Israel's conflicts over its identity were sharpened by the conflict in Lebanon. Iraq's war with Iran may have increased the salience of Iraqi, Arab, and Sunni identities, while its war with Kuwait may have undermined the latter two identities.

For many states in the region, Israel's behavior—in fact, its mere existence—has shaped the various identities in play. For Syria, the existence of Israel helps to define what it means to be Syrian and what it means to be Arab. Engaging Israel has critically influenced Egyptian identity, as such efforts weakened whatever remained of pan-Arabism's pull on the average Egyptian. Whether Jordan's

[43] I hesitate to label this strategic interaction as this category refers to more than just groups and states engaging each other.

[44] International economic changes also play a role, but the chapters pay relatively little attention to these forces, with the exceptions of the case studies of Syria and Egypt.

identity conflicts influence its relationship with Israel, the relationship shapes domestic and international disputes over Jordan's collective identity. While a complete and lasting peace and resolution to the Israeli-Palestinian conflict is hardly a foregone conclusion, such a situation would drastically alter the dynamics of identification in most Middle Eastern countries.

In part, a permanent resolution would alter the ability of transnational identities to influence the internal dynamics of states. Specifically, pan-Arabism and pan-Islamism have been important to the identity disputes of the region. Competition between elites for leadership of the pan-Arab movement significantly shaped the domestic politics of Egypt, Syria, Iraq, and others. Indeed, the effort to be the leader of the pan-Arab movement was akin to ethnic outbidding, which usually refers to competition within a polity by various elites for the support of a single ethnic group.[45] Because being Arab is important to citizens of nearly every country in the region, politicians' efforts to define what it means to be Arab and events that shape the content of the identity have broad ramifications. However, as the chapters suggest, efforts to increase the salience of pan-Arab identity tend to fail in the face of more local lines of conflict: city versus rural (Syria, Iraq), Sunni versus Shiite (Iraq), among others. Efforts to engage Israel, first by Egypt and then by others, also have challenged the meaning and relevance of pan-Arabism.

Despite Western fears concerning the rise of Islamic fundamentalism, the chapters suggest that Islam's ability to dominate a state's identity is highly contested. While powerful Islamic movements exist within several states in the region, these groups are encountering alternative definitions of community, based on divisions within Islam (Shia versus Sunni), race and language (Arab versus non-Arab), or clan and tribe (Somalia, Syria, Iraq). Even in Iran, political Islam competes with historical nationalism and anti-imperialism. While some of these movements and some states are trying to increase Islamic influence and identity in other countries, the success of these efforts is not assured.

Several contributors argue that both domestic and international dynamics influence which identities matter the most within in each country and for foreign policy. Lynch asserts that the public sphere, where debates influence preferences and even identities of actors, exists at both the domestic and international levels. Given the competition among Arab leaders for influence within the pan-Arab movement, Lynch's approach should apply beyond Jordan as he talks of an Arab public sphere. Clearly, the notion of public debate within and across boundaries is not unique to the Middle East. Competition to lead and to define the pan-African movement was important domestically and internationally in the 1960s, while similar dynamics played out in the Non-Aligned Move-

---

[45] Horowitz, *Ethnic Groups in Conflict*; and Rothschild, *Ethnopolitics*.

ment as well. Future work should consider how other national public spheres interact with transnational debates. Today, the existence of international public spheres interacting with domestic spheres may be an essential part of the development of a European identity, grounded in the European Union.

While a growing number of institutional analyses have examined Middle Eastern countries,[46] few of the contributions to this volume focus on the impact of political institutions, despite the trend in political science more generally.[47] A notable exception is Barnett's chapter as he stresses Israel's electoral system, how it empowers smaller parties and shapes coalition politics. Maloney discusses the existence of parallel sets of institutions, but does not develop how the nature and structures of these institutions shape subsequent political battles. Indeed, the existence of parallel institutions suggests that a variety of interesting interactions might occur, but Maloney does not really pursue this line of thought. The omission of institutions in the other chapters cannot be explained by the argument that institutions do not matter in authoritarian regimes.

First, Egypt and Iran have elements of democracy, even if they are fragile or weakly consolidated ones. One should expect that a variety of institutions should matter in at least these two states: party organizations, electoral systems, and the division of power between the executive and legislature. All of these potentially influence debates and conflicts over identity, and all could influence foreign policy. Thus, as explanations of identity and as rival explanations of foreign policy, future work on identity and foreign policy should consider institutions more seriously.

Institutions should matter in the study of authoritarian polities as well. While the new institutionalism has most clearly been applied to older, more established authoritarian regimes,[48] scholars should still consider whether authoritarian leaders face any institutional constraints or incentives. Such influences could include the ethnic composition of the military, the existence or absence of a secret police, and the extent of repressive institutions. Does Saddam Hussein have more or less freedom to maneuver than Hafiz al-Asad did? While institutions may be less binding in highly autocratic regimes, they are still significant, if only as additional costs for leaders when they are ignored.

[46] For instance, see Steven Heydemann, *Authoritarianism in Syria: Institutions and Social Conflict, 1946–1970* (Ithaca: Cornell University Press, 1999); and David Waldner, *State Building and Late Development* (Ithaca: Cornell University Press, 1999).

[47] In the discipline, much attention has been paid to the ways in which institutions create incentives for political actors to behave in certain ways and not others. Further, much work has focused on how institutions structure outcomes as they empower certain groups rather than others.

[48] For institutional analyses of the Soviet Union and China, respectively, see Philip G. Roeder, *Red Sunset: The Failure of Soviet Politics* (Princeton, N.J.: Princeton University Press, 1993); and Susan L. Shirk, *The Political Logic of Economic Reform in China* (Berkeley: University of California Press, 1993).

In this context, two key points about institutions deserve mention. First, institutions may determine which audiences are most important to various actors—who are the constituents? Knowing who politicians care about—those who pose a threat to remove incumbents from power; that is, the selectorate[49]—is a good first step for understanding which identities might matter. Once we know how constituents identify themselves, we can then see how leaders are constrained or how they might face various opportunities. Thus, studying institutions tells us something about the identities in play.

Second, institutions are the products of past political battles, compromises and debates. Consequently, they embody the policy implications of past identity conflicts. Politicians who seek to revise or to reform such institutions must not only battle self-interested partisans—those who directly benefit from the institution—but also those who find their identities challenged. Rather than being defined as a mild revision of an existing institution, a reform effort may be portrayed as a challenge to all of those who believe in religion X, speak language Y, or are historically privileged because of membership in group Z. Constructivists emphasize how agents shape structures, which then influence agents. One of the best examples of this process is when an identity shapes an actor's interests and perceptions, so that the agent creates an institution embodying the identity. Even after that actor passes from the political scene, the institution influences subsequent politicians, shaping their imagination about what is possible and what is legitimate. Further work should consider how particular identities are institutionalized while others are not. This might help to explain why some identities resonate over time while others fade. For instance, did pan-Arabism reside within significant institutions? As far as the cases suggest, pan-Arabism was never as institutionalized as other identities, such as Islam or tribal divisions.

In sum, the contributors have not arrived at a consensus on what shapes identity. The authors largely concur that multiple identities exist and that the salience of each one varies over time. However, the authors disagree about how much ability rulers have to manipulate or to emphasize particular identities at the expense of others. They also disagree somewhat about whether international politics shapes identities or is shaped by them. Given the complex nature of identity, it would be deceptive for this volume to push for an artificial agreement about what influences identity. Still, because the contributors find few points of convergence, determining the lessons we must draw for both policy and future research is difficult; however, the effort is still worthwhile. Therefore, I will suggest two conditions that shape identity more consistently and perhaps more powerfully than others do.[50]

[49] Roeder, *Red Sunset*.
[50] I am grateful to Michael Barnett for pushing me on this point.

The two conditions are domestic political competition and ethnic conflict. Transnational identities, while quite important, may be very limited in their long-term impact because politicians respond more strongly to domestic audiences than to opinions held by citizens of other countries. While outsiders can remove leaders, most threats to politicians' positions emerge from within their countries. Unless a transnational identity motivates domestic actors or demobilizes potential opponents, leaders may have to avoid costly stances on transnational issues. Leaders can even survive lost wars, as Sadat and Saddam Hussein demonstrated. Sadat, to be sure, paid the costs of engaging Israel, but, again, his opposition was domestic—the assassins were Egyptians. Elites must be concerned about those who can remove them from power, as being in a position of power is advantageous for shaping decisions and policies.[51] One does not need to be a rational-choice theorist to buy into this assertion (though it helps). For the constructivist, agents matter, but which agents matter the most may vary; leaders are important since they control resources, can set agendas, and frame events. Constructivists focus on the ability of leaders to frame issues or to persuade followers, but it is important to remember that these leaders need support (hence the framing or persuasion) to be effective. Even, or perhaps especially, the Asads and Saddams of the world need to appeal to some constituency to remain in power, and, in the end, this constituency is always a domestic one.

Just as domestic constituents are fundamental for understanding leaders' decision-making, competition among groups with different identities is a crucial influence on collective identity. Ethnic conflicts, by definition, implicate race, religion, language, and/or kinship. Leaders may try to develop or to buttress a non-ethnic collective identity (for example, civic nationalism), but as long as an ethnic conflict exists, the civic nationalism serves as only one way to define "us" and "them." Efforts to reinforce the nonethnic collective identity merely remind the populace of the alternative. As chapter 1 illustrates, state and national identities are "collective" in that they may not necessarily be shared by all but by a large portion of the populace.

Ethnic conflict can influence this collective identity in two ways. First, if the conflict is between those who share the collective identity and those who do not, the tensions and histories between the "us" and the "them" will shape the meaning, the content, and the implications of the collective identity. For example, Israeli identity is critically shaped by the existence of non-Israelis within the territory. Likewise, Jordanian identity is crucially shaped by the presence of Palestinians. Kurds within Iraq have been the "other" when Iraq was pan-Arab and when an Islamic identity has been offered as a common identity. Second, the ethnic conflict may foster a counter-hegemonic identity. For example,

[51] Mayhew, *Electoral Connection*.

conflict among Sunnis and Shiites in Iraq increased the salience of religious divisions, when the prominent divergence/identity centered on Arab versus non-Arab. As Barnett explains in chapter 3, tensions within the Israeli community may cause the dominant divergences of Jew versus non-Jew and Israeli versus Arab to be replaced by Russian versus non-Russian, Orthodox Jew versus less observant, and the like. Even if these identities do not replace the Israeli collective identity, they will continue to alter its meaning.

Despite other influences on identity, domestic political competition among leaders and ethnic competition among groups are consistently the most important dynamics shaping identity in these and other countries.

CHANGING CONTENT OF IDENTITY

Communal identity is relevant in foreign policy not just because of the existence or prominence of the identity but also because of its content. What does the identity imply for foreign policy or for domestic politics? What does it rule in or rule out?

Although pan-Arabism concerns a shared ethnic linkage, it means more than that, and that meaning has changed over time, as several of the authors indicate in their studies of individual countries. Indeed, the contest for leadership of the Arab nationalist movement was in part about the meaning of Arab nationalism. Likewise, Islam's implications for foreign policy have changed over time, in response to, among other events, the Iranian revolution. The definitions of enemy and ally have not been consistent, sometimes leading to conflict within the Islamic community and sometimes leading to cooperation.

Civic nationalism is subject to change over time. While Egyptian nationalism may have focused somewhat on Egypt's unique history in the Middle East, Sadat's separate peace with Israel made this aspect of Egyptian identity much more salient and meaningful than it was in previous years. The meaning of what it means to be a member of the Ba'thist party and what that means for relations with the outside world has also varied over time, as the chapters on Iraq and Syria indicate.

I highlight the content of identity because we often take for granted what it means for foreign policy. For instance, my work has focused on the ties and enmities between ethnic groups, their states, and potential supporters, but I have generally focused merely on the existence of ties and enmities without considering the deeper meanings of the identities at stake.[52] As this volume demonstrates, the contests among politicians and other actors is not only about which identity should be more salient and should shape domestic and foreign policies, but also about the meaning, the content, of identities. Without seriously considering the meaning of each identity, we might miss the real impact that identity has on foreign policy.

[52] Saideman, "Vulnerability vs. Ethnic Ties," "Inconsistent Irredentism," *Ties That Divide*.

Readers of this volume might conclude that identity matters in the Middle East, but is of less concern elsewhere. In this section, I discuss the similarities and differences between the Middle East and other parts of the world. Some aspects of this volume, including identity and ethnic politics, have broad applications, while others, such as transnational identities, may be more limited in scope.

Constructivist scholars are increasingly demonstrating the importance of identities for the foreign policies of many countries, in a variety of issue areas ranging from the environment to security.[53] These studies have indicated that identities may explain why Japan and Germany have followed foreign policies that differed from what realists and others might have expected,[54] and have shown that identity influences Chinese and French strategies and doctrines.[55] Scholars also have shown that identities have shaped how states have used and not used weapons of mass destruction.[56] Thus, the argument that identities are relevant for foreign policy is not region specific.

The idea that identities determine who are potential allies and who one cannot imagine as allies applies beyond the Middle East. This approach might help to explain why countries are not aligning against the most threatening country in the world—the United States. Stephen Walt, the most prominent realist to address alliance behavior in the Middle East, focuses on aggregate power, offensive capability, geographic proximity, and perceived intentions. The United States clearly possesses the first two, and, with its bases around the world and its ability to project power via its navy and air force, seems close to most of its enemies.[57] We are left with perceived intentions, which can be influenced by identity in two ways—shaping perceptions or determining intentions. Does the identity of the United States shape what others think? Does it constrain what the United States can do? There is little doubt that constructivist approaches can provide insights on a variety of issues around the world, so their contribu-

---

[53] Recent issues of *International Organization*, *International Security*, *International Studies Quarterly*, *Security Studies*, and *World Politics* testify to the increasing scope of constructivist accounts.

[54] Thomas U. Berger, "Norms, Identity, and National Security in Germany and Japan," in *The Culture of National Security: Norms and Identity in World Politics*, ed. Peter J. Katzenstein (New York: Columbia University Press, 1996): 317–56.

[55] Kier, *Imagining War: French and British Military Doctrine between the Wars* (Princeton, N.J.: Princeton University Press, 1997); and Alastair I. Johnston, *Cultural Realism: Strategic Culture and Grand Strategy in Chinese History* (Princeton, N.J.: Princeton University Press, 1995).

[56] Richard Price and Nina Tannenwald, "Norms and Deterrence: The Nuclear and Chemical Weapons Taboo" in *The Culture of National Security: Norms and Identity in World Politics*, ed. Katzenstein (New York: Columbia University Press, 1996): 114–52.

[57] Stephen M. Walt, *The Origins of Alliances* (Ithaca: Cornell University Press, 1987).

tion to the study of Middle Eastern politics should not be surprising. Further, we should not consider the value of constructivism here to be abnormal given its contribution to understanding the politics and policies of countries elsewhere.[58]

Still, one could argue that studying the role of identity in Middle Eastern conflicts is not a hard test for the constructivist approach.[59] Given the obvious importance of religious divisions and other forms of identity-based antagonism, identities should matter here and for security issues. Perhaps more challenging case studies would focus on Latin America, where identities are apparently not very important, and on economic issues, where profit motives might outweigh identity concerns.

While ethnic politics is, by definition, more limited in its applicability to a variety of issue areas, the approach is not limited by region or by levels of economic development. One might argue that ethnic politics matters in a region hotly contested for two millennia by world religions, but not in regions characterized by secular institutions and advanced political development. However, politicians play the ethnic card in a variety of countries, and this strategy is frequently successful around the world. American politicians resort to racial ties and antagonism to mobilize political support, while Canadian elites use linguistic divisions to bind supporters and to divide potential adversaries. The rise of right-wing nationalist parties in Western Europe during the past twenty years indicates that ethnic politics is in play, even in the most developed political systems. Of course, the question remains: Does ethnic politics influence the foreign policies of these states? Explaining Clinton's condoning of Greek policy toward Macedonia is difficult without reference to the Greek-American lobby, and addressing Germany's discriminatory policies toward Yugoslavia is difficult without taking into account the ethnic identities of the combatants.[60] While ethnic politics may be less helpful in explaining countries' foreign economic or environmental policies, it certainly shapes whom they support or oppose.[61]

Transnational identities are not unique to the Middle East, but their importance here is still remarkable. Pan-Arabism and Islam have played a central role in the domestic and international politics of Middle Eastern states. In the past, one could argue that pan-Africanism was to Africa what pan-Arabism was to the Middle East. In the 1960s, leaders of African states competed with each other to define and to lead pan-Africanism, in part to build an alternative identity to

[58] For instance, see *The Culture of National Security: Norms and Identity in World Politics*, ed. Katzenstein (New York: Columbia University Press, 1996).

[59] Walt, *Origins of Alliances*.

[60] Saideman, *Ties That Divide*.

[61] Of course, American sanctions of Cuba affect its foreign economic relations with many countries, and explaining this policy is difficult without reference to the electoral significance of Cuban-Americans.

more divisive ones at home.[62] As in the Middle East, the power and appeal of transnationalism declined over time, providing evidence that domestic audiences and concerns are of primary importance. Because domestic audiences (voters or the military) determine who governs, and because these audiences are more likely to care about their own condition than others' welfare, efforts to build transnational identities face obstacles that may be insurmountable. Eventually, African leaders had to focus on domestic problems as their constituents cared less about the plight of Africans elsewhere. In the world today, the only other region where a transnational identity plays such a role is Europe, where a European identity may be coming into existence, limiting what can be imagined and shaping what can be done. Still, it is too early to say what impact this identity will have.

Conclusion

To conclude, four issues must be addressed. First, can we distill a coherent theory out of the often conflicting chapters? Second, what does the focus on collective identity add to our understanding of foreign policy, particularly in the Middle East? Third, what additional research may clarify the relationships identified in this volume? Finally, what should policy makers glean from these chapters?

Clearly, there is no consensus among the authors producing a single theory of communal identity and foreign policy. While Lynch and Barnett develop compatible theories of identity and foreign policy, I cannot say the same for the other contributors. Despite the differences among them, however, we have some building blocks for a consensus. Identity may have the viscosity of used oil—it is fluid, but not as frequently imagined. Leaders are limited because they have only certain identities available to emphasize or to de-emphasize. Indeed, their efforts to place one identity at a higher level of salience and meaning often fails, even when the leader is quite powerful in other ways. A second point of consensus is that no single force shapes identities, as politicians, domestic conflicts, and international processes all influence the content of particular identities and the relative importance of each. Each of the chapters considers these three factors to be important influences of definitions of the political community, although the chapters may disagree about the weighting of each. The contributors agree as well that identities influence foreign policy although they may disagree on precisely how. This last point of agreement leads to the next question: What does identity add to debates about foreign policy?

[62] Catherine Hoskyns, *The Congo since Independence* (London: Oxford University Press, 1965); Touval, *Boundary Politics of Independent Africa*.

We must first note that the relationship goes both ways—collective identity influences foreign policy, and foreign policy influences collective identity. Identity can influence foreign policy in a variety of ways. It can be a tool for mobilizing support and for diffusing opposition. Islam and Persian nationalism were useful to Iranian elites as they sought more support in the war against Iraq. Identity can serve as a constraint on action or imagination; for example, Jordan's King Hussein could not cooperate with Israel as openly and as extensively as he would have preferred. Identity can be a device for justifying or legitimating policy, as Barnett asserts in his study of Israel. Identity also can provide an opportunity for destabilizing other countries, as Nasser, among others, understood quite well. Most powerfully, identity can define interests and threats, as Lynch demonstrates in his chapter. Thus, collective identity is a powerful concept for helping to explain why states do what they do.

Similarly, foreign policy influences identity in several ways. First, it can change the salience and meaning of some identities. Indeed, Lynch goes so far as to argue that foreign policy is a symbolic battlefield for identity conflicts. Foreign policy can alter the costs paid by politicians for particular ethnopolitical strategies, angering some groups and appeasing others. For example, the lost wars raised the costs for Nasser's pan-Arabism. External events and the consequences of foreign policies can change domestic agendas, causing some issues and identities to surface. External involvement in internal conflicts can prolong the conflicts, increase their costs, and advantage one group over others. War can weaken the state, empowering groups with alternative definitions of the political community. Iraq's failure in the Gulf War temporarily assisted the Shiites of the South and the Kurds of the North. Thus, identity matters as both cause and effect.

Because each chapter focused on a single case, drawing definitive conclusions about any approach is difficult. Future work must engage in comparative research to determine whether the role played by communal conflict is idiosyncratic to each state or applies more generally. Some interesting comparisons could focus on very different cases to see whether communal identity serves as a common factor.[63] For instance, a comparison of relatively homogeneous Saudi Arabia with very heterogeneous Lebanon might prove interesting. Likewise, it would be interesting to compare Middle Eastern states with those elsewhere to determine whether the impact of communal identity is merely the consequence of Israel, Islam or Arabism, or whether identity may be a factor in most countries' foreign policies. On the other hand, comparing very similar cases might

[63] For the benefits of most different comparisons, see Theodore W. Meckstroth, "'Most Different Systems' and 'Most Similar Systems': A Study in the Logic of Comparative Inquiry," *Comparative Political Studies* 8, no. 2 (1975): 132–57.

also be useful for determining the impact of identity on foreign policy. For instance, one could compare Iraqi and Syrian policies toward Kurds in other states. Another interesting comparison would be Egypt and Jordan toward Israel in the 1990s. Comparing Lebanon before the civil war to afterwards might provide interesting findings.

Finally, we need to consider the policy relevance of this project.[64] Why should policy makers care about communal identity and foreign policy? To address this, we must consider two perspectives: When making foreign policy, decision makers need to know what constraints or influences they face within their own country and what influences the situations and policies of other countries. In making foreign policy, policy makers need to be aware of how identities influence their policies. An identity may cause a policy to have more or less support, to have intended or unintended consequences at home, or to be more or less legitimate. Elites should consider how their imaginations are constrained by their identities and by those of their country.

Likewise, leaders need to understand the roles of communal identities in other countries—both how identities influence foreign policy and how international processes shape communal identity. Understanding identity's impact would help politicians to predict what other countries might do, to understand their preferences and their constraints, and to manipulate situations so that identities leading to favorable outcomes increase in salience. This is not easy, particularly as this book does not provide a clear causal mechanism, but it is something that scholars and policy makers should consider.

In sum, we now have answers to some questions but leave several important issues for future research. The contributors to this volume have shown that identity does shape foreign policy in the Middle East in systematic ways, and that foreign policy in turn influences the content and salience of various identities. The chapters indicate that identity conflicts do not constrain states as much as vulnerability arguments suggest. We have evidence that identity works at deep levels, constituting interests, among other things, and we have reason to believe that rationalist approaches focusing on strategic politicians can enhance our understanding of identity politics in the region. The volume shows that the content of a communal identity is not fixed, but has great relevance for the identity's policy implications. Future research should determine when politicians will succeed as they grapple with identities, although the chapters provide some clues about which conditions facilitate their efforts. More study is also required to determine at what point internal ethnic conflicts challenge the identities of the state. Finally, the chapters suggest that we should pay attention to the roles that institutions play in shaping identity and its impact on foreign policy.

---

[64] Policy relevance was not the aim of the project but is something we should consider anyway.

Index

Islam (*continued*)

    universalism of, 100, 102
    See also Shiites; Sunnis
Islamic conservatism, 140
Islamic fundamentalism, 191
Islamic Republican Party (Iran), 105, 106n.42
Islamic utopianism, 99–100
Ismail I, Shah, 94
Israel, 57, 64–65, 77
    effect on identity of neighbors, 55, 180,
      190–91
    and Egypt, 162–63, 166–67, 180–81, 190
    elections in, 58, 71, 74–75, 80–83, 86–87
    historical narratives of, 65–68
    historical revisionists, 76
    identity of, 24, 58–60, 63–65
    importance of religion to, 175–76
    and Iran, 104, 108, 111
    and Jordan, 37–38, 49–56, 190–91
    and Lebanon, 14, 164–65
    political fragmentation of, 58, 70–71,
      80–82, 86–87
    political system of, 70–72
    recognition by Arab states, 72–73
    Six-Day War, 159–60
    and Syria, 149, 190
    See also Netanyahu, Benjamin; Peres, Shimon; Rabin, Yitzhak; Shamir, Yitzhak
Israeli-Jordanian peace treaty, 49–54
Israeli Labor Party, 71, 73–74, 75, 80, 86

Japan, 196
Jazira, al- (TV), 21
Jervis, Robert, 162
Jewish identity, 63
Jordan
    Arabism within, 35–38
    economy of, 53–54
    identity of, 7, 23, 30, 32–34, 39–40, 55,
      190–91
    integration of Palestinians, 38–39, 47–48
    and Israel, 37–38, 49–56, 190–91
    media in, 34–35, 54
    and PLO, 39–40, 41–43, 45–46
    position on Gulf War, 37
    public sphere of, 34–35, 36–37, 44
    and West Bank, 26, 40–41, 43–44
    See also Abdullah I, king of Jordan; Hussein, king of Jordan; Transjordan
Jordanian-Israeli peace treaty, 49–54
Jordanian National Charter (1991), 44
Jordanian-Palestinian agreement, 42–43
Jordanian-Palestinian confederation, 45–46, 48
Justification, public, 31–32, 171, 177–78

Kabariti, Abd al-Karim al-, 48
Karawan, Ibrahim, 23, 182, 185, 188
    on Egyptian identity, 14, 25, 172, 187, 190

Karsh, Efraim, 107
Kedourie, Elie, 10
Kerr, Matthew, 16
Khaddam, Abd al-Halim, 145–46, 151
Khalaf, Rima, 48
Khameini, Ali, 110
Khatami, Mohammad, 113–14, 115
Khomeini, Ayatollah Ruhollah, 20, 97–100,
    101
    death of, 88, 109–10
    propaganda during Iran-Iraq War, 131–32
    response to Soviet invasion of Afghanistan,
      105–6
Khomeini, Hossain, 106n.42
Korany, Bahgat, 162
Kurds, 93, 132, 173, 189, 194, 199
    identity of, 120
    rebellion by, 128
    response to Fertile Crescent Union, 124–25
Kuwait, 127, 190

Labor Zionism, decline of, 65
Laitin, David, 187
League of Arab States, 125
Lebanon, 14, 149–50, 164–65
Levy, David, 80–81
Levy, Yitzhak, 81n.79
Likud-Gesher-Tsomet alliance (Israel), 80
Likud Party (Israel), 71, 74, 75, 80, 82–83, 86
Lubotzky, Alex, 81n.79
Lynch, Marc, 7, 179–80, 188, 199
    on factors influencing identity, 189, 190, 191
    on Jordanian identity, 17, 23, 114, 182

Mahapach (political reversal), 75
Majali, Abd al-Hadi al-, 47n.59, 48
Makhluf, Rema, 143
Maloney, Suzanne, 170–71, 176, 180, 181, 188
    on factors influencing identity, 190, 192
    on Iranian identity, 23, 24, 179, 182, 184
Marx, Karl, 148n.40
Masada, 67
"Masada complex," 64
MAS business group, 143–44
Materialism. *See* Rationalism
Media, 21
    in Egypt, 164–65, 166
    in Iran, 113
    in Jordan, 34–35, 54
    and political legitimation, 164–65
    role in influencing identity, 189–90
    state repression of, 54, 168
    in Syria, 143
Meretz (Israeli political party), 75, 76
Mesopotamia, 135
Middle East North Africa (MENA) economic summits, 52, 53
Military conscription, 146–47n.36, 153
Mina, Hanna, 147
Misha'al, Khalid, 53

Mithaq al-watani, al- (1991), 44
Mojahedin-e Khalq (Iranian political party), 101
Moledet Party (Israel), 75
Mordechai, Yitzhak, 84
Mossadeq, Mohammad, 95
Mubarak, Hosni, 57, 166–67
Muslim Brotherhood, Jordanization of, 44–45
Muthana, al- (magazine), 124
Mutual identification, 19, 22
Myths, national, propagation of, 93

Nabulsi, Sulayman al-, 36
Nagorno-Karabakh, 112
Nahhas, Sa'ib, 141, 143
Narratives, Israeli historical, 65–68
Nasif, Muhammad, 146
Nasir, Jamal Abd al-, 20, 125–26, 199
  failure to influence identity, 178, 187
  state Arabism of, 157–60
National Constitution Party (Jordan), 48
National identity. *See* Identity, national
National interest, 17
Nationalism
  cultural, 122
  modernization theory of, 152
  Persian, 95–97
  role of military conscription to, 146–47n.36
  state versus Arab, 19–20
  Syrian, 148, 152–54
  See also Arabism; Zionism
National Religious Party (Israel), 80
Netanyahu, Benjamin, 45, 53, 59, 80
  compared to Rabin, 85–86
  criticism of, 54, 55, 61, 82–84
"New Historians," 76
Nixon Doctrine, 96
No Ruz (Zoroastrian New Year), 97

Occupied territories, 26, 40–41, 43–44, 64–65, 72, 78, 79
October 1973 war, 161, 162
Oil, political impact of, 95–96, 130, 142, 165
Ollapally, Deepa M., 108
Orientalism, 3
Orthodox Jewry, rising power of, 65
Oslo Accords (1993), 77–78, 80, 82, 86
  threat to Israel's identity, 59, 71

Palestinian Liberation Organization. *See* PLO
Palestinian National Council (PNC), 42
Palestinians
  identity of, 33–34, 39–40, 41
  integration into Jordan, 38–39, 47–48
  in occupied territories, 64–65
  representation in Geneva conference, 162
Pan-Africanism, competition for leadership of, 191, 197–98

Pan-Arabism, 184–85
  competition for leadership of, 20, 191, 195
  See also Arabism
Pan-Islam, 184–85. *See also* Islam
Peace
  Israel-Egypt, 162–63
  Israel-Jordan, 37–38, 49–54
  Israel-Lebanon, 164–65
  See also Oslo Accords
"People Apart Syndrome," 64
Peres, Shimon, 75n.61, 80
Persian carpet, metaphor of, 94
Persian nationalism, 95–97
Perthes, Volker, 143, 147
Picard, Elizabeth, 141
Pipes, Daniel, 150
PLO, 14, 17
  recognition by Israel, 77
  relationship with Jordan, 41–43
  support for, 39–40, 42, 45–46, 160
  support of Saddam Hussein, 73
  See also Oslo Accords
Political consciousness, Arab, 19
Political identity, 12–13, 93
Popular Front for the Liberation of Palestine, 157
Primordialism, 134–35, 186
Public justification, 31–32, 171, 177–78
Public spheres, 29–30
  interaction between domestic and international, 191–92
  international system, 30–31
  in Israel, 57
  and Israeli-Jordanian peace treaty, 49–54
  in Jordan, 34–35, 36–37, 44
  state repression of, 30–31

Qabbani, Nizar, 147
Qabus, Sultan of Oman, 130
Qaddisiya, battle of, 132
Qasim, Abd al-Karim, 126–27, 135

Rabat summit (1974), 37, 42
Rabin, Yitzhak, 74–75, 79, 82
  assassination of, 59, 61, 79
  compared to Netanyahu, 85–86
  vision of Israeli identity, 61, 75–77
  on withdrawal from occupied territories, 78, 79
Rafsanjani, Akbar Hashemi, 109n.50, 110, 111
Ranger, Terence, 118
Raouf Rawabdeh, Abd al-, 35, 48
Rationalism, 2–4, 170–71, 189–90
  compared to constructivism, 5–6, 27–29, 182–83, 189–90, 194
Renan, Ernest, 121
Restricted political pluralism, 168
Return of Consciousness, The (al-Hakim), 157
Reza, Shah Pahlavi (father of Mohammad), 94–95

Reza Shah Pahlavi, Mohammad, 88, 95–97
Rifa'i, Zayd, 43n.48
Rogers initiative, 160
Rothschild, Joseph, 187
Rubin, Barry, 32
Ruggie, John, 18
Rumi, Majda, 147
Rushdie, Salman, 109–10
Russians, immigration to Israel, 81

Sa'dabad Pact, 123
Sadat, Anwar, 12, 14, 56–57, 115
    peace initiative with Israel, 160–63,
    180–81
Sadowski, Yahya, 25, 93, 171–72, 188
Sadr, Imam Baqr al-, 131
Said, Edward, 6
Sa'id, Nuri al-, 124
Saideman, Steve, 11–12, 25
Samet, Gideon, 58
Samman, Ghada al-, 147
Saudi Arabia, 111, 112
Savafid dynasty, 94
Sawt al-Arab (radio broadcast), 20
Security Threatened (Arian), 64
Selectorate, 174, 176, 193, 194, 198
Separatism, 172–73
Settlers, Jewish, 74, 77, 79
Shahnameh (Ferdowsi), 92
Shahrur, Muhammad, 140
Sham, al- (Syria), 145
Shamash (god), 127n.34
Shamir, Yitzhak, 73, 74, 82
Sharansky, Natan, 80
Shariati, Ali, 99
Shariatmadari, Ayatollah Kazem, 99n.25
Sharon, Ariel, 55
Shas (Israeli political party), 80, 81, 86, 87
Shia Islam, 98, 99. *See also* Islam
Shiites, 124–25
    Iranian, 93
    Iraqi, 107, 120–21, 124–25, 130, 199
Shubaylat, Layth, 51
Sidqi, Bakr, 123, 124
Six-Day War, 159–60
Smith, Anthony D., 8–9, 118, 134
Social identity, 62n.8
Socialist Youth Organization (Egypt), 157,
    158
South Africa, 104
Soviet Union
    collapse of, 111
    invasion of Afghanistan, 105–6
    and Iran, 96, 100–101, 103, 105–6
State identity. *See* Identity, state
Stein, Janice, 117
Steinberg, Blema, 117
Suez crisis, 125
Suleiman, Hikmat, 123–24, 135

Sunnis
    Iraqi, 121, 124, 132
    Syrian, 138, 140
Swidler, Ann, 68
Syria
    Arabism in, 139–40, 147–48, 158–59
    business community of, 141, 143–44
    decline of ideology in, 139–40
    foreign policy of, 139–40, 150–52
    identity of, 4, 25, 137–39, 149–50, 190
    intermarriage in, 145–46
    and Israel, 149, 190
    and Lebanon, 149–50
    liberalization of economy, 140–43
    nationalism of, 148, 152–54
    rural-urban conflict in, 144–45
    See also Asad, Hafiz al-

Taifel, Henry, 62n.8
Tajik civil war, 112, 113
Tal, Tariq al-, 26
Talas, Firas, 143–44
Tamir, Zakariya, 147
Tarawnwh, Fayz, 38
Tawtin (resettlement), 47
Tekumah (television program), 67
Telhami, Shibley, 3, 5, 27, 180, 184
Thawra, al- (newspaper), 133
Theory of Alliances (Walt), 3
Theory of International Politics (Waltz), 2
Timman, Jafar Abul, 123
Transjordan, 36, 40. *See also* Jordan
Transnational identity, 19, 184–86, 194,
    197–98
Tribalism, 119
Tudeh Party (Iran), 101
Tueni, Ghassan, 149
Turkey, 37–38, 111

Ulema (Iranian clergy), 98
Umma (Islam community), 105, 111
United Arab Emirates, 112
United Arab Kingdom (UAK), 42
United Arab List, 80
United Arab Republic (UAR), 126, 127
United States, 111, 196, 197
    and Iran, 89, 96, 100, 103, 105–6, 112, 113

Vatikiotis, P. J., 10
Velayet-e faqih (guardianship of religious ju-
    rist), 98
Vulnerability, effect on foreign policy, 172–73

Wafd Party (Egypt), 157–58
Walt, Stephen, 3, 10, 196
Waltz, Kenneth, 2
Wannus, Sa'adallah, 147
Washington Declaration (1994), 53
Wendt, Alexander, 18, 28, 62n.8